Long Corridor Paintings
at Summer Palace
颐和园长廊彩画故事精选

Summer Palace Administrative Office   颐和园管理处

Foreign Languages Press   Beijing   外文出版社·北京

The Summer Palace in Beijing　北京颐和园

Members of Editorial Board: Liu Baojun, Sun Shuming, Yang Mingqing, Geng Liutong, Xu Fengtong, Lan Peijin

Director of Editorial Board: Liu Baojun

Deputy Director of Editorial Board: Sun Shuming

Stories Selected by: Jing Tong, Li Zhang

Photographs by: Yao Tianxin, Yang Yin, Bai Zhaoxian, Yin Renjie, Sun Shuming, Liu Chungen, Lan Peijin

Bookcover Designed by: Cai Rong

Plates Designed by: Ye Zhongyue, Gu Chenglin

Edited by: Lan Peijin

编　委　会： 刘宝军　孙树明　杨明庆　耿刘同　徐凤桐　兰佩瑾

编委会主任： 刘宝军

编委会副主任： 孙树明

故事选编： 敬同　李章

摄　影： 姚天新　杨茵　白兆贤　尹仁杰　孙树明　刘春根　兰佩瑾

封面设计： 蔡荣

图版设计： 叶中岳　顾成林

编　辑： 兰佩瑾

Home Page:
  http://www.flp.com.cn

E - mail Addresses:
  info@flp.com.cn
  sales@flp.com.cn

First edition 1996
Second printing 1998

Long Corridor Paintings at Summer Palace

ISBN 7 - 119 - 01859 - 0

© Foreign Languages Press
Published by Foreign Languages Press
24 Baiwanzhuang Road, Beijing 100037, China
Printed in the People's Republic of China

Long Corridor at Summer Palace 颐和园长廊

In 1990, China was informed by *The Guinness Book of Records* that the Summer Palace's long corridor, already famous for its traditional architecture and paintings of historical scenes, was determined to be the largest painted corridor in the world. This newly-won recognition brings even more appeal to an already well-loved cultural monument.

If all the architectural and aesthetic features of the Long Corridor were described in writing, we would have a long essay rich with details concerning arrangement, measurement, structure, outlook, color, aesthetics and mechanics. And perhaps the most significant component of the essay would be the large number of color paintings depicting famous cultural figures.

The Long Corridor in the Summer Palace was first built in 1750, the 15th year of Emperor Qian Long's reign. In 1860 it was destroyed by British and French soldiers who invaded Beijing. During the reign of Emperor Guang Xu (in the end of 19th century), the Long Corridor was reconstructed according to the original pattern. This 728-meter-long art gallery starts from Greeting the Moon Gate in the east and ends at Stone Man Pavilion in the west. It has 273 sections in all. In between, there are four octagonal pavilions with double roofs, named as Liuzhui, Jilan, Qiushui and Qingyao, symbolizing the four seasons. This ingeniously conceived, intricately patterned and uniquely styled corridor is like a long colorful ribbon linking the scenic spots scattered in front of neighboring Longevity Hill. Using special painting techniques, the corridor's artwork expresses the Chinese nation's search for beauty from various levels and angles. While walking on the Long Corridor, you'll see Longevity Hill with its lofty pines, to the north; to the south is peaceful Kunming Lake, ripples softly breaking on the surface. However, the paintings on the corridor can bring people into an even more fantastic world.

On the beams of each section of the Long Corridor there are over forty color paintings, each one with a unique story and painted in various styles and sizes. These color paintings can be divided into four categories: human figures and stories, landscapes, flowers and birds, and architecture. Among these, the most fascinating part is certainly the over 200 paintings depicting historic figures, folk and fairy stories and scenes from traditional opera. These works cover thousands of years of history, from the first emperor of China (c. 2100-2000 BC) to the last feudal dynasty which ended early in this century. The long span of history depicted, large scale and rich contents of these paintings are rare in the world. For this album we have selected the best and most representative works.

Landscape painting 山水彩画

Except for some folk stories, most of the Long Corridor's paintings center on the Chinese classic novels, including, the *Three Kingdoms, Journey to the West, Outlaws of the Marsh, A Dream of Red Mansions, Strange Tales from Make-Do Studio.* In this album you'll enjoy lively scenes from all of these classic works.

Painting of human figures 人物故事彩画

Three Kingdoms recounts the breathtaking war at the end of the Han Dynasty and Three Kingdoms (220-280) in China—Wei Kingdom, the strongest, and the Shu and Wu kingdoms. Each vied to unify China and destroy the other two. During this dozen year war, many respected historical figures emerged, including Liu Bei, Zhuge Liang, Guan Yunchang, Zhang Fei, Cao Cao, Sun Quan, Lü Bu, Zhao Yun and Diao Chan. These figures continue to captivate.

Journey to the West is one of the most popular and loved novels in China. The novel relates the adventures of the Tang Dynasty (618-907) Buddhist monk Xuanzang as he travels west with his three disciples, Monkey, Pig and Friar Sand (to today's India and Nepal) in search of Buddhist scriptures. During his prigrimage, Xuanzang met all kinds of monsters and spirits who wanted to eat him. Only the courage and watchfulness of his disciples saved him from death. Finally they reached the west and obtained the scriptures. The paintings on the Long Corridor depict how Xuanzang and his disciples evaded or defeated the many monsters and spirits that hindered their journey.

The Long Corridor paintings also depict *Outlaws of the Marsh*, a classic novel which portrays the peasant uprising at the end of the Northern Song Dynasty (1110-1121). The heroes in the novel include Song Jiang, Wu Song, Li Kui, Lin Chong, Lu Zhishen and Shi Qian. The Long Corridor paintings, and these pages, depict in lively fashion these much-loved characters.

A Dream of Red Mansions presents the indulgent life of nobles in the middle of the Qing Dynasty, the last feudal dynasty. The love affairs of Jia Baoyu and Lin Daiyu, the hero and heroine, spawn many interesting stories. The

Long Corridor paintings follow the plot of the story.

A collection of short novels, *Strange Tales from Make-Do Studio*, with the help of various fox spirits, disclose the ugly faces of officials and bullies of feudal China, while attacking arranged marriages and other irrational practices and systems of this period.

Flower and bird painting 花鸟彩画

Many Chinese and foreign tourists who have visited the Summer Palace feel that the Long Corridor is just like a history and culture museum—it displays not only traditional Chinese art but also brings to life the essence of China's several-thousand-year history and culture. In this album we've culled the essence of this essence.

Dear readers, it is our wish that this book brings you the fragrance of Chinese culture and conveys the power of its wisdom.

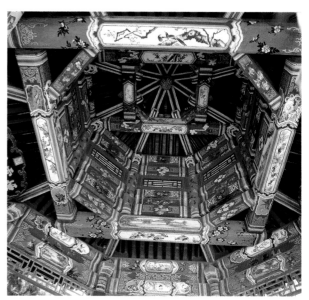

Ceiling paintings inside the pavilion 亭子内彩绘藻井

1990年,设在英国伦敦的《吉尼斯世界大全》总部,向中国有关部门发来一条重要消息:

"中国北京颐和园的长廊,经过各方面权威人士的认真评估,以建筑独具特色,绘画数量多、内容丰富多采,而被评为当代世界上最长的画廊。"这是中国被海外权威机构较早承认的既具有很高文化价值又适于参观游览的世界之最。从此,颐和园的长廊,以她独有的建筑艺术魅力更被世人所厚爱。

长廊的建筑艺术,包括布局、体量、结构、外形、色彩、美学、力学等,如果要把长廊的建筑艺术展开来叙述,肯定会成为一篇内容丰富而又独特的大文章,而长廊上那大量的内容不同色调各异的彩画,则是她建筑艺术中最重要的组成部分。

颐和园的长廊,始建于乾隆十五年(1750年),1860年被入侵北京的英法联军焚毁。光绪年间(十九世纪末)又按原样重建。长廊东起"邀月门",西止"石丈亭"。全长728米,共有273间。中间建有"留佳"、"寄澜"、"秋水"、"清遥",象征春夏秋冬的四座重檐八角亭子。长廊建筑构思巧妙,布局完整,形式独特,内涵丰富。她似一条

Painting of traditional Chinese buildings 建筑风景彩画

长长的彩带,把万寿山前山分散的景点建筑连在一起,使它们像点点繁星洒落在自己身旁。长廊彩画以中国绘画的独特技巧,把中华民族追求美的意趣,多层次多角度的表现出来。在长廊漫步,向北望去,是高阁耸立青松环绕的万寿山,向南望去,是碧波荡漾堤岛争辉的昆明湖。而观赏长廊上的彩画,则又把人们带入了一个更加迷人的世界。尤其是在娇阳似火的夏暑和遇上雨雪天气,由于长廊能起遮阳避雨的作用,丝毫不会影响人们的游兴,所以,长廊更成为人们非常喜欢游览的地方。

在长廊每间廊子的上方,根据建筑形式不同,画师们在四周的梁、枋等处,分别绘有四十多幅大小不同、内容各异、形式多样的彩画。这些彩画如果按内容来划分,基本上可以分为四大类。一是人物故事,二是山水画屏,三是花卉翎毛,四是建筑风景。其中最为引人入胜的是在廊子的内外被称作"包袱画"的二百多幅人物故事彩画。这些彩画有历史人物,民间传说,神话故事,戏曲片断等。时间跨度,从中国的三皇五帝(公元前21世纪至20世纪),到中国最后一个封建王朝,上下绵延达数千年之久。其历史之长、范围之广、内容之丰富,在当今世界上确实少有。这本画册,就是从长廊上数百幅人物故事彩画中精选而成的。

长廊上的人物彩画,除了一部分是来源于中国的民间故事以外,其余大多选自中国的古典文学名著。其中以《三国演义》、《西游记》、《水浒传》、《红楼梦》、《聊斋志异》五部文学著作占的数量最多。

A pavilion on the Long Corridor 长廊中的亭子

Paintings on the pavilion's beam 亭内梁枋上的彩画

《水浒传》是一部描写北宋末年(公元1110至1121年)农民起义的文学著作。书中的不少人物曾被人们津津乐道。如宋江、武松、李逵、林冲、鲁智深、时迁等。长廊上的彩画,把这些历史人物描绘得既很有个性又非常生动有趣。

《红楼梦》是描写中国最后一个封建王朝清朝中期(18世纪前后)贵族生活的文学名著。在那座大观园里,那些男男女女们,眼看着即将衰落下去的家业,正在无可奈何的消磨时光。书中的贾宝玉和林黛玉是两个男女主人公,围绕着他们二人的爱情瓜葛,又衍生出许多很有意思的故事来。长廊上许多有关《红楼梦》内容的彩画,都是围绕着这些情节而展开的。

《聊斋志异》是一部短篇小说集。它以谈狐说鬼的形式,揭露官吏、豪绅恶霸的丑行,抨击包办婚姻和不合理的制度。

《三国演义》是描写中国汉朝末期及公元190至280年间的故事。当时的华夏大地,有魏国、蜀国和吴国,三国并立。魏国的势力最为强大,蜀国和吴国较弱。三个国家为了扩大自己的势力,削弱对方,从而最后达到消灭对方,实现统一中国的目的,三国之间展出了既惊心动魄又妙趣横生的角斗。在这场长达数十年的较量中,出现了众多的被后人传颂的历史人物。如刘备、诸葛亮、关羽、张飞、曹操、孙权、吕布、赵云、貂蝉等。长廊上那些有关三国的人物彩画,就是叙述那段历史故事的。

《西游记》是一部在中国影响最广的神话故事著作。说的是中国唐朝(公元618—907年)一位叫玄奘的僧人,带领孙悟空、猪八戒、沙僧三位弟子,不怕艰难险阻,不远万里去西天(现在的尼泊尔、印度一带)取经。一路之上,师徒四人遇到了不少妖魔,这些妖魔鬼怪都想活吃这位僧人的肉,多亏了随从他的三位弟子与妖魔勇敢机智地奋力拼搏,才使这位僧人生命转危为安,最终实现了他们去西天取经的宏愿。长廊上那些有关《西游记》的彩画,就是描绘这师徒四人是如何战胜这些妖魔鬼怪的。

Paintings on the corner beams of the Long Corridor
长廊拐角处梁枋上的彩画

在参观过颐和园的中外游客中,不少都有这样的体会,他们说,在长廊漫游,如同走进一座建筑别致的历史博物馆,不仅能观赏到独特的中国传统绘画艺术,还能领略不少中国数千年历史文化中的精华。

This story is an ancient Chinese fairy tale. The Eight Immortals refer to the following people: Li Tieguai, Han Zhongli, Lan Caihe, Zhang Guolao, He Xiangu, Lü Dongbin, Han Xiangzi and Cao Guojiu. According to legend, one year there was a plague in the world. The Eight Immortals decided to go to Yingzhou in the East Sea to collect some herbal medicine to cure people. They decided to cross the sea by starting from picturesque Laoshan Mountain on China's east coast. Han Zhongli, Cao Guojiu and Zhang Guolao would travel together, while Lü Dongbin, Han Xiangzi and Lan Caihe would form another group. Li Tieguai and He Xiangu would travel together dressed up as father and daughter.

The Eight Immortals started from the Kunlun Mountains in western China and agreed to meet again on the top of Laoshan Mountain on August 15. The Eight Immortals got together at Laoshan Mountain at the appointed time. Every one brought along his own unique charms which could protect them in crossing the sea. Facing a vast expanse of misty, rolling waters and fresh breeze, the Eight Immortals set out across the sea, chatting and laughing all the way. From then on, this proverb was spoken: "The Eight Immortals cross the sea, each one showing his or her special prowess." It means that when people do something together or compete with each other, each displays his or her own ways and skills.

八仙过海是一个神话故事。八仙指的是：铁拐李、汉钟离、蓝采和、张果老、何仙姑、吕洞宾、韩湘子和曹国舅八人。相传有一年天下闹瘟疫，八仙想到东海瀛洲采药解除人间的瘟疫。共同商定，渡海时从山明水秀的崂山开始。汉钟离、曹国舅、张果老一起，吕洞宾、韩湘子、蓝采和结伴，铁拐李和何仙姑扮成

父女，八位仙人从昆仑山出发，约定八月十五在崂山山顶会面后，各自拿出自己的宝物，倚物渡海。面对烟波浩淼的大海，徐徐清风扑面而来。八位仙人说说笑笑向大海彼岸漂去。之后民间流传谚语"八仙过海，各显神通"，比喻干成某件事或互相竞赛时，各自都有一套办法或本领。

Qin Xianglian was married to Chen Shimei, a scholar from an impoverished family. As Chen's mind was on academic study and passing imperial exams some day, the entire family burden was on Qin, a gentle and hardworking girl who waited attentively upon her aged and sick parents-in-law and reared her children. To save for her husband's travel fare to the capital for imperial exams, Qin cooked meals and labored in field during the day and spun cotton into yarn and wove cloth by oil lamp deep into the night. Everybody in the neighborhood praised her virtues.

Several years later, Chen placed first in the imperial exams. The emperor, fond of this young scholar's handsome looks and talents, married his daughter to him. Living the high life of an imperial family member, Chen soon forgot his family back home. Later, his home area suffered severe draught and crops failed for many years in a row. Both of Chen's parents died of hunger. Qin, the virtuous daughter-in-law, wept in the streets selling her long hair that she had kept to cover their burial cost. Then, as she had nobody else to turn to, she went all the way to the capital with the children to look for her husband. After much suffering Qin met Chen, but the ungrateful husband disowned her and the children and turned them out of his house. Wang Yanling, the old and kind-hearted prime minister tried to help. He brought Qin, disguised as a singsong girl, to Chen's birthday party in the hope to rouse Chen's sympathy. Even he was humiliated by Chen's verbal abuse. Chen even sent soldiers to kill Qin and the two children. Qin, in despair, brought a law case to Kaifeng Court against Chen. She finally won the case.

《包公案》中的故事。秦香莲嫁给书生陈士美,丈夫一心想求取功名,只管读书,家庭重担,全部落在香莲身上。温顺、勤劳的秦香莲,上要服侍年老多病的公婆,下要教育一双儿女。为了给丈夫积攒进京赶考的路费,她白天干活做饭,晚上纺线织布,辛勤劳作。方圆百里,都知道陈家有一个好媳妇。

数年后,陈士美进京应试,一举中了状元。皇上见陈士美才貌双全,即招为驸马。陈士美贪图荣华富贵,早把家人忘得一干二净。后来,连年灾荒,颗粒不收。陈士美的父母饿死,香莲剪掉头发长街叫卖,换钱埋葬了公公和婆婆。她实在走投无路,便带儿女上京寻夫。香莲母子经过千辛万苦找到了陈士美,丈夫忘恩负义,不但不认妻子儿女,反将他们赶出门去。耿直的丞相王延龄让香莲扮艺人随他一起去给陈士美祝寿,想顺便劝说陈士美,反被骂出陈府,并派人暗杀香莲母子。香莲无奈,被逼告到开封府。

This is a story from the classical novel *Three Kingdoms*. Toward the end of the Eastern Han Dynasty (25-220) China was war-stricken. After a royal edict to recruit soldiers in Zhuozhou, three heroes surfaced. One was Liu Bei, a descendent of Liu Sheng, Prince Jin of Zhongshan during the Han Dynasty. Liu Bei was sighing while reading the posted edict when he heard an impatient voice behind, "What use is just sighing, without a man's devotion to his country?"

Then the man introduced himself: "I'm Zhang Fei and my livelihood is selling wine and slaughtering hogs."

"I do want to devote myself to the country," Liu explained after telling Zhang his name. "But how can I help if I'm empty handed?"

"You needn't worry," said Zhang. "I'm willing to give up my fortune to build an army and embark on this new career with you."

While the two talked merrily over cups in a small restaurant, in came a martial looking, handsome man with a huge build and a red complexion. Liu and Zhang invited him to join them. They learned that the man was named Guan Yu. As he had upheld justice by killing a local tyrant, he had fled home and wandered about for many years. During an amiable conversation the three found that they shared a common ambition and the next day in a peach garden they swore brotherhood to heaven and earth before lit candles and joss sticks, Liu Bei the eldest, Guan Yu the second-oldest and Zhang Fei the youngest. They vowed devotion to China. Later, the three sworn brothers had successful career. Liu Bei ascended to the throne of the State of Shu in 221 A.D in present-day Sichuan.

《三国演义》中的故事。　东汉(25－220 年)末年,天下大乱。朝廷发布文告,下令招兵买马。榜文到涿县,引出了三位英雄。刘备,是汉朝中山靖王刘胜的后代。一天,他一边看榜文一边长叹,忽听背后有人说:"男子汉大丈夫不思为国出力,在这里叹什么气?"并自报姓名说:"我叫张飞,靠卖酒杀猪为生。"刘备说出自己姓名后说:"我想为国出力,又感到力量不够,故而长叹!"张飞说:"这没什么可难的,我可以拿出家产,招兵买马,创建大业。"刘备听后非常高兴。二人来到一个小店,边喝酒边谈,正说得投机,门外突然来了一个红脸大汉,威风凛凛,相貌堂堂。刘备、张飞请他一同饮酒。交谈中得知,此人名关羽,因仗义除霸有家不能归,已流落江湖五、六年了。他们各自抒发自己的志向,谈得十分投机。

隔日,三人来到一个桃园,点燃香烛,拜告天地,结为兄弟。按年龄刘备为大哥,关羽为二哥,张飞为三弟。并发誓:"同心协力,报效国家。"此后,三人果然作出一番惊天动地的事业。

The Tang Priest's Journey for Scriptures　唐僧取经

A story from *Journey to the West*. During the reign of Emperor Tai Zong (627-649) of the Tang Dynasty, at his request, esteemed Buddhist Monk Xuan Zang was sent to India, the birthplace of Buddhism, for scriptures. From Chang'an (present-day Xi'an), the capital of the Tang Dynasty, the monk journeyed west. When he eventually fulfilled the mission and returned, seventeen years had passed. From that time forward, Buddhism spread across China.

As this legendary trip was told and retold by later generations, many embellishments were zealously added. Wu Cheng'en, using popular versions of the story along with his own fictional details, created the intriguing classical novel *Journey to the West*. The Tang Priest, Monkey, Pig and Friar Sand characters from the book are popular images among Chinese people.

Note: Wu Cheng'en (1500-1582), was a Ming Dynasty novelist.

《西游记》中的故事。　唐贞观年间(公元 627 - 649 年)，唐太宗重视佛教，派僧人玄奘到佛教发源地去取真经。唐僧离开长安，一直西行。用了长达十七年的时间，终于实现了自己的伟大宏愿，到达天竺国(今印度)取回了真经。从此，佛教在中国弘扬、传播。

玄奘取经事，历史上确有其人其事，《西游记》就是根据这段历史而写成的一部文学著作，小说家吴承恩在民间口传的基础上，又加进了不少神话色彩，更增强了故事的可读性和趣味性。小说中的唐僧、孙悟空、猪八戒、沙僧等人物形象，在中国家喻户晓，老幼皆知。

This is a story from *Outlaws of the Marsh*. After killing the local tyrant Zhen Guanxi, for fear of being jailed, Lu Zhishen fled to Mount Wutai where he stayed in a temple as a monk. After breaking the temple rules by drinking, he was sent by the abbot to the Monastery of Great Assistance to State, where he was put in charge of a vegetable garden. The property had been plagued by a band of local hooligans who frequently came to steal. None of the previous watchmen could stop the theft. Now, on hearing that a new watchman had been employed, the hooligans came again, only to be welcomed by a good beating: the two leaders were kicked into a manure pit and the rest dropped to their knees and kowtowed for mercy.

The next day they came again, but this time to apologize with wine and food. While they were enjoying the food, crows up in a tree cackled nonstop. A bad omen, the hooligans claimed. They were about to fetch a ladder to destroy the bird nest, when Lu Zhishen stopped them. He sized up the tree and said, "No need for the trouble." He stripped off his coat, bent down and grasped the trunk. Then he yanked the tree right out of the ground. The hooligans gasped in disbelief and went down on their knees and begged Lu to teach them martial arts.

《水浒传》中的故事。 鲁智深打死恶霸镇关西后,怕吃官司,逃往他地。他先来到五台山文殊院出家,因不守佛规,喝酒闹事,方丈又把他介绍到大相国寺看菜园子。菜园子附近住着二、三十个泼皮,他们常来菜园子偷菜,已换了几个看园子的人都管不了他们。这次听说又换了个新人,便来闹事,没想到被鲁智深把两个领头的踢到粪坑里,吓得他们跪地求饶。第二天,泼皮们买些酒菜向鲁智深赔礼。大家正吃得高兴,听到门外大树上的乌鸦叫个不停,泼皮们说这叫声不吉利,吵得人心烦,便欲搬梯子拆掉鸟巢。鲁智深上前把那棵树上下打量了一下说:"不用了,待我把树拔掉。"说完,只见他脱掉外衣,用左手向下搂住树干,右手把住树的上半截,腰往上一挺,那棵树竟然连根拔起。众泼皮惊得个个目瞪口呆,忙跪在地上拜鲁智深为师。

Seeking Plum Blossoms in Snow　踏雪寻梅

This is a story from *A Dream of Red Mansions*. Betrothed to the son of a Imperial Academician surnamed Mei, Baoqin stayed in Jia Residence waiting for her wedding date. In the depth of winter, the earth was draped with a cloak of snow. Li Wan invited cousins over to chant poems and enjoy the snowy scene. She told Baoyu to fetch some plum blossoms from Miaoyu's place. Baoyu did as he was bid and soon returned with crimson flowers in fine bloom. Then Li Wan bid three of her cousins to compose poems, each taking "red," "plum" and "flower" as a subject matter. Amid the excitement, old Lady Jia came in a sedan chair to join them. She praised the flowers and drank cheerfully in the company of the merry girls around her. Suddenly, Lady Jia noticed that out in the snow stood an ethereal, beautiful young lady in a fur drape, accompanied by a servant girl holding a branch of plum blossoms. It was a scene just like a picture. It was Baoqin on her way back from a plum-fetching trip from the same place. Lady Jia appreciated Baoqin's beauty and talents, and thought of making a marriage proposal on behalf of Baoyu. On learning that the girl had been betrothed to Young Lord Mei and that the wedding would soon happen, the old lady reluctantly quit the idea. This picture shows Baoqin in the snow with flower blossoms.

《红楼梦》中的故事。薛宝钗的堂妹薛宝琴,许配给都中梅翰林之子为妻,进京待嫁,来到贾府。此时正值隆冬,刚好下了一场大雪,给大地披上了一层银装。李纨组织姐妹们以"雪"为题办起诗社,大家在芦雪庭赏雪吟诗。李纨命宝玉去栊翠院向妙玉要一枝红梅。宝玉欣然从命,很快就折回一枝红梅。李纨又命邢岫烟、李纹、宝琴分别以红、梅、花三个字各赋诗一首。一时间,芦雪庭内热闹非常。贾母高兴,背着王熙凤等人坐轿来到芦雪庭,边夸梅花开的好,边饮酒取乐,大家陪着贾母玩笑。突然贾母见白雪之中,宝琴身披凫裘,旁边丫头抱着一瓶红梅,竟像画中的天仙一般。原来宝琴看栊翠院红梅开得好看,非常喜爱,也去栊翠院折了几枝。贾母见薛宝琴长得美如天仙,又很有才气,心中十分喜欢,有意为宝玉求婚。一问薛姨妈,才知早已许给梅翰林家,而且很快就要完婚,贾母只好作罢。这幅画描绘宝琴折梅回来的情景。

This is a story from *Strange Tales from Make-Do Studio*. Lady Fan was gentle and beautiful. One day, accompanied by an attendant on an outing to the Water and Moon Monastery, she encountered the warm and equally beautiful Lady Feng. As they found an affinity between each other, on departing Lady Fan invited Lady Feng to visit her home some day. Back home Lady Fan missed her newly made friend terribly and soon fell ill. On the ninth day of the ninth month of the lunar calendar, the Double Ninth Festival, Lady Fan and her attendant came to the family garden to enjoy flowers. There she saw Lady Feng looking at her from outside the garden wall. Overjoyed, Lady Fan invited her in to stay. Her illness was gone.

One day next spring, on an outing, Lady Fan met Meng Anren, a young, handsome and talented scholar from a impoverished family. Helped by Lady Feng, Lady Fan and the young scholar entered betrothal. Unfortunately, a rich local bully also had his eyes on Lady Fan and forced a marriage proposal on Lady Fan's parents, who saw no choice but to accept. The day before the wedding, Lady Fan hanged herself in her room. The heartbroken young scholar, on hearing the news, rushed to her tomb and wailed uncontrollably. Suddenly, he heard Lady Feng's voice from behind, "If you dig up the tomb, I can bring her back to life." He did as she said, and carried the dead Lady Fan back to his place. With Lady Feng's magic medicine Lady Fan indeed came to life and the two lovers married. Before Lady Feng left, she disclosed her real identity—a fox fairy.

《聊斋志异》中的故事。 范十一娘,心地善良,有倾国倾城之貌。一日在丫环的陪同下去水月寺游玩,遇上美丽热情的封三娘,二人见面都很喜欢对方。分别时,十一娘约封三娘去她家玩。十一娘回家后,日夜想念封三娘,日久天长,郁郁成疾。重阳节这天,丫环扶十一娘在花园赏花,忽见封三娘正攀墙向园内张望,于是被请进园来,并住下。十一娘的病就此好了。

来年春天,她俩结伴郊游。十一娘碰见年轻英俊的贫寒秀才孟安仁,在封三娘帮助下,订了婚约。有一显贵相中十一娘,十一娘父母惧怕权势,同意了这门亲事。就在迎亲前一天,十一娘自缢。孟安仁听到噩耗,万分悲痛,夜晚到十一娘坟上大哭。忽听三娘在背后说:"你快挖开坟,我有办法。"孟安仁挖开坟将十一娘背回家中。经封三娘调药相救,十一娘苏醒了,二人遂成婚,封三娘辞别时说出自己是狐仙。

This is a story from *The Generals of the Yang Family*. During the Northern Song Dynasty (960-1127) the State of Liao in the north attacked the central part of China. Yang Yanzhao, the famous Song warrior, was guarding the Waqiao Pass. He held back several onslaughts by the invading Liao Army. But Liao gathered more troops, about 300 thousand, and formed a unique Heavenly Gate Battle Formation to challenge the Song Army. Failing to recognize the formation and unable to break it, Yang Yanzhao hurriedly sent for his capable fifth brother, a monk in a Mount Wutai temple. The fifth brother was willing to help, however, his weapon failed —the shaft of his axe had rotten after years of storage and the wood could only be replaced with the magic dragon-subduing wood native to Mount Muke.

Meng Liang, a general, was sent on the mission to obtain the wood, only to return embarrassed, for he had proved no match for Mu Guiying, the young female martial arts expert from the Mu family's mountain fortress.

Then the warrior's son Zongbao was dispatched to get the job done. The arrogant young man was sure of a quick success. Upon first encountering Mu Guiying, he raced forward on his horse like the wind and lanced at the girl. Learning that the young man was the young lord of the famous Yang family, the girl asked in surprise, "Why are you here, in stead of fighting the Liao Army at the front?" The young man simply said, "I came for the magic dragon-subduing wood to break the Liao battle formation." As the young man charged, she lifted her weapon and the two were locked in a fierce but even combat. Overcome by the young man's handsome looks, outstanding martial skills and noble family background —his grandfather was a hero known nationwide—Mu Guiying fell in love. After 50 rounds of combat, she became fearful that the young man would be injured. She had an idea: retreat in a feigned defeat. Failing to recognize the trick, the arrogant young man chased behind, only to be caught by a red net that the girl threw back over her shoulders. The young man was brought up on the mountain, and thus started a perfect marriage.

《杨家将》中的故事。北宋(公元 960－1127 年)时期,辽国侵扰中原,朝廷派抗金名将杨延昭为帅,镇守瓦桥三关。杨延昭打败辽军的数次进攻,辽军不甘失败,又调集三十万人马,在龙谷口摆下"天门阵"。杨延昭因不识天门阵,派人去五台山请哥哥杨五郎。五郎出家日久,久不用的武器——金镶斧斧柄已坏,需用穆柯寨之镇山之宝降龙木修复。孟良前去强取降龙木被穆桂英打败。杨延昭之子杨宗保争强好胜,不把穆桂英看在眼里,拍马挺枪来战穆桂英。穆桂英经盘问才知道是杨家将的先锋官杨宗保,忙问:"你不在阵前打仗抗辽,到我山寨来干什么?"杨宗保喝道:"要降龙木破天门阵。"说完,不容桂英回话,策马向前,举枪直取穆桂英。穆桂英是武将之后,平时专爱舞棒耍枪,她见宗保一枪刺来,急忙应战。两人各自施展自己的本事,一时打得难解难分。穆桂英看宗保年轻英俊,武艺高强,又是忠臣之后,顿生爱慕之情。斗了五十回合,她怕伤着宗保,虚晃一枪,佯装败阵。宗保不知是计,紧追不放,穆桂英悄悄取出红罗套,猛一回身,将宗保套住,擒上山来。从此,成就了一段好姻缘。

This is a story from *Tale of the White Snake*. At the Pure Brightness (5th solar term) time, Lady Bai and her attendant Xiao Qing came to enjoy the beautiful West Lake, where, by the famous Dilapidated Bridge they saw a handsome young scholar with whom Lady Bai immediately fell in love. She revealed her feeling to Xiao Qing who then held up her small finger towards the sky. At once a dark cloud came from the west and rain began. The young man, not expecting this sudden change of weather, hurriedly boarded a boat. Lady Bai and Xiao Qing called to the boatman, "We have no umbrella with us. Please let us board too." With the approval of the young man, who had rented this boat, the boatman asked the girls where they were heading and invited them aboard. After expressing gratitude, Xiao Qing managed to strike up a conversation with the scholar learned that his name was Xu Xian and his parents had both died, and most importantly, that he was still single. At this, the two girls gave each other a knowing smile.

When the two girls were about to disembark at Taiping Bridge, it was still raining. "May we use your umbrella?" Xiao Qing asked. "You may come to our residence tomorrow to pick it up. Our young lady will be very grateful." Xu Xian happily agreed. The next day, Xu Xian did come for the umbrella. He was treated to a tableful of delicious food and excellent wine. While eating, Lady Bai and Xu Xian sent love messages back and forth with their eyes. With the help from the outspoken Xiao Qing the two soon were married.

《白蛇传》中的故事。　清明(每年的四月上旬)这一天,白娘子和小青来到西湖边游玩。她俩在断桥亭旁看到一英俊后生,白娘子顿生爱慕之情,并把心事告诉了小青。小青有心成全白娘子和这后生的婚事,便生出一计来。小青用手一指,只见西北方向飘来一片乌云,不一会便渐渐沥沥下起了小雨。那后生急忙租了一条船,钻进船舱。这时,小青和白娘子也急忙跑到岸边,小青高喊:"船家慢开船,雨下得这么急,我们没带伞,让我们搭一程吧!"船家征得后生同意,把船靠岸,问明了姑娘去的地方,让她俩上了船。上船后,小青借感谢后生的机会问其姓名,才知道这个英俊后生叫许仙,父母双亡,孤身一人。白娘子和小青会心地笑了。

船到太平桥,白娘子和小青该下船了,天仍然下着雨,小青忙说:"许相公,请你把伞借给我们用一下,屈尊你明天来我们宅上取,我们小姐会感谢你的。"许仙答应着把伞递给了她们。第二天,许仙来取伞,小青热情地设酒席招待了许仙。席间,白娘子和许仙含情脉脉,在小青地撮合下结为伉俪。

During the Song Dynasty, after placing first in the imperial examinations and marrying the princess, Chen Shimei plotted to kill his legal wife Qin Xianglian and his two children. As nobody dared to help Qin with her written complaint against Chen, she brought her case to Lord Bao by stopping the latter's sedan chair on the street. Lord Bao instructed his men to write the complaint and then sent for Chen Shimei. Chen came, and the two took seats in the hall before Lord Bao mildly brought up the matter in the hope Chen would mend his way and accepted his legal wife and the children. Instead of accepting the accusation, Chen unsheathed his sword meaning to kill Qin, but was stopped by the angry Lord Bao. Seeing this unfavorable situation, Chen meant to leave. At an order from Lord Bao, soldiers rushed up to rope Chen. Just then, the emperor's mother and aunt announced their arrival. They pleaded for mercy for Chen's sake, and when refused, raised a havoc. At end of resource, Lord Bao turned to Qin and pleaded with a sad look, "I give you money and you bring your children back home and forget what has happened." "People say," the tearful Qin lamented, "that you have upheld justice and respected only law, not power. Now I see that it's really not true. You're just like the others. All officials shield one another. You want me to swallow my grievance and leave!"

An upright person by nature, Lord Bao felt shamefaced. These words whipped his conscience. He made up his mind: it's better to lose his office than leave law unenforced. Resolutely, he took off his headwear, the symbol of officialdom, and held it high in the air. In the face of the emperor's mother and aunt, he issued an order. A specially made cutter was brought and Chen was executed.

Note: Lord Bao, named Bao Zheng, held the office of Kaifeng Court, the highest judge of the Northern Song Dynasty (960- 1127).

《包公案》中的故事。宋朝状元陈士美被招为驸马后，前妻秦香莲想状告他忘恩负义，杀妻灭子，无人敢替她写状纸，香莲只好在开封府尹包拯(999－1062年，人称包公)回府的路上拦轿喊冤。包公命手下人帮她写好状纸并派人去找陈士美。公堂上，包公劝陈士美认下香莲母子，陈士美不但不听，反抽剑要杀香莲，被包公喝住。陈士美见势不妙，想马上回府，包公立即拦住，并命衙役们将陈士美捆绑起来。这时，国太、皇姑赶来为陈士美说情，见包公不准，便以权威大闹公堂。包公实在没有办法，只好劝说香莲："我给你些银子，带着孩子回家去吧。"香莲看到此情此景，哭诉道："包大人，老百姓都说你不畏权势，执法如山，看来你也是官官相护，民妇只好含冤走了。"性格刚直的包公，听了香莲的话无地自容。他觉得宁可官不当，也要秉公断案。于是，当着国太和皇姑的面，摘下自己的乌纱帽高举在手，让刽子手抬来虎头铡，将陈士美依法处斩。

This is a story from *Three Kingdoms*. While the Han court was in chaos Dong Zhuo marched his 200,000 battlewise Xiliang troops into the capital of Luoyang. He forced Liu Bian to quit the throne and made Liu Xie the Emperor Xian and himself the prime minister. As he rode roughshod over the emperor, manipulated power for personal ends, and had acted extremely cruelly, all ministers and generals wanted to get rid of him.

Cao Cao, a wise and resourceful army officer, had long wanted to kill Dong Zhuo. One day, he came to see Dong Zhuo with a borrowed blade. The latter was sitting in his bedroom, his brave step-son Lü Bu standing by his side. Inquiring why he had been late, Cao Cao said, "My horse was slow." Dong Zhuo immediately sent Lü Bu to pick a steed from his stable for Cao Cao. As Lü Bu left, Cao Cao thought: "Dong Zhuo, now it's your time to die." But fearful of resistance from the old but still strong Dong Zhuo, Cao Cao waited for the right moment. As

Dong Zhuo was a very large man, a while of sitting tired him and he lay down facing inward. Taking the chance Cao Cao unsheathed the knife. It so happened that Dong saw his move in a mirror. He looked back and asked Cao Cao what he was doing. Just then Lü Bu returned with a horse. The quick-witted Cao Cao made up a story, "I chanced to secure a very unusual blade which I would like to present to you." So saying he handed the knife to Dong Zhuo. Sure enough, the blade was extremely sharp, and about twenty some centimeters long. Delighted, Dong Zhuo told Cao Cao to have a look at the chosen horse. Outside, Cao Cao pleaded for a test ride. He then leaped onto the horse and sped away. "He must have come to murder me," said Dong Zhuo to Lü Bu. "I agree," the latter chorused. They sent soldiers to give chase, but by then, Cao Cao had fled out of the eastern gate.

《三国演义》中的故事。 统帅二十万西凉大军的刺史董卓，乘朝野之乱进军洛阳，废少帝刘辩，立刘协为献帝，自封为相国。他欺主弄权，残暴凶狠；朝中正直的大臣们都想除掉他。

校尉曹操，足智多谋并早有杀董卓之心。一日，曹操借王司徒宝刀一口，藏刀来到相府。他走到小阁，见董卓坐在床上，义子吕布侍立于侧。董卓问曹操为何来迟，曹操说："马走不快，所以迟了。"董卓听后，命吕布选一匹西凉好马送给曹操，吕布答应着出去了。曹操心想，老贼该死，欲刺他，又怕董卓力大，没敢妄动，只好站在一旁等待机会。董卓身体肥胖，不能久

坐，不一会，即侧身而卧。曹操见他躺下，急抽刀欲刺，董卓在穿衣镜内看见了曹操的动作，转身急问："你要干什么？"这时吕布也牵马回来。曹操急中生智说："我得一口宝刀，欲献恩相。"董卓接刀一看，长有盈尺，锋利无比，果然是一口宝刀。董卓引曹操出阁看马，曹操谢道："愿借马一试。"然后快马加鞭往东南疾去。吕布对董卓说："曹操有行刺之举。"董卓说："我也怀疑。"于是派人去追。此时曹操已飞马奔出东门，逃得无影无踪了。

A story from *Three Kingdoms.* Toward the end of the Eastern Han Dynasty (25-220), state power fell into Dong Zhuo's hand, a very cruel and manipulating person. Yuan Shao, the leader of an opposition force, led a punitive expedition to Luoyang, the capital. Dong Zhuo sent a very battlewise general named Hua Xiong to meet the expedition army. Hua killed several generals in run from Yuan Shao's side. Guan Yu volunteered to meet Hua Xiong, saying if he failed to kill him he would kill himself. At this, Cao Cao, in admiration, poured a cup of heated wine for Guan Yu for encouragement. But Guan said, "Keep the cup here until I come back." When Guan Yu returned with Hua Xiong's head, the wine in the cup was still warm. Dong Zhuo was alarmed at the news that his brave general Hua Xiong had been killed.

He dispatched Lü Bu with 150,000 troops to guard the Hulao Pass outside the capital. Yuan Shao sent eight armies to attack. When the two sides met, no generals from Yuan Shao's side seemed able to withstand Lü Bu; several generals had been killed by him. Zhang Fei charged Lü Bu, but after fifty rounds of fierce combats he still did not succeed. At the sight of his sworn brother Zhang Fei unable to gain an upper hand, Guan Yu lifted his crescent-moon shaped sword to join the battle. After thirty more rounds, their elder sworn brother, Liu Bei unsheathed his sword and charged up too. The three brothers closed in. This proved too much for Lü Bu, who feigned a lance attack and while one of the three dodged, ran back to Hulao Pass for his dear life.

《三国演义》中的故事。　东汉末年，董卓把持朝政，凶狠专横。各诸侯，举袁绍为盟主，带各路兵马杀向洛阳，讨伐董贼。董卓派华雄迎战，连杀数将。关羽立下军令状，愿去斩华雄的首级。曹操佩服关羽，敬一杯热酒，关羽说："酒先放在这里，我去战罢再喝。"说完，拍马出阵。当关羽提华雄人头进帐时，那杯酒还微微烫手。董卓听说华雄被杀，派吕布领十五万兵驻守洛阳城外的虎牢关。袁绍派八路大军前去攻打。虎牢关下吕布连杀数位将领。这时，张飞冲杀上去，连战五十回合。关羽见张飞胜不了吕布，便舞动青龙偃月宝刀前去助战。三匹战马，丁字摆开，厮杀三十回合，仍胜不了吕布。刘备见状，掣宝剑，骑黄鬃马斜刺过来，三个人把吕布围在当中，走马灯般的轮流厮杀，吕布毕竟难敌三人，渐渐觉得难以招架，便朝刘备虚晃一戟，拍马冲出了包围圈逃回虎牢关。

This story describes two characters from *Journey to the West*. Inside the Country of Aolai, east of the ocean belonging to the Continent of Superior Body, there was the Mountain of Flowers and Fruit. On its peak stood a magic stone. Through years of cultivation the stone turned into a stone monkey. After it learned how to crawl and walk it bowed to each of the four quarters. As its eyes moved, two beams of golden light shot towards the heavens. The Jade Emperor was alarmed. He hurriedly sent two subjects, Thousand-mile Eye and Wind-accompanying Ear outside the Southern Gate to listen and observe. The two went out of the gate and soon reported back what they had observed. "Creatures down below are born of the essence of heaven and earth," remarked the Jade Emperor, now assured. "There's nothing remarkable about him." Later, many things happened because of this monkey: it raised havoc in the heavens, and was subdued and asked to assist Tang Priest to fetch scriptures from the Western Heaven.

This scene shows how Thousand-mile Eye and Wind-accompanying Ear observe and listen carefully outside the Southern Gate.

千里眼和顺风耳是《西游记》中的两个人物。东胜神洲的傲来国中,有一座山,叫花果山。山顶有一块仙石,日久天长化作一个石猴。石猴学走学爬,拜了四方,从眼内发出两道金光,直射到天庭,惊动了玉皇大帝。玉皇大帝即命千里眼、顺风耳开南天门观看。二将奉玉皇旨意出南天门。千里眼手搭凉棚,仔细观看,顺风耳伏耳细听,很快查明了情况,向玉帝汇报。玉皇大帝说:"原来是下方之物,他乃天地精华所生,没有什么可奇怪的。"由此,才引出了孙悟空大闹天空,以致后来收服悟空,让他帮助唐僧去西天取经的故事。此幅画,是千里眼和顺风耳出南天门后,按住云头,仔细观听的场面。

This is a story from *A Dream of Red Mansions.* As Jia Baoyu, Xue Baoqin, Xing Youyan and Ping'er had birthdays on the same day, the young ladies held a hilarious drinking party in the hall of the peony garden for them. When it was Xiangyun's turn to compose a verse amid a drinking game, she made fun of the service maids by saying, holding a duck head in hand, "This *ya tou* (referring to the duck head in hand) is not that *ya tou* (referring to the service maids around, as both are homophones in Chinese), for this *ya tou* has applied no hair oil...." Everybody roared with laughter. Some service maids protested, laughing, "You made fun of us, so you have to drink another cup. Let's pour a full cup for her...." As the party went on drinkers' games continued with ceaseless laughter and people suddenly noticed that Xiangyun had disappeared. While they looked this way and that, a service maid rushed in laughing, "Young ladies. Hurry to have a look at the Lady Xiangyun. She's sleeping on the stone bench over there." The group tiptoed over, and sure enough, saw Xiangyun sleeping soundly. Fallen flowers scattered on her body, her hair and her face. Her fan had dropped on the ground aside. Bees danced in the air around her. Under her head was a make-shift pillow of peony flowers wrapped with her handkerchief. Amid laughter service girls gently woke her up and helped her—she was still mumbling something drunkenly—get inside the room.

《红楼梦》中的故事。　贾宝玉、薛宝琴、邢岫烟、平儿四人同一天过生日。众小姐带上自己的丫头们借机在芍药栏中红香圃三间小敞厅内饮酒行令，一时敞厅内热闹非凡。轮到湘云说酒令时，她想拿丫头们取笑，她喝了一口酒，夹了一个鸭头，举起来说："这鸭头不是那丫头，头上没有桂花油。"众人笑了起来，惹得晴雯等一帮丫头说："云姑娘拿我们开心，快罚她喝酒。"大家都来敬酒，一时猜拳行令，呼三喝四，过了一会，大家突然发现湘云不见了，便各处去找。不一会，一个小丫头笑嘻嘻跑来说："姑娘们，快去看看，云姑娘吃醉了，在山石后面石凳上睡着了。"众人听后，便轻轻走过去，果然看到湘云在石凳上已入梦乡，四面的芍药花飞落了一身，满身满头都是花瓣。扇子落在地上，也被花瓣埋了一半。一群蜜蜂蝴蝶在她周围飞舞。湘云枕着用手帕包着花瓣的枕头。众人看了又是爱，又是笑，忙上来搀扶。湘云仍酒醉不醒，还嘟嘟噜噜地说着，众人笑着推醒她，拥着湘云回屋里去了。

This is a story in *Strange Tales from Make-Do Studio* about "Drunken Tao," a unique species in the chrysanthemum family. The Ma family was a scholars family and a family of chrysanthemum lovers. In this story, the lord of the present generation, Ma Zicai, was more fanantical about the plant than those of previous generations. On hearing of a unique species available in Jinling City, he rushed there and bought two. On his way back he saw a handsome young man on a horse behind a canopied cart. He was surnamed Tao and the girl inside the cart was his sister Huangying. They were moving away from Jinling and looking for a new place to live. At Ma's invitation, the two settled down in the south court-yard of the Ma residence. The girl often picked up the withered plants Ma discarded and would replant them in front of her room. The next day these withered plants would bloom splendidly and fragrantly. Before long, Huanying's flowers became known in the area and many people came to buy them.

Before long Ma's wife died of illness and Ma married the flower-loving Huangying. Every day Ma drank and played chess with her brother beside chrysanthemum flowers. One day, after getting drunk, the young man tripped and fell. Ma couldn't believe his eyes when the young man fell and turned in a huge, man-sized chrysanthemum plant. He ran to report to his wife, who rushed out and plucked a flower that she kept inside her dress. By dawn, Ma saw the young man again, lying on the ground fast asleep. He realized that the brother and sister were both chrysanthemum spirits.

But the second time the brother turned into a plant after getting drunk, the young man failed to change back to human form. His sister reserved a length of root from the plant. Before long, a unique species sprouted, grew up and bloomed with a smell of wine aroma. Later generations called this species "Drunken Tao."

《聊斋志异》中的故事。 有一种菊花叫"醉陶",此花名流传着一个故事。从前,有一家姓马的,历代爱菊。到了马子才这一代,更有过于前辈。一次,子才在金陵买了两株菊花佳品。回家路上遇到一位英俊少年,骑驴紧跟着一车前行。少年自称姓陶,车内坐的是姐姐黄英。因姐姐住不惯金陵,想移居他地。于是,在子才的邀请下,姐弟俩住进了马家南院。陶家姐弟经常把子才扔掉的残谢菊花种到自己住的南院。今日种下,隔日开花,姿色绝美,香气袭人。从此,前来买花者不断。不久,马

子才的妻子病死,娶黄英为妻。陶弟天天和子才在菊圃下棋饮酒。一日,陶弟喝醉,在回屋时,不小心被菊花绊倒,即化为一株菊花。子才急忙告诉黄英,黄英急出,拔菊放入衣下,待天亮时,见陶弟在地上酣睡。子才这才知道黄英和陶弟都是菊仙。一日,陶弟又醉酒,倒地化菊再未能转回。黄英说我弟弟没命了,立即掐一段根,回屋精心护植,不久开花,飘出浓烈的酒香。后来,人们把这种菊花叫"醉陶"。

"Lord Jiang angles for the fish only those that are willing are caught." This proverb comes from a story in history. Towards the end of the Shang Dynasty (about 11th century B.C.), a recluse by the name of Jiang Ziya believed he was talented and able to be a great success in his career. Every day he angled for fish by the Weishui River, actually awaiting a chance to meet a wise ruler. The way he fished was strange—he used a straight hook without bait, with the line hovering a meter above the water surface. This eccentricity had aroused many laughters, but Jiang minded not. "My catch will not be fish," he said, "but a wise ruler." Later, King Wen of Zhou planned to sent a punitive expedition army against the King Zhou of Shang Dynasty and needed capable men. Through recommendation, he met Jiang and made him prime minister. Though eighty years old already, Jiang didn't let down expectations and assisted King Wen to overthrow the rule of Shang and establish the Zhou Dynasty.

　　"姜太公钓鱼,愿者上钩"这句成语出自古代一个故事。商朝末期(公元前11世纪),有一名隐士叫姜子牙,他深信自己很有才干,并能干一番事业,便每天在渭水河边垂钓,等待圣贤的君主来赏识他。姜太公钓鱼用直钩,无鱼饵,而且钩离水面三尺多高,故此常常被别人取笑。而姜太公却说:"我名为垂钓,意不在鱼而在圣君。"后来,周文王伐纣迫切需要人才,经人推荐,得知渭水河畔的姜子牙很有才干,拜他为相。年已古稀的姜子牙不负众望,果然辅佐周文王之子周武王消灭了商纣,建立了周朝。

Lord Jiang Angles for Fish　姜太公钓鱼

This story is about Ruan Ji, Ji Kang, Ruan Xian, Shan Tao, Xiang Xiu, Wang Rong and Liu Ling, the seven outstanding literary men at the turn of the Wei and Jin dynasties. Dissatisfied with society, they often met to play chess, musical instruments and drink.

Ruan Ji, a literary man of Wei and once a holder of a high office, asserted the alliance of nature and the Confucian ethical code. He was quite fond of drink, and often used it as an escape from pending political trouble. Ji Kang was also a Wei literary man and once held an office too. He had a profound and wide range of knowledge, and had a great respect for Laozi's path of self-cultivation. An expert in musical instruments, chess, calligraphy and painting, though, he had a strong objections to Confucian doctrines. Ruan Xian, the nephew of Ruan Ji and thus called Ruan the Junior, was also famous for his literary talent. Once an official, he was a master in music knowledge and a good *pipa* player. Unlike others, Shan Tao during the Western Jin period failed to quit his office though he had tried several times. Xiang Xiu, a metaphysician of the Western Jin period, served in different offices successively. Wang Rong was a minister of the Western Jin and had successively held many offices. He owned many excellent farming fields back home but was still unsatisfied. Liu Ling was a famous literary man at the turn of Wei and Jin, and was once an official too. His philosophy was to abandon the Confucian ethical code and return to nature. He often went out for fun drinking, traveling. As these seven shared many common values and interests, they often withdrew to a secluded place to sing and play music and drink to their heart's content. Their names have come into history as the Seven Sages of the Bamboo Grove.

She used all her strength trying to tear the handkerchiefs but she was too weak to do it. Then she asked Xueyan to light the fire basin at once. Zijuan and Xueyan thought she felt cold and hurriedly moved the fire basin to her. Before they noticed, she had already thrown the handkerchiefs and poem notebooks into the fire and burned them into ashes. Completely cutting off her devoted love for years, she left the world with hatred against feudal society.

Note: Xueyan and Zijuan were Daiyu's two maids.

竹林七贤指的是魏末晋初(公元三世纪)的阮籍、稽康、阮咸、山涛、向秀、王戎、刘伶七位文坛上的优秀人物。他们都不满意当时的社会,经常聚在一起下棋、抚琴、饮酒。

阮籍,魏国文学家,曾受封过关内侯之职。他主张把"自然"和封建名教相结合,嗜酒如命。经常以纵酒佯狂避祸。稽康,魏国文学家,曾官至中散大夫。他博学多才,很喜欢老子的气养之术,琴棋书画无所不能,他反对儒家繁琐的礼教。阮咸,魏晋名士,阮籍之侄,和阮籍有大阮小阮之称,官任散骑侍郎。他精通音律,善长弹琵琶。山涛,西晋名士,曾任冀州刺史、吏部尚书,多次辞官,都没批准。向秀,西晋玄学名士,曾任黄门侍郎、散骑常侍等职。王戎,西晋大臣,仕途通畅,曾作过中书令、光禄大夫、尚书左仆射、司徒等,家中广置四方良田,仍不满足。刘伶,魏晋名士,曾任过建威参军之职。提倡放弃名教,返朴归真。常乘鹿车,提酒壶外出游玩。他们七位,志同道合,情趣相仿。经常在僻静的竹林一起高谈阔论、弹琴作歌,肆意酗酒,以酒消愁,被世人称为"竹林七贤"。

This is a story from *Three Kingdoms*. The manipulation of state affairs by the prime minister Dong Zhuo towards the end of the Eastern Han Dynasty (25-220) aroused strong anger in people, but nobody dared to air it. Upright ministers wanted to but failed to think of a way to get rid of him. Deep at night and alone in his garden, Wang Yun, a minister, sighed at these worries, his tearful eyes cast up at the moon. Suddenly, he heard a sigh from the pavilion nearby. He went over to see Diao Chan, the sixteen-year-old, very beautiful singsong girl in his family. Upon enquiry, the girl went down on her knees and said, "Your excellency has treated me so nice after I came. How could I repay your kindness? I have noticed your knitted eyebrows. You must have big worries that I dare not ask. I sighed, because I wish I could help you·in some way."

Who could believe, thought Wang, that the destiny of the Han Dynasty lies in this girl's hand. He helped the girl up, then he himself prostrated and kowtowed to her. "Why do you bow to me?" the puzzled girl asked. She repeated her offer to help in any way.

Convinced of her resolute attitude, Wang Yun was straightforward: "Both Dong Zhuo and his stepson Lü Bu love women. I'll take you as my step daughter, then I'll betroth you to Lü Bu before I present you as a gift to Dong Zhuo. You will seek opportunities to sow discord between them and make Lü kill Dong. In this way we can preserve the Han Dynasty." "If I fail to do as you say," she vowed, "I will die a violent death." These were the interlocking stratagems laid by Wang Yun and Diao Chan.

《三国演义》中的故事。　东汉末年，太师董卓专权，朝野上下敢怒不敢言。正直的大臣们都想除掉他，但又苦于无好计可施。司徒王允，深夜独自到花园，望着天空一轮明月，心想着国家大事，不觉悄然泪下，他忽然听见牡丹亭处有人长叹，走过去一看，原来是家中十六岁的美丽歌女貂蝉。问她为何长叹，貂蝉跪道："我自入府，大人待我恩重如山，我不知如何报答才好。最近见大人总是愁眉不展，一定是有难办的大事，但又不敢问，故而长叹，如果我能与大人分忧就好了。"王允一听，猛然醒悟说："没想到汉朝天下，竟在一个女子手中啊！"他把貂蝉领到亭内，跪在地上给貂蝉叩头。貂蝉忙问："大人，你这是干什么？有用我之处，尽管吩咐。"王允见貂蝉十分坚决，就说："董卓和吕布都是好色之徒。我收你为义女，先把你许给吕布为妻，然后再献给董卓为妾，你在他们二人之间周旋，见机行事，挑拨离间。设法让吕布杀掉董卓，以保住汉朝江山。"貂蝉听后，满口答应，并发誓说："如果我不按大人说的去做，不报大义，我当被乱刀砍死！"这就是王允和貂蝉共同定下的连环计，最后除掉了董卓。

This story refers to Su Shi, Qin Guan and Xie Duanqing of the Song Dynasty (960-1127). All of the three had outstanding literary talents and were very knowledgeable in history and excellent in classical learnings. They often met to drink and compose verses. On most of these occasions, prompted by Su and Qin, Xie would drink too much while the other two were still sober.

Xie had met Su when he first time came to sit for the imperial examinations. Since then, Su often invited him over for drinking and poetry parties. That year, after a severe draught, the emperor ordered that an altar to pray for rain be set up and had Su write a prose piece to be chanted on the ceremony. Longing for a chance to see the emperor, Xie pestered Su to bring him along. That day, dressed in his priest robes, Xie and other priests waited in front of the hall. After the ceremony was over, at the order to present tea, Xie sent a cup of tea in. The emperor had a sudden fancy for this pleasant-looking priest. He asked Xie a few casual questions, to which Xie answered in a fluent and pleasant manner, "I came from Jiangxi, your majesty. It is my greatest honor to meet you." Delighted at the answer, the emperor gave him a Buddhist name on the spot—*Fo Yin* (meaning Buddhist mark). Since then, Xie indeed walked into the gate of Buddhism and became a monk. Su felt guilty. Each time they met, Su would plead in vain that Xie return to secular life.

宋代(公元 960－1127 年)大文豪苏轼(苏东坡)、秦观(秦少游)、佛印(谢端卿)三人,名噪文坛,被誉为"文人三才"。这三位文人,博经通史,文辞盖世。三人常在一起饮酒作诗。但经常是苏轼、秦观二人合伙把佛印灌醉。佛印学识渊博文才出众,当他来京赶考时,苏轼经常约他饮酒作诗。这一年天旱,皇帝要设坛求雨,让苏东坡写祈天祭文代官主斋。佛印得知后很想借机一睹龙颜,请求苏轼无论如何设法带他进去。祈雨那天,苏东坡让他身披袈裟,假装添香剪烛和其它小僧一起来到殿前。皇帝来后,斋仪完毕。佛印听叫献茶的声音后,捧茶来到皇帝眼前。皇帝看这小僧生得方面大耳,眉清目秀,便问他家住哪里,来寺里几年了。这一突如其来的问话,使佛印一点思想准备都没有。只得随口道是江西人,新来寺里,今天有幸见到皇上,不胜欣幸。皇帝见他口齿伶俐,非常高兴,当即赐法名了原,号佛印,从此真出了家。苏东坡总认为是自己连累了他,每次饮酒时总劝他还俗,但佛印心如磐石。

Xiang Ling in Grass Game　香菱斗草

This is a story from *A Dream of Red Mansions*. On Baoyu's birthday the young ladies held a drinking party in which they composed poems and had much fun. Their service maids started a game of their own. Xiang Ling, Xue Fan's concubine, collected some flowers and grass and began a grass game with the others. "This one is bodhisatva willow," one said. And another one would say, "I have arhat pine." Suddenly, Dou Guan said she had a sisters flower. While the rest of them failed to find a matching term, Xiang Ling said, "I have a husband-and-wife flower." "Never heard of that," the previous girl protested. "Why," Xiang Ling explained. "One flower on a stem is called *lan*, and several flowers on a stem make *hui*. Two on one stem , one up and one down, is a brother flower, and two flowers side by side is certainly a spouses one." The other girl, however, did not easily give up. Laughing, she challenged, "Well, then if one flower is big and the other one small, then it's a father and son flower; and if two flowers face different ways it's probably an enemies flower. Is that right? Xue Fan is gone for over half a year. I guess because you miss him you made up that husband and wife flower." Blushed, Xiang Ling rushed up meaning to pinch the sharp-tongued girl, who laughed and begged for the other's help. At the sight of the girls' laughing, poking and punching each other in a friendly manner, Baoyu came to join their excitement with grass in hand.

《红楼梦》中的故事。　宝玉生日那天，众姐妹们忙忙碌碌地安席饮酒作诗。各屋的丫头也随主子取乐，薛蟠的妾香菱和几个丫头各采了些花草，斗草取乐。这个说，我有观音柳；那个说我有罗汉松。突然豆官说，我有姐妹花，这下把大家难住了，香菱说，我有夫妻蕙。豆官见香菱答上了不服气地说："从来没有什么夫妻蕙!"香菱争辩道："一枝一个花叫'兰'，一枝几个花叫'蕙'。上下结花为'兄弟蕙'，并头结花叫'夫妻蕙'，我这个是并头结花，怎么不叫'夫妻蕙'呢?"豆官一时被问住，便笑着说："依你说，一大一小叫'老子儿子蕙'，若两朵花背着开可叫'仇人蕙'了。薛蟠刚外出半年，你心里想他，把花儿草儿拉扯成夫妻蕙了，真不害臊!"说的香菱满脸通红，笑着跑过来拧豆官的嘴，于是两个人扭滚在地上。众丫环嘻戏打闹，非常开心。这时，宝玉也采了些草来凑热闹。

This is a story from *Strange Tales from Make-Do Studio*. Old man Gan had two sons. He died when the second was only five. After his death, the parrot he had kept flew away. The second son grew up into a very handsome young man. His brother and sister-in-law decided to choose a suitable girl for him. One day, the second son met a very beautiful girl in the fields. Looking around to make sure that nobody was about, the girl said in a low voice, "Your father betrothed us when he was alive. Why are your brother and sister-in-law looking for somebody else?" Having never heard of this, the second brother rushed back to tell his elder brother, who was ignorant of this too. Several days later the elder brother met a tearful, beautiful girl on his way. On inquiring, the girl said, "My name is A'ying and I was betrothed to the second son of the Gans and now they want to break off the betrothal." The elder brother hurriedly dismounted and said, "I'm the elder son of the Gans. I really didn't know my father had betrothed my brother to you. Please come with me to my home." When they met at home, the

second brother saw that she was the girl he had met in fields. So, the two married. One year, on the Mid-autumn Festival, the sister-in-law sent for A'ying. Despite repeated prompts by her husband A'ying didn't go. The next day, the sister-in-law came asking why A'ying had become so sad the previous night. By then, the second brother realized his wife had magic power. Also, he believed she was not a human being, so he told her to leave. "Yes," A'ying explained. "I'm not a human being. I'm a parrot, your father's parrot. Your father betrothed me to you when you were very young. As I can't bear you children,... I have long wanted to leave. I was only held back by the kindness you have shown to me. Now I'm leaving. Take good care of yourself." So saying, she turned into a parrot and flew away.

When old man Gan was alive, he had often joked to his second son, "When the parrot grows up you take her as your wife." And when he wanted the boy to feed the bird he would say, "Go and feed your wife." The bird had come to fulfil his wish.

《聊斋志异》中的故事。 甘翁膝下二子。大儿叫甘玉，二子名甘珏。甘珏五岁那年甘翁谢世，他生前最喜爱的一只鹦鹉也随之飞走。甘珏长大后，风姿秀美，哥嫂一心要为他选一美貌姑娘为妻。一天，甘珏在郊外遇到一绝色女子，少女四顾无人，便低声对甘珏说："你家令尊，为我俩订下婚约，你哥嫂为什么还四处为你说亲？"甘珏说不知道订婚一事。回家后问哥嫂，都说不知道。隔了几日，甘珏骑马外出，途中见一美丽女子垂泪，便上前问话，女子说："我叫阿英，曾许甘家二郎，现在甘家想赖婚。"甘玉听后，急忙下马说："我是甘家大郎，先人许婚，实在不知，快请到家里。"到家后才知，这就是甘珏遇到的那女子。

于是，二人成婚。一年中秋，嫂嫂派人来请阿英，丈夫催促阿英快去，但阿英始终没动身。第二天，嫂嫂来问，昨晚见阿英，不知为什么不高兴。甘珏大吃一惊，这才知阿英有分身术，怀疑她是妖怪，请她离去。阿英说："我本不是人，是你令尊给我订的婚约，我不能生育早想走，但你们对我太好，我不忍心离去，今天告辞，望多保重。"说完变作一只鹦鹉飞去。全家人这才醒悟，甘翁在世时，曾对甘珏开玩笑说："鹦鹉长大给你作媳妇。"还经常对甘珏说："快喂喂你媳妇。"仙鸟不悔前盟，变少女嫁给甘珏。

Following the interlocking stratagems they had laid, Wang Yun betrothed his step daughter Diao Chan to Lü Bu, then, to sow discord between the two, presented the girl to Dong Zhou as a concubine. Lü Bu was furious, and each time he met Diao Chan, the latter feigned a sad tearful look. One day, while Dong Zhuo was in court, Lü Bu rushed back to Dong Zhuo's residence to see the girl. In the Fengyi Pavilion the girl said to him with a desperate look, "I have prolonged my life in disgrace simply so I could have a final meeting with you and let you know my feelings. I should have waited upon you but unfortunately Dong Zhuo took me by force. We can only meet in the next life...." So saying she meant to throw herself into the lotus pool. Lü Bu hurriedly held her back and swore, "How can I be a man if I fail to marry you?"

Suddenly aware of Lü Bu's absence, Dong Zhuo, suspicious, rushed back to his residence to see Diao Chan was nowhere. The service maids told him the girl and Lü Bu were in the back garden. Dong Zhuo rushed there and at the sight of the two, roared with anger. Lü Bu fled. When Dong Zhuo got back to his bedroom he saw Diao Chan's face was tearful. Being demanded for an answer, the girl said, "I was enjoying flowers in the back garden when Lü Bu stole in to take my liberty. I tried to escape but he drove me to the pavilion with his lance...." Before long the interlocking stratagems worked out—Dong Zhuo was killed by Lü Bu.

《三国演义》中的故事。 按着王允和貂蝉商定的"连环计",王允先把貂蝉收为义女许给吕布为妻。为挑拨董卓与吕布的关系,后来又把貂蝉送给董卓为妾。吕布见貂蝉被董卓霸占,心中愤愤不平。貂蝉在吕布面前也假意伤心落泪。一日,董卓上朝议事,吕布忙跑回相府来会貂蝉,二人来到凤仪亭,貂蝉凄凄切切地说:"我忍辱偷生是为了见将军一面,表白我的心意,我本应该服侍将军,现在却被董卓霸占,今日见面,我心意已了,今生不能作夫妻,再等来世吧!"说完纵身要往荷花池跳。

吕布上前抱住说:"我今生不娶你,绝非英雄!"董卓在殿上正议事,回头不见吕布,心中疑惑,急忙回府。进后堂找不到貂蝉,问丫环才知貂蝉、吕布在后花园。董卓急赶到后花园,向二人大吼一声,吕布转身就跑。董卓回到卧室,见貂蝉哭得泪人一般,责问貂蝉说:"你为什么私通吕布!"貂蝉哭诉道:"我在后花园看花,吕布进来调戏我,我急忙躲开,他提画戟把我赶到凤仪亭……,"后来,董卓找吕布追问貂蝉被调戏之事,吕布反目刺死了董卓。

This is a story from *The Generals of the Yang Family*. Because of Yang's family tradition, Yang Paifeng, a vigorous kitchen maid, had also developed into a martial art expert. One year, troops from the Xixia State invaded the central plain areas. Mu Guiying, the daughter-in-law of the Yang family was recommended by the old minister Kou Zhun to the Song emperor to lead the army in resistance against the Xixia troops. Yang Paifeng was made the vanguard. The arrogant Yin Qi, the Xixia general, planned an ambush with large amount of troops in the hope to wipe out the Song army. But Mu Guiying, a very experienced general, saw through the trick. She turned Yin's trick against him by devising an ambush of her own in the nearby forests while she sent a small number of troops to challenge the Xixia army. When the two sides met, the Song troops feigned retreat, luring Yin Qi and his main force into hot pursuit, only to be caught off guard when Yang Paifeng and her troops appeared from the forest. At a frightening roar from the girl, the Xixia general almost fell off his horse. After a dozen or more rounds of combat, Yin Qi proved no match for the girl. He hastily fled all the way back to his state, with what was left of his army.

Note: Xixia is a regional state established by the Dang Xiang people between 1038-1227 in present day Ningxia areas.

《杨家将》中的故事。 杨府的烧火丫头杨排风性格泼辣, 受杨家的熏陶, 同男孩子一样爱弄枪舞棒, 并练就了一身好武艺。有一年, 西夏国元帅殷奇率兵侵犯中原, 老臣寇准保举杨家女将穆桂英挂帅出征。穆桂英命杨排风为先行, 日夜兼程, 赶往边关。殷奇目中无人, 见穆桂英带领的全是女将, 便调来大批人马, 设下重重埋伏, 想使杨家将全军覆灭。其实, 他布的阵, 早被久经沙场的穆桂英看破。穆桂英将计就计, 让杨排风埋伏在密林之中, 然后派人叫阵, 把敌人主力引出后便佯装败走。殷奇信以为真, 拍马猛追。这时, 杨排风猛然从密林中跃出, 拦住去路, 大喝一声说:"西征将军杨排风在此, 殷寇快快下马投降吧!"话落枪到, 殷奇受惊, 差点落下马来。双方战十余回合, 殷奇力尽臂乏, 落荒而逃, 带领残兵败退西夏国。

注:西夏国, (公元 1038 – 1227 年)党项羌所建, 位于今宁夏一带。

Love Renewed by the Dilapidated Bridge 断桥解冤

This is a story from *Tale of the White Snake*. Xu Xian and Lady Bai, after getting married, brought Xiao Qing to Zhenjiang where they settled down and opened a Chinese medical herb business. That year, the city was plagued by a seasonal febrile disease. Instead of going to the Monk Fahai's temple to pray before Buddha's statue and burn joss sticks, people went for Xu Xian's medicine with which they soon recovered. The old monk Fahai, out of jealousy, burned with hatred against Lady Bai. Monk Fahai had been in his previous life a giant turtle in the Western Heaven. With three treasure items that he stole from the Buddha, he came to the human world and settled down in Jinshan Temple. He loved the beautiful scenes around. He had spread this febrile disease to strike awe into people's minds so that they would favor him. Now seeing his scheme foiled by Lady Bai, and realizing the girl was a snake spirit from the Mount Emei, he made

a vicious scheme: he lured Xu Xian to his temple on the fifteenth of the seventh month, where he told Xu of his wife's true identity—a snake spirit. Scared, Xu Xian fell into his trap and agreed to stay in the temple. After a long and vain wait for her husband to return, and realizing what was happening, Lady Bai and Xiao Qing came to the temple for Xu Xian, but the two girls were no match for the old monk. After a fierce fight they retreated in defeat. By the West Lake they wept bitterly, and faulted Xu Xian for his fickleness. Xu Xian had seen how his wife and Xiao Qing fought with the monk for his sake. The little monk who had watched him, moved by the scene, released Xu Xian. When he met his wife by the Dilapidated Bridge, the angry Xiao Qing meant to kill him, only to be stopped by Lady Bai, whose heart softened at Xu Xian's self accusation and the memory of their past happy matrimonial life.

《白蛇传》中的故事。白娘子与许仙结婚后，带着小青一块来到镇江，开了一家药店。正赶上这一年镇江城内闹瘟疫，人们纷纷到白娘子的药店里看病抓药，而不是去寺庙烧香拜佛，病势很快得到了控制。这下可把老和尚法海气坏了，于是他千方百计地迫害白娘子。法海和尚原本是西天的一只大龟，偷了如来的金钵、袈裟和青龙禅杖三件宝贝来到人间，他看到金山寺山青水秀就住下来了。为了让这里百姓信服自己，他散布了这场瘟疫，没想到让白娘子破坏了自己的计划。后来，法海认出白娘子是峨嵋山上一蛇仙，便设下一条毒计，悄悄约许仙七

月十五到金山寺烧香。在金山寺里，法海告诉许仙，白娘子是蛇妖，许仙听了很害怕，便同意藏在寺内。白娘子见丈夫不回家，知道许仙信了法海的谗言，便和小青去寻找。因白娘子身怀有孕体力不支，在和法海激烈的较量中败下阵来，她们回到西湖边上，边哭边骂许仙。金山寺内的小和尚被白娘子对爱情忠贞不渝所感动，便偷偷放了许仙。许仙在断桥亭与白娘子相遇，小青要杀这个负心汉。许仙百般认错，善良的白娘子怀念以往夫妻恩情，劝小青饶了许仙。

This is a story from *Three Kingdoms*. At Cao Cao's instruction, Liu Bei was about to set off for a punitive expedition against Yuan Shu. Before he left, Liu Bei worried about the defence of Xuzhou City. When Zhang Fei volunteered to take the task, Liu said, "How can I feel assured, when you're so fond of drinking and after drinking you always flog your soldiers for no reason? And you're such a hot-tempered person and frequently you refuse to take advice." He entrusted the task upon Zhang only after the latter's repeated entreatments and resolutions to mend his ways. For safety, he left consultant Chen Deng to assist Zhang. One day Zhang invited his subordinate officers over. "My elder brother instructed me before he left to stay away from wine for fear I may fail my duties to guard the city. Let's have an final

drinking party today, and starting from tomorrow, we will quit drinking and concentrate on the job." With these words said, he began toasting everyone. When neither of his toasts was accepted by Cao Bao, Zhang flared up. By then, Zhang was already drunk. He had Cao flogged fifty times. After the party was over, the resentful Cao sent one of his men to Lü Bu, the enemy general, asking him to attack the city that night while Zhang was drunk. Lü came with 500 horsemen. They successfully took the city. When Zhang woke up with a start, the city was gone. He fought his way out of the enemy troops and fled the city, leaving his elder brother's family behind. When he met Liu, he felt so shame-faced that he unsheathed his sword meaning to commit suicide, only to be stopped by his elder brother.

《三国演义》中的故事。　曹操命刘备伐袁术，刘备临行时为由谁留守徐州拿不定主意。这时，张飞请求留守徐州。刘备却说："你一是爱喝酒、耍威风、鞭打士兵，二是办事草率不听人劝。让你留守，放心不下。"张飞愿改过并再三请求，刘备答应张飞，并派陈登协助。一日，张飞请留守各将赴宴，说："我大哥临走时不让我喝酒，怕酒后误事，今天请你们来一醉方休，从明天起全都戒酒，帮我守好城池。"说罢便轮番敬酒，当二次到曹

豹面前劝酒时，遭曹豹拒绝。这时张飞已醉，命鞭打曹豹五十鞭。散席后，曹豹怀恨在心，便连夜派人送信给吕布，让他今夜乘张飞大醉偷袭徐州。

吕布当夜领五百轻骑取得徐州。呐喊声震醒张飞，知徐州已失，顾不得刘备的家眷，边战边逃。后张飞见到刘备，悔恨万分，欲抽剑自刎，被刘备死死拦住。

Qing Wen Mends the Cloak　晴雯补裘

This is a story from *A Dream of Red Mansions*. As Xi Ren, the leading service girl who had taken care of Baoyu was away to visit her home, the duties, and the charge of Yihongyuan Court, fell on Qing Wen. A girl anxious to excel in everything, Qing Wen did everything personally. For the special occasion of his uncle's birthday party, Baoyu put on a very unique Russian-made cloak woven with threads from peacock feather, a gift from his grandmother. That evening, he returned with a sad look: the cloak had a hole burnt in it. Fortunately it was evening and the grandmother and the ladies in the house failed to notice. One servant hurriedly brought the cloak out to professionals to be mended over night, for Baoyu had to wear the cloak the next morning. But the servant returned to report that no craftsman dared to take the job, as none of them was able to identify what material the cloak was made of. While everyone was upset, Qing Wen managed to sit up from her sick bed, and after a look she claimed the material was peacock gold thread. "Mending with our similar peacock gold threads," she said, "the cloak will look as good as new." Even with the proper thread, no one dared to take the job. Therefore, Qing Wen, with a coat draped over her shoulders, began to mend. Due to sickness, she felt dizzy and saw stars. She bit her lips and continued. She had to stop for a break every few stitches. It was in the small hours of the morning when she finally finished the job. People marveled at the mending she had done—the damage was almost invisible.

《红楼梦》中的故事。　宝玉的大丫头袭人回娘家，怡红院诸事交丫环晴雯料理。晴雯事事要强，带重病操持宝玉的一切。宝玉为舅舅过生日，特穿上贾母送他的一件俄罗斯人用孔雀毛线织成的毛氅去赴宴。但晚上回来后，只见宝玉唉声叹气，一问才知毛氅烧了一个洞，幸好天黑，贾母和太太们都没有看到。丫头连夜叫嬷嬷拿出去补，让天亮前补好，因为明天还得穿。嬷嬷们去了半天回来说："工匠们不认识这是什么，不敢揽这活。"大家都很着急。因病卧床的晴雯，听说此事，忙硬挺着身子坐起来，拿过来一瞧说："这是孔雀金线，咱们用孔雀金线织密点，就能混过去。"虽有孔雀金线，大家都说不会织。晴雯只好披衣，但因身子虚，刚要动手，觉得头重脚轻，眼前冒金星，又怕宝玉着急，只得咬牙拼命撑着，缝几针，歇一会，一直到后半夜才补完。大家拿过来一看，简直和原来的一模一样。

This is a story from *Three Kingdoms*. Yuan Shu sent 100 thousand troops, led by General Ji Ling, to attack Liu Bei. For fear of Lü Bu in Xuzhou who might lend Liu a hand, Yuan wrote Lü a letter, together with many food supplies as gifts, asking him not to help Liu. Liu, on the other hand, wrote Lü a letter asking for assistance. "If I remain an onlooker with folded arms," thought Lü, "I will be in danger after Yuan defeats Liu. But if I help Liu, Yuan will be resentful to me." So Lü invited both Liu Bei and Ji Ling to a banquet.

Lü sat between Liu and Ji at the banquet. After a few rounds of toasts Lü began, "Please grant me a favor by stopping the fight." When Ji Ling refused, Lü shouted for his long lance to be brought over. Both Liu and Ji got a fright. "I'll stand my lance 150 steps away outside the gate. If my arrow hits its edge you two will stop your fight. And if I miss the target you have your own way." Ji secretly hoped that he would miss the target, while Liu crossed his fingers wished Lü succees. Lü had wine brought up to him. After each one had a cup Lü arched his bow, aimed and shot with a big shout. The arrow flew like lightening toward the target, and hit right on the edge of the lance. A big applause rose from everybody around. Lü dropped his bow and laughed, saying, "You see, even the heavens wish that you stop fighting." With his excellent archery, Lü averted a fight between the two sides.

《三国演义》中的故事。　袁绍之弟袁术派大将纪灵率领十万大军攻打刘备。袁术担心在徐州的吕布救援刘备，派人给吕布送去粮草和密信，要吕布按兵不动。刘备考虑到自己兵力不足，也写信求助吕布。吕布收了袁术的粮草，又收了刘备的求援信，他想：我若不救刘备，袁术得逞后我也危险；若我救刘备，袁术必恨我。于是，吕布让人把刘备和纪灵同时请来赴宴。

吕布坐在刘备和纪灵中间，吩咐开宴，刚吃几杯酒，吕布说："看在我的面上，你两家不要打了。"纪灵不肯。吕布大叫一声："把我的画戟拿来！"刘备、纪灵都吓了一跳。吕布又说："我把画戟插到辕门外一百五十步地方，如果我一箭射中画戟的枝尖，你们两家就不要打了。如果我射不中，打不打我就不管了。纪灵希望射不中，刘备希望能射中。吕布叫人端上酒来，各自饮了一杯，酒毕，取出弓箭，搭箭拉弦，只听"嗖"的一声，吕布大喊："着！"那箭不偏不倚，正中画戟的枝尖。在场的人无不喝彩。吕布把弓扔在地上，笑着说："看来老天也不愿意让你们打仗啊！"就这样，吕布以他精湛的箭法平息了一场厮杀。

The Boar Wood 野猪林

A story from the *Outlaws of the Marsh*. Lin Chong and Lü Zhishen were sworn brothers. One day, Lin's wife, a very pretty woman, suffered sexual harassment from the son of Gao Qiu, a very high official, when she was praying in a temple. At the news, Lin rushed over, giving Gao Qiu's son a good beating, thus offending Gao Qiu. Gao framed Lin with a false accusation, then had him flogged and banished him to Cangzhou. Gao secretly instructed the two guards to kill Lin on the way.

On the way Lin had a very hard time, bruised and flogged almost every day. Seeking an occasion, the two guards scalded Lin's feet with boiling water. Lin walked each step with unbearable pain.

One day, they came to a densely wooded place, where sunshine was unable to penetrate the leaves. The two guards told Lin to stop by a tree for a rest. They tied him fast to the tree, saying that it was for safety concerns. Only after they finished did they reveal their real purpose: "We have been instructed by Gao Qiu to kill you," they said. While one of the guards lifted his cudgel and Lin lowered his head waiting for the fatal blow, Lü Zhishen jumped from nowhere and fended off the blow. Lü had heard of how Lin was framed and had followed all the way there, thus saving Lin's life. Lin asked him to spare the two guards. Lü agreed, but instructed that they wait upon Lin attentively all the way to Cangzhou.

《水浒传》中的故事。 林冲和鲁智深是结拜兄弟。一日，林冲的妻子在庙中烧香，被权臣高俅（？－1126年）的儿子调戏，林冲得到报信后，把他们打跑，为此得罪了高俅。高俅设计陷害林冲，将林冲打二十军棍并发配沧州，还叮嘱解差董超、薛霸在路上结果林冲性命。押解的路上，董超、薛霸百般折磨林冲，林冲本来就有棒伤，二解差故意用开水将林冲的脚烫肿，林冲行走非常困难。

有一天，他们来到了野猪林，这里柏树参天，老藤缠绕，林中见不到一丝阳光。二解差假意让林冲休息，说怕他逃跑又用绳子把林冲绑在树上，林冲动弹不得。这时两人露出狰狞面目说："我们奉了太尉的命令，要杀死你。"当薛霸刚举起水火棍要打，没想到棍子被突然跳出来的鲁智深打飞。原来，鲁智深听说林冲被害，前去搭救，一问才知道已发配沧州，便一路上追赶才保住了林冲的性命。在林冲讲情下，鲁智深饶了两个解差，要他们好好服侍林冲，并一直送到沧州。

A story from *A Dream of the Red Mansions*. One day, Tanchun, Li Wen, Li Qi and Xing Youyan came to a pond. "Let's test our luck for the new year by fishing," Tanchun suggested to the rest of the girls. "Whoever has a catch will be lucky throughout the year." Everybody agreed. Tanchun started first. She lowered the line into the water and before long, a fish bit her hook. She hurriedly lifted the line: a bouncing fish, though small, dropped on the ground. She handed the pole to Li Wen, who lowered the line, and raised it when she felt a jerk, only to see an empty hook. She dropped the line again, and lifted it when the pole gave another tug: another empty hook. Upon careful inspection, she saw that the hook was damaged. After having the hook changed, she baited it before she threw it into the water. Before long, she caught a small fish too. Suddenly, Tanchun cried merrily, "Look, many fish have come to the Third Sister's place. Let her fish quickly." As soon as Li Qi took the pole and lowered the line she had a catch. Xing Youyan was the last one. Secretly she hoped for good luck. Sure enough, as soon as she lowered the line a fish came to her hook. They were all happy for a catch, a symbol of good luck for everyone.

"四美"是指《红楼梦》中的探春、李纹、李绮和邢岫烟四人。一天，她们闲暇无事，来到湖边钓鱼取乐。探春说："咱们用钓鱼卜算全年的运气，谁要是钓得着鱼，谁今年就运气好。你们说怎么样？"大家一致同意，让探春先钓。探春把丝绳扔到水里，不一会就有一条小鱼上钩，探春急忙把竿挑起，一个活蹦乱跳的小鱼掉在地上。探春把竿交给了李纹，李纹急忙把竿垂下，觉得丝儿一动，忙挑起一看是个空钩。又垂下去，忽然丝一动，挑起一看又是空钩。李纹拿下钩一看，原来钩已坏了，她忙让丫头调换鱼钩，挂上鱼食，很快就钓上了一条小鱼。突然，探春叫到："你们看，鱼都游到三妹妹那边去了，快让三妹妹钓吧！"李纹把竿递给李绮，竿刚垂下，就钓上了一条小鱼。这回该邢岫烟钓了，她见大家都钓到鱼了，希望自己也能如愿，果然，刚下钩没有一会儿，也钓上一条鱼来。四美钓鱼卜运，皆有所得，都很高兴。

Mi Heng was recommended to Cao Cao when the latter, to expand his influence, needed someone to lobby Liu Biao. But Mi was slighted. Mi took his anger out on almost all of Cao Cao's subordinates. One day, at a banquet in honor of distinguished guests, Cao bid Mi to work as a drummer, just to insult him for fun. Mi came dressed in rag, and when asked why he simply stripped off what was on him to proudly stand nude before the public. Guests shut their eyes in embarrassment. To rebut the angry blame by Cao Cao, Mi said, "You said I'm shameless? Not me but someone who has misled his majesty. Let people view my clean conscience." "If you're clean," Cao roared, "Who's dirty?" "You!" Mi sneered. "Your eyes are dirty for being unable to tell good men from bad, your mouth is dirty because you do not read, your ears are dirty because you refuse to listen to advice, you know nothing about history because of your dirty body, and you tolerate nobody because of the dirt in your belly." Cao, infuriated, ordered him to the battle front, hoping the enemy's sword would kill him.

《三国演义》中的故事。 曹操为了扩大自己的势力,想请人去刘表那里游说,孔融就推荐了他的好朋友祢衡。祢衡被召来后,曹操对他不以礼相待,惹得祢衡当面骂遍了曹操手下的谋士和大将。第二天,曹操大宴宾客,让祢衡击鼓取乐。祢衡身穿破衣上堂,有人责问祢衡为何不更衣,祢衡当场脱衣,光着身子站立,吓的宾客以手捂眼,气得曹操大骂祢衡无耻。祢衡反唇相讥说:"什么叫无耻,欺君才叫无耻。我光着身子,是让大家看看我的清白。"曹操怒指弥衡说:"你清白,谁肮脏?"祢衡冷笑道:"你就是一个肮脏的人。你不分好人坏人,是你的眼太脏;你书也不读,是因为你的嘴太脏;你不听人劝,是因为你的耳朵太脏;你不懂历史,是因为你的身体太脏;你容不得别人,是因为你的肚子太脏。"曹操一气之下,命他立即出征,借敌人的刀杀了祢衡。

This is a story from *Strange Tales from Make-Do Studio*. One day a scholar named Wang Sheng in Taiyuan met, on his way out, a beautiful girl. He brought her back to be kept in his study. The girl asked him not to tell anybody. Days later, Wang met a Taoist priest, who asked, "Did you have any peculiar encounter?" "No," Wang firmly denied. "But you have an evil air in your face," the priest said with a worried look. "And your blood is about to be drained by a monster." Back home, before he entered the room, Wang looked into his study through the window lattice. He saw a fierce-looking devil was painting a hide. Upon hearing his footsteps the devil hurriedly draped the hide and became the beautiful girl

again. Frightened almost to death, Wang broke into a run, but it was too late. The devil caught him, cut open his chest and ate his heart. Wang's wife saw this. The grieved woman fled to seek help from the priest. To see if the woman was sincere about saving her husband, the priest made fun of her. He even bid the woman to eat what he had vomited. To save her husband, she endured everything. The priest laughed before he left. Back home, the wife wailed with Wang's body in her arms. Suddenly she felt like vomiting. Something from her mouth dropped into her husband's cut chest. Slowly, her husband regained his life.

《聊斋志异》中的故事。　太原王生，早晨出门遇见一位年轻漂亮的女子，便把她带回家，藏在书房。女子告诉他，对谁也不要说这件事。一天，王生外出碰见一老道，老道见王生忙问："你最近遇到什么了？"王生撒谎说："什么也没遇到。"老道说："你身上有一股妖气，你的血快被妖精吸干了。"王生回到家中，隔窗往书房内看去，只见一狰狞厉鬼，正用一支彩笔画人皮，听到人的声音后，又忙把人皮往身上一披，立刻变作一位美丽的少女。王生吓得魂飞魄散，拔腿就跑。厉鬼赶上，拉住王生，挖

出了他的心。王生妻子陈氏，亲眼看到丈夫被害，悲痛欲绝，她急忙找到道士，跪地哀求道士救她丈夫。老道为考验陈氏救夫的决心，百般戏弄陈氏，并从口中吐出东西让陈氏吃。陈氏一心想救丈夫，什么都忍受了，道士见状哈哈大笑而去。陈氏回到家里，抚着丈夫的尸体大哭，在抱尸收敛时，她突然呕吐，所食的东西一下子从口中飞出，落入丈夫腔中，丈夫慢慢地苏醒过来。

Making Havoc in Heaven 大闹天宫

This is an episode from the novel *Journey to the West*. Though Monkey was versatile and boasted supernatural powers, Great Sage Sun as he was called, was fooled into coming up to heaven by the Great White Planet. The Jade Emperor conferred upon Monkey the title of Protector of the Horses. When Monkey realized that his job was to look after the horses he became so angry that he returned to his Mountain of Flowers and Fruit. Upon returning, he put up a sign which declared himself "the Great Sage Equalling Heaven." The Jade Emperor swiftly ordered two heavenly generals to command some heavenly troops to capture Monkey. Li Jing and Ne Zha served as the commanders of the heavenly troops. When they arrived at the Mountain of Flowers and Fruit, they ordered the Mighty Magic Spirit to challenge Monkey. Great Sage Sun asked the Mighty Magic Spirit to forward his message to the Jade Emperor that if he was conferred the title of "the Great Sage Equalling Heaven," he would refrain from attacking the Heavenly Palace of the Jade Emperor.

The Mighty Magic Spirit was too headstrong to flaunt his superiority but he was bitterly defeated by Monkey. Ne Zha changed into a fighter with three heads and six arms each holding a different weapon. Just as he was charging at Great Sage Sun, Monkey also changed into three heads and six arms wielding three gold cudgels. The two were soon engaged in a heated battle. Cudgels and spears were wielded while swords and broad swords emitted flashes of light in front of a water-covered cave at the Mountain of Flowers and Fruit. The troops in either camp shouted and waved flags to express support for Great Sage Sun and Ne Zha. The sky was darkened by the sand and stone stirred up by their bitter fight. When Monkey saw that it was hard to win the battle, he pulled out a thread of his hair and made it become an image of himself while his real body leapt behind Ne Zha for a surprise attack. Monkey wielded his cudgel and hit Ne Zha from behind. Ne Zha was forced to withdraw.

When Li Jing, also known as Heavenly King, saw that two of his generals were defeated, he sent out the signal to retreat. The Jade Emperor was thus forced to confer the title of "the Great Sage Equalling Heaven" upon Monkey.

The picture depicts the battle between Great Sage Sun and Ne Zha.

《西游记》中的故事。 神通广大的孙猴,被太白金星骗到天上,玉皇大帝封他为"弼马温"。当他得知"弼马温"只是个看马的小官后,一气之下跑回花果山水帘洞,并挂起了"齐天大圣"的旗帜。玉皇大帝召两路天神捉拿孙猴,李靖和哪吒领旨前去。他们来到花果山,令巨灵神前去叫阵,孙大圣叫巨灵神去给玉帝报信:若依他作"齐天大圣",不动刀枪,否则打上灵霄宝殿。巨灵神逞强好胜,被大圣打得丢盔弃甲。哪吒上阵后,变作三头六臂,手持六种兵器,朝大圣打来。大圣随即也变成三头六臂,把金箍棒变作三条,和哪吒厮杀起来。水帘洞前刀光剑影,枪来棍去。两边阵中,摇旗呐喊,孙大圣、哪吒各显神通。直杀得天浑地暗,难解难分。孙大圣略施小计:拔根毫毛变作他的本相,真身提棒跳到哪吒脑后,一棒打下,哪吒躲闪不及,被大圣打下阵来。托塔天王李靖见两将俱败,不能取胜,便急忙鸣金收兵。玉帝一时也没有了主意,只好按孙猴的要求,准他作了"齐天大圣"。这幅画是孙大圣大战哪吒的场面。

Stealing A Medicinal Herb to Save Her Husband 盗草救夫

This is a story from *Tale of the White Snake*. After getting married, Xu Xian and the Lady Bai settled down in Zhenjiang. That year, at the Dragon Boat Festival, as is the custom, every household hung up Chinese mugwort and drank realgar wine. As snake spirits, they could not drink alcohol because it would reveal their true identity. To protect her, Lady Bai told Xiao Qing to stay in the depths of the mountains for a while while she stayed behind to keep Xu Xian company. Knowing nothing about their secret, Xu Xian insisted Lady Bai drink some realgar wine. After drinking just one cup, the girl felt her stomach in pain. She struggled to her bed for a rest. Xu Xian, out of concern, sent tea for his wife, and when he lifted the bed's curtain, he saw a giant serpent coiled in bed. He was frightened dead on the spot. When Xiao Qing returned and woke up Lady Bai, the latter was heart-broken at the dead Xu Xian. Prompted by Xiao Qing, Lady Bai tried to think of a way to bring Xu Xian back to life. Lady Bai felt his bosom and knew Xu Xian still had some life. She told Xiao Qing to keep watch at home while she went to Mount Kunlun for a magic medicinal herb. Up on Mount Kunlun, just as she had picked the herb and was about to leave, she was seen by the guarding crane and deer spirits. While the three of them were locked in a fight, the South Pole God came, to whom Lady Bai prostrated and begged for help. Sympathetic with her, the god let her have the herb and return. Thus Lady Bai was able to bring Xu Xian back to life.

Note: At the Dragon Boat Festival (the 5th day of the 5th lunar month), the traditional Chinese festival, customs of hanging up mugwort grass to keep off evil spirits and drinking realgar wine are still observed today.

《白蛇传》中的故事。 许仙和白娘子成婚以后,迁到镇江住下。这一年的端午节,家家户户挂艾叶,备雄黄酒。白娘子和小青是蛇仙,雄黄酒能使她们显出原形,本应去深山躲避。为了与许仙团聚,白娘子让小青去深山。不知根底的许仙硬要白娘子喝酒,白娘子刚喝一杯,便觉腹中难忍,挣扎着上床休息。许仙给白娘子送茶时,撩帐子一看,床上盘着一条大蛇,当时吓得昏死在地。小青回来,叫醒白娘子,白娘子见丈夫被吓死,悲痛欲绝,小青劝白娘子快想办法。白娘子一摸许仙心口还有气,告诉小青看守许仙,自己去昆仑山取仙草救许仙。当白娘子盗得仙草刚要离开时,被守山护草的白鹤仙和鹿仙发现,三位仙人,兵器相见,双方厮打得难解难分。这时,南极仙翁赶到,白娘子跪下哭着央求仙翁送仙草救丈夫,仙翁同情白娘子的遭遇。白娘子用仙草救活了许仙。

During the reign of the Emperor Wu Di of the Han Dynasty (140-88 B.C.), Su Wu, as an official, was sent with an imperial edict to Xiongnu, a nomadic ethnic group in the northern part of China. But as soon as he arrived he was detained. The ruler of Xiongnu tried to win him over to his side to help with his tribe's administration. He tried every way to turn Su's loyalty from Han to him. When the wealth and high officialdom he offered were firmly refused, he beheaded Su's assistant to intimidate him. Failing again, the ruler sent a Han traitor with a nimble tongue to work on Su. But Su was firm. "Live as a Han man," he vowed, "and die a Han spirit. Take my life if you want, but I'll never surrender." The ruler began to torture Su, leaving him in an icy dungeon in winter. Su managed to stay alive with a leather belt and goat hide as food. Later, he was sent to herd sheep in a wild place (present day Lake Baikal) with very little grain. While herding the sheep Su held in reverence the plate bearing his identity as a Han envoy, his eyes cast afar, thinking of his homeland. Later, Li Ling, a former Han general who had surrendered to Xiongnu, came, trying to talk him out of his loyalty to Han. "Let others be fickle," he said. "I won't disgrace my ancestors." Moved, Li sent him domestic animals as food and a Xiongnu girl to look after him. Later the girl married him. After 19 years of hardship, during the reign of Emperor Zhao Di, the relationship between Xiongnu and Han was getting better. When Su Wu eventually returned to Chang'an, the capital of Han, his hair and eyebrows were as white as snow.

汉武帝(公元前 140 – 前 87 年在位)时,苏武(? – 前 62 年)奉命出使匈奴,他一到匈奴,就被扣押。匈奴的单于要苏武帮助治理朝政,以高官厚禄引诱,千方百计劝降,苏武全然不动。为达目的单于斩了副使威胁苏武,苏武临危不屈。之后,又派汉降将卫律劝降,苏武发誓:生为汉朝人,死为汉朝鬼,要杀要剐随便,就是不投降。单于便百般折磨苏武,隆冬季节,把苏武扔进灌满雪的地窖,苏武餐冰吞雪,用皮带、羊皮碎片充饥。后来,单于又让他到荒无人烟的北海(今贝加尔湖)牧羊,天寒地冻,给很少的粮食。牧羊时,苏武总拿着汉朝符节,眼望远方,深深怀念父母之邦。这时,已投降匈奴的李陵又来劝降,苏武说:"宁让人负我,我也不负列祖列宗。"李陵很受感动,叫人送去牛羊,又派一匈奴姑娘服侍他。姑娘敬慕苏武的气节,便嫁给苏武。汉昭帝(公元前 86 – 前 74 年在位)时汉匈和好。须发皆白的苏武历经十九年磨难终于回到长安。

This is a story from *Three Kingdoms*. Liu Bei captured an excellent horse in a battle. When Liu Biao marveled at the steed, Liu Bei gave it to him as a gift. Under Liu Biao, there was a horse expert who said, "This horse, though excellent, tends to harm its owner; you'd better return it to Liu Bei." Following the expert's advice, Liu Biao returned the horse to Liu Bei. Liu Biao's wife Cai and her brother had long wished to kill Liu Bei. One day, Liu Biao invited Liu Bei over to Xiangyang to meet some officials. Cai and her brother decided it was an good opportunity. They sent troops to guard every city gate except the western one, for outside that gate, the wide Tanxi River, with its rapid water, blocked the road. At the banquet for officials, a man hinted to Liu Bei that Liu Biao planned to kill him. Liu Bei followed the man to the back garden, where he whispered into his ear the details of plan Cai and her brother had set. "Every gate but the western one is heavily guarded," the man added. "The western gate is your only chance." Alarmed, Liu Bei mounted the horse and fled. Outside the gate the river blocked his way. Soldiers were fast approaching. Liu Bei whipped the horse like mad, the animal moved forward, but after just a few steps into the river it stumbled. "Surely you harm your master," Liu Bei cried in despair. At this, oddly, the horse made a vigorous leap to the other side of the river, leaving the soldiers behind.

Note: Liu Biao was a governor of Jingzhou and a Han royal family member.

《三国演义》中的故事。 有次打仗,刘备缴获一匹名叫"的卢"的千里马。荆州刺史刘表看后禁不住连声称赞。刘备见刘表如此喜欢,将此马送给了刘表。刘表手下有一人颇懂相马术,言此马有妨主之相,劝刘表将马还给刘备。刘表的夫人蔡氏和其兄蔡瑁早有杀害刘备之心。一次,刘表请刘备代替他到襄阳去会见百官,蔡氏兄妹觉得这是杀害刘备的好机会。该城西门外有一条檀溪河,河宽水急,不易通过。蔡氏兄妹在东、南、北门派重兵把守,只留西门,等待下手。席间,一个叫伊籍的人来到刘备面前暗示,刘备假借更衣来到了后花园,伊籍附耳告诉刘备:"蔡瑁设计害你,已在东南北三个门派人把守,你只能出西门,快逃!"刘备大惊,策马跑出西门,行数里被檀溪河阻住去路,这时追兵赶来,刘备急打马过溪,没走几步,马失前蹄。刘备大呼:"的卢,的卢,今日果然害我!"话音刚落,只见马从水中一跃数丈,飞身上了西岸,摆脱了追兵。

This is a story from *Complete Biography of Yue Fei*. After killing his rival in a martial-skill competition on the royal drilling grounds. Yue Fei went back home to Henan. Afterwards, Yue Fei's name spread afar as a martial arts expert and strategist. One day, Wang Zuo, a general from the rebellion army at Dongting Lake, came with gifts, asking Yue Fei to join them. "I live as a Song subject and die as Song ghost." Yue said to Wang with a stern look. "Please take your gifts and leave."

Yue told his mother about this. The old lady lit joss sticks and candles in the living room, and prayed to heaven, the earth and her ancestors. She then told her daughter-in-law to prepare ink and a needle. When both were ready, the old lady instructed Yue to kneel down, saying, "I feel happy at your loyalty to the country. You were able to resist the lure of wealth. But I'm not sure of your fate after I die. What if you fail to resist the temptation of fortune and join those outlaws? I have prayed to heaven, now I'm going to tatoo the following words on your back: 'Remain loyal to and die for the country.' You should be a loyal subject and die for the country when necessary. By this your name will go down in history. Then I will be happy after I die." Then, with tears in her eyes, the old lady pricked her son's back and rubbed ink into the wounds. The words would stay forever. After she finished, Yue got to his feet and gave thanks to his mother for her teaching.

The stories of Yue Fei's resistance against the Jin army were popular among Chinese folks, as is this story of his mother tattooing on his back.

Note: Yue Fei (1103-1142) was a well-known army general who fought against Jin troops during the Southern Song Dynasty.

《说岳全传》中的故事。 岳飞(1103－1142年)在校场比武,枪挑小梁王后,便回河南老家闲居。一天,岳飞家中有人叩门,原来是洞庭湖起义军将领王佐。他早知岳飞文武双全,特带来厚礼,前来招贤。岳飞退回聘礼正色道:"我生为宋朝人,死是宋朝鬼!"王佐只好收拾聘礼走了。

岳飞对母亲细说了王佐来的目的,岳母听罢,就让岳飞在中堂摆上香案,点上灯烛,拜过天地祖宗后,岳母叫媳妇研墨,让岳飞跪地。岳母说:"娘见你不叛国,不为贼作事,甘守清贫,我很高兴。但恐怕我死后,你经不起不肖之徒诱惑而作出不忠之事,我已祝告上苍,要在你背上刺下'精忠报国'四个字,愿你永作忠臣,尽忠报国,流芳百世,这样,我就可以含笑九泉了。"说完,岳母含泪刺字,又将墨涂上,使其永不退色。岳飞起身,叩谢母亲教训之恩。岳母刺字和岳飞抗击金兵的故事,一直在民间流传。

Legend has it that Guan Lu was a prophet who knew everything. One day, on an outing, he saw a lad plowing a field. After looking at him for a while, Guan asked the lad his name and age. "My name is Zhao Yan," the lad said, "I'm 19 years old."

"My name is Guan Lu," Guan said, "You have a lump of death air between your eyebrows and you will die within three days." The lad rushed home to report this to his father, then both of them begged Guan for help. "He's my only son," the father, on his knees, wept. "And we depend on each other so much. Please save his life." The lad pleaded between sobs. Guan was sympathetic. "Bring a pot of wine and a piece of deer meat," he said to them. "Go to the South Mountain, where you will see two men playing chess under a tree: an ugly one in white and handsome one in blue. While they are engrossed in their game, present them with the wine and meat. They will take it without looking up. After they finish eating and drinking it, tearfully cry for a longer life-span."

The lad did as Guan had said. When he kneeled down and entreated them for a longer life-span, the two men were alarmed. The one in red said, "It must be Guan Lu who told him about us. But we have taken his food and drink, so we must take pity on him." The one in white took out the book of life and changed the lad's life-span from 19 to 99. Then he said to the lad, "Return to bring these words to Guan Lu: if he discloses Heaven's wish one more time he'll be doomed." Since then, bearing this warning in mind, Guan never made life and death predictions for others.

相传，管辂是一位无事不晓的神卜。一日，他到郊外去游玩，见一少年耕地，管辂在旁看了一会问："你叫什么名字？今年十几岁了？"少年说他叫赵颜，今年十九岁了。管辂又说："我是管辂，我看你眉间有团死气，三天之内必死"。赵颜听后，急忙回家告诉父亲。父子追上管辂，跪地哭求："先生，我只有这么一个儿子，我俩相依为命，救救我的儿子吧！"赵颜也在一旁哭求。管辂看这父子实在可怜，对赵颜说："你准备一壶酒和一块鹿肉，去南山之中，在大树下有二人下棋。一人穿白袍，相貌丑恶；一人穿蓝袍，长得很美。你趁他们棋兴正浓时，把鹿肉和美酒给他二人，他们只顾下棋，不会理会，待他们吃完后，你跪在地上哭拜求寿。"

赵颜按管辂说的去做。当赵颜跪地哭求时，二人大惊。穿红袍的说："这必定是管辂教他的。我们吃了人家的东西，就可怜可怜他吧！"说毕，只见穿白袍的拿出生死薄，把赵颜的十九岁改成了九十九岁，并对赵颜说："你回去一定要告诉管辂，如果他再泄露天机，必遭天谴。"赵颜回来后，把此事告诉管辂。从此，管辂很少给人卜卦。

This is a story from *Three Kingdoms*. Xu Shu was much valued by Liu Bei for his strategic talents. After several victories on the battleground against Cao Cao, Xu was made the chief military advisor. At the news, Cao Cao was begrudging. "If you want this person," one of his advisors said, "you can bring his mother to Xuchang and send a forged letter in his mother's handwriting, asking Xu Shu to desert Liu Bei and come here. As Xu is well-known for a strong filial affection, surely he will come." This plot worked, for Xu, on receiving the letter, cried tearfully, asking Liu Bei for an immediate departure. Feeling sad, though, Liu persisted in his stay for another night, during which the two aired their sad feelings.

The next day Liu laid a banquet outside the city for Xu. Holding the latter's hand, Liu said, "After we separate today, only heaven knows when and where we will meet again." He wept bitter tears. After setting off on his way, Xu suddenly turned his horse and returned. "I almost forgot an important matter," he said to Liu. "Ten kilometers from Xiangyang City, in a place called Longzhong, there lives a very capable man named Zhuge Liang. Do you want to meet him?" Liu expressed his willingness at once, but also aired doubt about whether Zhuge Liang was as talented as Xu. "He tells configurations of stars in the heavens," Xu assured him, "and recognizes everything on earth. He knows a person's real nature at the first meeting—the number one talent under the heaven. If you have him as your military advisor, you'll have the country under your name." Liu suggested a visit to Zhuge by Xu on his behalf, at this, the latter shook his head in disapproval. "You must go and offer your invitation personally, and his acceptance depends entirely on your sincerity." With these words said, Xu turned his horse and left. Later, Liu paid three trips to Zhuge's straw house, another favorite story among Chinese people.

《三国演义》中的故事。　徐庶投奔刘备后，很得刘备重用。曾帮助刘备几次打败曹兵，被封为军师。曹操得知此事很惊讶。曹操的谋士程昱献计说：丞相如果想用此人，召来不难，徐庶是个孝子，丞相派人把他母亲接到许昌，再仿他母亲的笔体写信让他来许昌，他必来。"徐庶接信，果然大哭一场，拿信找刘备辞行。刘备见信也哭，强留徐庶叙情一夜。第二天，刘备在城外排宴替徐庶饯行。刘备拉着徐庶的手说："先生这一走，你我天各一方，不知何时才能再见？"说完又痛哭流涕。徐庶行数里又拍马返回对刘备说："忘了一件大事，襄阳城外二十里的隆中，有一位天下奇人叫诸葛亮，将军想不想见他？"刘备说："我当然愿意见他，不知他能比上先生吗？"徐庶说："他抬头能知天文，低头能察地理，见面能识人心，是天下第一才人，如他能出来帮助你，将军就可以稳坐天下了。"刘备见徐庶这样了解诸葛亮，想请徐庶辛苦一趟把诸葛亮请来。徐庶摇头说："这样的人才，只能将军亲自去请，他愿不愿出来，还得看将军的诚意。"徐庶说完，策马离去。之后引出刘备三顾茅庐的故事。

Laozi's real name is Li Dan, a great thinker during the Spring and Autumn Period (770-476 B.C). He is the founder of the Taoist school, a great reader and a scholar who had a thorough understanding of nature. His ideology and doctrines gained much following at the time. It is said that Confucius once consulted Laozi about a question. After he returned to the State of Lu, Confucius voiced his admiration of Laozi to people.

Hangu Pass was located in Lingbao County, Henan, a place heavily guarded day and night. One day, the guards on the pass noticed in the southeast a lump of purple air slowly moving towards them. The officer in charge of the garrison, a Taoist follower, was extremely delighted, "It must be a sage coming up." So he refrained from eating and drinking and waited patiently. Laozi appeared on an ox. After greeting the officer sincerely, he asked Laozi for teachings. So Laozi stayed for a while and wrote his spiritual classic *Dao De Jing* (often *Dao De Ching*). After he finished the book, Laozi exited the pass and people lost track of his whereabouts.

老子，姓李名聃，是春秋(公元前770－前476年)时的大思想家、道家学派的创始人。他潜心于书籍之中，学到了很多知识，使他对万物有了更加深刻的认识。他的思想和学说在当时已经有相当的影响。相传，孔子曾拜访请教过老子。孔子回到鲁国后，经常向人们赞美老子。

函谷关是河南灵宝县境内的一个关卡，日夜有人把守。一天，卫士登上城楼，向四周观看，发现函谷关东南有一股紫气缓缓向函谷关飘来，守此关的小吏尹喜高兴地说：紫气飘来，定有圣人过关。于是，他不吃不喝，耐心等待。果然，老子骑青牛很快就来了。尹喜很喜欢道术，见老子来了，就诚心诚意地请教老子，并请老子住下"讲学"。据说，老子著名的"道德经"就是在这里写成的。写完后，老子出关隐居，从此再没人知道他的下落了。

Wen Yanbo, a native of Jiexiu, Shanxi, was a minister during the Northern Song Dynasty (960-1127). Because of his excellent administration skills, he was entitled "the Lord of Lu Guo." Despite his high status and power, he was a very friendly person and hospitable host. His door was forever wide open to visitors. In childhood, one day, the ball he and his little friends were playing with rolled into a hole in a tree trunk. Some, sleeves rolled up, reached their arms into the hole, some used sticks as chopsticks to try to snatch the ball—but none of these efforts worked. While everybody was dejected, and the owner of the ball began to bawl, Wen rushed back home and returned with a basin of water. He poured it into the hole and the ball floated out. This story is used in the Chinese primary school textbook.

文彦博，山西介休人，是北宋的大臣，因治国安民有方，被封为"潞国公"。他虽地位高、权力大，但从不骄横，使人感到平易可亲，家中经常高朋满座。

这幅画讲述的是文彦博小时候的一个故事。一天，他和很多小朋友一起玩球，一个小朋友把球踢到树洞里去了，大家都很着急；有的卷起袖子去掏，但树洞很深够不着；有人出主意拿棍夹，但因球是圆的，滚来滚去夹不上来；大家一时没有了办法。球的小主人因取不出球来，急得哇哇直哭。文彦博想出个好办法来，他回家端了一罐水，把水倒进树洞中，结果球浮出洞外。这个故事现被中国小学语文课本录用。

This is a story from *A Dream of Red Mansions*. Third Sister You, a very pretty and strong character, was the sister of Jia Zhen's wife. When Jia Zhen, a playboy by nature, was tired of his wife, his eyes fell on the beautiful Third Sister. Collaborated with his cousin Jia Lian they tried to seduce the girl, only to be met with a harsh telling-off. The two playboys, scared by this virtuous but unyielding girl, tried to marry her off as soon as possible. When the Third Sister fell in love with Liu Xianglian, an actor who had once played opera in the residence, her sister, Jia Zhen's wife, told her that the young man had left town. But the Third Sister was determined. "I'll wait for him, one year or ten, it doesn't matter," she said. "And if he dies I'll shave my hair and become a nun." On a business trip in the capital, Jia Lian chanced to meet Liu. Jia told Liu of the Third Sister's wish. Liu aired his willingness on the spot. He asked Jia to give his mandarin duck sword to the girl as a token of his betrothal. Feeling assured of her marriage and future, every day the girl looked several times affectionately at the sword she had hung by her bed. A few months later, Liu returned. When he saw the girl's beautiful looks, he grew suspicious of her virtue. "The men in the Jia family are all promiscuous," he thought. "Why would this girl fall in love with me when she and I have never met?" He stepped back on the betrothal on a pretext that his aunt had betrothed him to somebody else and he came to retrieve his sword. Third sister knew what was on his mind. Heart bleeding, she took the sword from the wall, unsheathed it and committed suicide before Liu, an act to show her virtue and unyieldingness. The regretful young man cried bitterly over her corpse. He spent the rest of his life as a priest in a Taoist temple.

《红楼梦》中的故事。　尤三姐是贾珍之妻尤氏的妹妹，她花容月貌，性格刚烈。贾珍玩腻了尤二姐，就串通贾琏打尤三姐的主意，却被尤三姐狠狠地责骂一番。从此二人很怕尤三姐，一心想快点把她嫁出去。尤三姐看中了曾来贾府唱过戏的柳湘莲，姐姐告诉她湘莲现在不在京城。尤三姐说："他一年不回我等一年，十年不归我等十年，人死了，我情愿剃头当尼姑去。"贾琏离京办事，遇上柳湘莲，说了尤三姐的事，湘莲应允，并取"鸳鸯剑"作聘礼，转交给尤三姐。三姐觉得终身有靠，将剑挂在床头，每天看几次。数月后，湘莲回京，得知尤三姐是天下无双的美人，他认为宁府的人品行不端，三姐和我素不相识，为何钟情于我，对尤三姐产生了怀疑，便假称姑妈已给定婚，想要回宝剑。尤三姐猜想湘莲一定是把自己当成下流女子了，心如刀绞，于是，摘下宝剑，当着湘莲的面自刎以表清白。湘莲后悔，抚尸大哭离去，后出家当道士去了。

This is an episode from the novel *Three Kingdoms*. After they had become sworn brothers at Taoyuan, Liu Bei, Guan Yu and Zhang Fei made concerted efforts to restore the Han Dynasty. But they felt that it would be impossible to do it without the help of a smart adviser. The Liu-Guan-Zhang alliance later won one battle after another thanks to the advice of Xu Shu. But before long, Xu had to surrender to the opposing camp of Cao Cao in order to save the life of his mother who was abducted by the Cao troops. Before he left, Xu Shu recommended Zhuge Liang to the brothers.

Accompanied by Guan Yu and Zhang Fei, Liu Bei went to Wolonggang in Longzhong in the hope of inviting Zhuge Liang to be their military adviser. But Zhuge's servant said: "The Mentor left in the morning." Liu Bei asked the servant to forward to Zhuge Liang his message that the brothers had come to visit him. After that, Liu rode his horse away, returning home sullenly. A few days later when he learned that Zhuge Liang was at home, Liu Bei went for another visit along with Guan Yu and Zhang Fei. The servant said: "The Mentor is reading books at his thatched cottage." Liu requested to see him.

When they learned that the one reading books at the thatched cottage was not Zhuge Liang himself but his brother Zhuge Jun, the Liu-Guan-Zhang brothers left a letter to express their admiration and then braved heavy snows to return home.

Not long after they returned to their barracks at Xinye, Liu Bei wanted to visit Zhuge Liang's thatched cottage once more. But Guan Yu dissuaded Liu from going by saying that perhaps Zhuge Liang was not as smart as expected and that he was simply dodging the visiting brothers for that. Zhang Fei said: "You don't need to go. I'll tie him up and force him to come and see you instead." Liu Bei lost no time in telling his brothers the story of King Wen bent on visiting one of his subjects called Jiang Ziya. Liu, Guan and Zhang, therefore, paid a third visit to Wolonggang. They had no sooner arrived than the servant said: "The Mentor is sleeping." Liu Bei waited until Zhuge Liang was awake and dressed. Finally, he consented to see the brothers. Liu Bei paid three visits to the thatched cottage without complaint. He finally succeeded in inviting Zhuge Liang to be his military adviser and to help the brothers in their cause.

《三国演义》中的故事。 刘备、关羽、张飞自桃园结义后，虽整天东奔西跑，但因缺少谋士，总觉得恢复汉朝天下无望。后来得徐庶帮助，连打胜仗。徐庶为救母无奈去了曹营。临走推荐了诸葛亮。

一日，刘备带关羽、张飞来到隆中卧龙冈，想请诸葛亮出山。小僮说："先生今早出去了。"刘备让僮子转告先生说他来访，然后拉马闷闷地回去了。又过了数日，刘备探得诸葛亮已回家，便同关、张二次来访。僮子说："先生正在草堂看书。"刘备求见后得知不是诸葛亮，而是其弟诸葛均。于是留下一封信，表达敬慕之情。兄弟三人又冒雪回去了。

回到新野不久，刘备想再次去请诸葛亮。关羽劝说：可能诸葛亮没本事，怕见我们。张飞则说：你们别去了，我用绳子捆来。刘备忙讲了当年文王访姜子牙的故事。兄弟三人又第三次来到卧龙冈。他们一到，小僮忙说："先生在睡觉。"刘备一直等到诸葛亮睡醒后更衣相见。刘备不辞劳苦，三顾茅庐，终于请出诸葛亮出山辅佐，共图大业。

Ying Ning with Plum Blossoms   婴宁拈梅

This is an episode from the novel *Strange Tales from Make-Do Studio*. His father died while Wang Zifu was very young. His mother gave her whole heart to bringing Zifu up. After he was grown, the mother decided which girl was to marry her son. But before the marriage took place, the chosen girl died.

On the day of the Lantern Festival, Zifu's cousin, Wu Sheng, invited him for an excursion. Wu had to return home early to attend to something else. Zifu stayed and whiled away the time alone. Suddenly, Zifu spotted in the crowd a girl with bright eyes. The girl was carrying a twig of plum blossoms and was walking delicately slowly. Zifu could not help but glue his sight on the girl. When the girl saw what was happening, she left her twig of blossoms on the ground and walked away smiling.

Zifu picked up the flower and returned home. He put the flower under his pillow. He missed the girl so much so that he would not eat or drink. Zifu soon became so weak that he was not able to support himself. When Wu Sheng learned of this he came to ask about the reason. Zifu told the truth to his cousin. To comfort Zifu, Wu Sheng lied, saying that the girl was one of Zifu's cousins living in the mountains some 15 kilometers to the southwest. He promised that they would go and look for her after Zifu got well. After hearing Wu's words, Zifu felt so happy that he soon fully recovered. Since he was lying, Wu Sheng was reluctant to see Zifu again and made himself scarce.

Wu Sheng made excuses every time Zifu asked him to help him go look for the plum blossom girl. Zifu could wait no longer, so he went alone in accordance with the description of Wu Sheng. In the mountains, he found a door made of branches of wood. It was the home of a girl called Ying Ning. Zifu stayed in Ying Ning's home for a few days before taking her home to marry her. After marriage, Zifu and Ying Ning loved each other very much and they lived a happy life. One day Ying Ning told Zifu that she had been the daughter of a fox-immortal. She was brought up to be a human by a ghost mother. Zifu was not at all put off by this news.

《聊斋志异》中的故事。 王子服从小失去父亲，母亲非常疼爱他。子服长大后，母亲为他订下一位漂亮姑娘，还没娶过门，姑娘就死了。元宵节那天，子服表兄吴生约子服郊游，后因吴生家中有事，留下子服一人游玩。在游人中，子服忽见一女子秋波盈盈，手拈一枝梅花，冉冉而来，子服目不转睛地盯着这女子，少女发现后扔下梅花，笑着走了。子服拾花回家放在枕下，因思念这位美丽的少女，不吃不喝，身体瘦弱难以支撑。吴生知后问其原因，子服实话告诉。吴生撒谎说：这女子是你的姨妹，住在西南山中三十里处，等你病好咱们一块去找。子服听后高兴，病很快就好了。吴生因是撒谎，便不愿来见子服。一日，子服等不及吴生，自己按吴生所指来到那个地方，见一柴门，正是郊游时所遇少女婴宁家。子服住了几天，便带婴宁回家成亲。婚后夫妻恩爱，日子过得幸福美满。一天婴宁对子服说，自己原是狐仙生的女儿，托鬼母抚养成人。子服知道她的身世后，并不介意。

It was said during the Song Dynasty there was a poor fisherman called Wang Hua. Both his parents died while he was young. He grew up fishing for a living. Wang Hua was an honest man and always offered help to his fellow fishermen. One day after he sold his catch in the market and was returning home, Wang Hua saw an old man surrounded by a crowd of people. The old man was wearing dirty, shabby clothes and shouted: "Whoever buys me as his father will become rich in the future!" Some of the onlookers were laughing at the old man; others were scolding him; and others were even throwing stones at him. Wang Hua felt pity for the old man. All he thought of was saving the old man from insults and injuries. He never thought of getting rich with the old man. Wang Hua edged his way into the crowd and told the old man: "Father, I would be your son. Let's go home." After that, he carried the old man on his back and went home.

No sooner had he arrived home than he washed and dressed the old man. He asked his children to recognize the old man as their grandfather. He also told his wife to treat the old man as her own father. Every time when Wang Hua came home from fishing voyages, he chose the best fish to feed the old man. Wang's family lived peacefully and harmoniously.

After several months passed the old man said: "I have stayed in your place and you have treated me just like your own father. I am really reluctant to part from you but I have to go. When I am gone, please come and look for me according to the address I give you."

When Wang Hua, his wife and children came to look for the old man as they were told, they found that the old man was the eighth nephew of the ruling emperor. The old man, known as the Eight-Thousand-Year-Old prince, rewarded the Wang family which lived a happy life thereafter.

相传宋朝时，有个穷苦的渔民叫王华，他从小失去父母，长大后靠打鱼为生。他心地善良，为人忠厚，经常帮助有困难的渔民。一天，王华卖完鱼要回家时，看到街上很多人围着一个老头。老人穿的又脏又破，高声喊着："谁买我做亲爹，将来能富贵。"围着的人们，有的笑，有的骂，还有的用石头打老人。王华看到老人非常可怜，他不考虑将来能不能富贵，只是不愿让老人受人打骂，便分开众人，走到老人面前说："爹，我愿意做你的儿子，跟我回家吧！"说完背起老人就回家了。

一到家，王华亲自给老人梳洗更衣，叫孩子出来认爷爷，告诉媳妇要像对待亲爹一样地对待老人。王华每次打鱼回来，总把最好的鱼留给老人吃。全家人和和睦睦地生活。几个月过去了，有一天，老人突然对王华说："我在这里住了这么多日子，你们对我像对亲人一样，我实在舍不得离开你们。但我该走了，我走后，你们按我写的地址去找我吧！"后来，王华带着妻儿，按老人留下的地址找到老人，才得知是当朝皇帝的侄子"八千岁"。王华得到老人的回报，过上了好日子。

Fresh from Thatched Cottage 初出茅庐

This is an episode from the novel *Three Kingdoms*. Liu Bei visited the thatched cottage three times and finally succeeded in inviting Zhuge Liang to be his military adviser. Yet his sworn brothers, Guan Yu and Zhang Fei, did not take Zhuge seriously. Before long, Cao Cao dispatched an army of 100,000 to attack Liu Bei's headquarters at Xinye. Cao's troops were at the command of General Xiahou Chun. When Liu Bei turned to Zhuge Liang for advice, Zhuge said: "I have to borrow your majesty's sword of authority in that I am afraid that Guan Yu and Zhang Fei will not listen to me." Liu lost no time in lending his sword of authority to Zhuge who then started to dispatch Liu's army for the defence.

Zhuge ordered Guan Yu to lurk and wait at Mount Yushan with 1,000 troops. Guan was not to attack the enemy but rather let them pass. He would charge at the enemy as soon as he saw fire break out in the enemy procession. Zhang Fei was ordered to lurk and wait in the valley with another 1,000 troops. Zhang was to attack the town of Bowang as soon as he saw fire break out in the enemy procession. Guan Ping, adopted son of Guan Yu

and General Liu Feng were ordered to each guide 500 troops to wait behind the slope of Bowang. They would set fire to the enemy procession as soon as the enemy arrived at the slope. Zhuge recalled Zhao Yun from Fancheng to be the vanguard of Liu's army. But Zhao was ordered not to defeat the advancing enemy but rather pretend to be defeated. Liu Bei was given 1,000 troops as the backup force.

Guan Yu was so curious that he asked: "We all go out to fight the battle. But what will you do?" Zhuge Liang answered smiling, "I will sit and wait here in town." Zhang Fei burst into laughter and said: "We all go out to risk our lives while you enjoy your time carefree inside the town!" Zhuge said: "I have the sword of authority. Those who disobey my orders will be executed." Guan and Zhang had nothing more to say, but they walked away sneeringly.

Since the generals carried out Zhuge Liang's orders to the letter, the enemy was routed. Zhuge's first military advice turned out to be smart and farsighted. Guan Yu, Zhang Fei and other generals in the Liu camp soon came to respect the new military adviser.

《三国演义》中的故事。 刘备三顾茅庐请出诸葛亮并拜为军师。而关羽、张飞对此不以为然。没过多久,曹操派大将夏侯惇领十万大军打新野,刘备找诸葛亮商议,诸葛亮说:"怕众将不听我令,愿借主公印剑一用。"刘备忙将印剑交给诸葛亮。诸葛亮开始集众点将。命关羽带一千人马埋伏在豫山,放过敌人先头部队,看到起火,迅速出击。张飞带一千人马埋伏在山谷里,待起火后,杀向博望城。关平、刘封带五百人马,在博望坡后面分两路等候,敌军一到,立刻放火。又把赵云从樊城调来当先锋,只许败不许胜。刘备带一千人马作后援。关羽忍不住问:"我们都去打仗,先生干什么?"诸葛亮说:"我在城中坐等。"张飞大笑说:"我们都去拼命,先生你好逍遥!"诸葛亮说:"印剑在此,违令者斩!"关羽、张飞无话,冷笑着走了。在战斗中,各将按诸葛亮吩咐行事,直杀得曹兵丢盔弃甲。诸葛亮初次用兵,神机妙算,大获全胜。使关羽、张飞等佩服得五体投地。

This is an episode from the novel *A Dream of Red Mansions*. Just as the whole family was busy preparing the birthday ceremony for Jia Zheng, Jia was summoned to report to the imperial court. His family did not know why and felt uneasy about it. The family members waited for quite a while before the butler came back to say that Jia Yuanchun (Jia Zheng's eldest daughter) was conferred the title of highest-ranking imperial concubine. The emperor had granted that Yuanchun would pay a visit to her parents at the upcoming Lantern Festival. The Jia family relaxed after hearing the news. In order to welcome the homecoming imperial concubine, the Jia family became busier and built a garden of grand views for the occasion.

On the day of the Lantern Festival, Jia Zheng's mother led all members of her clan to wait by the main entrance to the garden. Accompanied by a swarm of imperial maids, Yuanchun came back on a sedan chair which was draped with an embroidery of a phoenix and tiny gold bells. Eight men carried the sedan chair on their shoulders. The imperial concubine was shown around the garden, in which there were pavilions with gorgeously-painted beams and pillars. There were also patches of bamboos and strangely-shaped stones. The trees in the garden were decorated with flowers made of silk cloth while lanterns made of conches and clams were placed aside a pond. The garden was decorated so majestically that even Yuanchun thought it to be too luxurious.

After Yuanchun was seated, Jia Zheng's mother and Madam Wang (Yuanchun's grandmother and mother) met with her. They faced one another in silence: the mother and grandmother couldn't speak a word; they just sobbed. Yuanchun finally said: "It is not easy for me to come back from a place where I can see no family members. But now that I'm back, you just sob away and have nothing to say to me. I'd better return to the palace. I don't know when I will be allowed to come home again." After that, all continued to cry.

After the banquet was ready, Yuanchun was marshaled to her seat. The imperial concubine invited her sisters and Bao Yu to recite poems, and she bestowed gifts to everyone at the table. When the time came to leave, Yuanchun held the hands of her grandmother and mother and asked them to keep fit. She requested that they not squander money on her next homecoming, if there was one. The imperial concubine then turned away from her parents and left mournfully.

《红楼梦》中的故事。 贾政生日那天，正在热闹之际，忽然传贾政入朝。全家老小不知出了什么事，心情不定地等了好一阵子，才见管家报信说，贾政的大女儿贾元春被封为贵妃娘娘了，皇上恩准明年元宵节回家省亲，这时全家才放下心来。为迎接元妃省亲，贾府上下开始忙碌，还专修了一座大观园。元宵节那天，贾母率荣宁两府老少，一清早就在大门口迎候。元春坐八人抬绣画栋金碧辉煌，佳木怪石竹林掩映，转了一圈。只见园内雕梁画栋金碧辉煌，佳木怪石竹林掩映，树上挂满各种绢花，池中有螺蚌制成的彩灯。贵妃看后觉得"太奢华糜费了"。元春落座，贾母、王夫人等相见。大家相对无言，只是抽泣，最后还是元春强说："当初送我到那不得见人的地方，好不容易才回家，大家不说笑只顾哭，我回去了，不知何时才能再见……"说着又哭起来。宴会齐备，请贵妃入席。贵妃请姐妹们与宝玉咏诗。元春对每个人都有赏赐。临走时，拉住贾母、王夫人的手，要她们保重身体，并叮嘱，如下次省亲，切不可浪费，说完悲悲切切地转身而去。

Three County Sheriffs 三个县令

In the Song Dynasty there was a county sheriff surnamed Shi. His wife died and left him a young daughter called Yue Xiang. The middle-aged county sheriff did not marry again for fear that the stepmother would abuse Yue Xiang. Shi was an honest man and treated all cases fairly. When he took up his office, Shi learned that a businessman, Jia Chang, had been framed and sentenced to death. The new county sheriff went out to find evidence and acquitted the businessman of his conviction. Jia Chang was set free in the end.

A raging fire burned down the grain warehouse of the county. The sheriff was held responsible for the incident. His properties and his daughter were auctioned to compensate for the loss of the granary. Shi was deeply shocked by the fire and the ensuing events and soon died of illness. Businessman Jia Chang redeemed the sheriff's daughter. He treated her as his own daughter. But Jia Chang's wife was vicious by nature. Whenever Jia was out doing business, his wife would abuse Yue Xiang. To protect the county sheriff's daughter, Jia Chang refrained from doing business elsewhere for five years. But

the Jia family soon became impoverished.

When Yue Xiang turned 15, the new county sheriff, Zhong Liyi, was preparing to marry his daughter to County Sheriff Gao's son. But Zhong could not find a maid to serve as a dowry. As her husband went out to do business, the vicious woman sold Yue Xiang to the needy county sheriff as a servant. While she was sweeping the courtyard one day, Yue Xiang burst to tears after she saw a small hole on the ground. She recalled scenes of her childhood in the sheriff residence playing with marbles around the hole. After the new county sheriff learned why the servant was crying, he felt so sympathetic that he took the girl as his adopted daughter. Zhong's in-law, County Sheriff Gao, also felt sympathetic about the life experience of Yue Xiang. He decided to marry the bereft daughter to his second son. The two county sheriffs arranged the two marriages for the same day, on which two sedan chairs sent the two daughters of County Sheriff Zhong to the residence of County Sheriff Gao to marry his two sons.

宋朝时,有一个姓石的县令,中年丧偶,膝下只有一女,名唤月香,他怕女儿受气,不再续娶。石县令为人正直,办事公平,他新上任时,查得本县商人贾昌被人诬陷判了死罪,他四处寻访,查清案子,放了贾昌。

一次大火烧了县里的粮仓,上边向下罪来,石县令的财产、孩子都被拍卖充公,县令惊吓成疾,不久去世。贾昌赎回石小姐月香,视为亲生女儿一样。无奈贾昌老婆心地狠毒,趁贾昌不在时,常常虐待月香。为了这事,贾昌一连五年不外出做生

意,家景日渐衰落。那年,月香十五岁。新来县令钟离义给女儿办婚事,缺少一个陪嫁丫环。贾昌老婆趁丈夫做买卖外出,把月香卖到钟县令家。月香清扫院子时,看到自己小时候在这里玩球时,抛球进洞的洞口,便触景生情,不觉伤心地哭了起来。当钟县令知道她原是石县令的女儿很是同情,遂收为义女。钟县令亲家高县令也很同情月香,决定把月香给二儿子作媳妇,并安排二个儿子同一天举行婚礼。成亲那天,钟家两顶花轿抬走两位小姐,高家迎来两位新娘。

This is a story about the five sons of Dou Yujun at Yuyang in the late Five-Dynasty Period (907-960). Dou Yujun was a court official. His family enjoyed a well-to-do life. But Dou never pampered his sons. In educating his sons he stressed hard work and diligence. Dou invited a learned tutor to teach his sons. The boys all delved into reading the family's rich collection of books and all became learned and well-mannered.

All the five sons of the Dou family had passed the highest imperial examination. The eldest son, Dou Yi, also studied in the Imperial Academy before being appointed to serve as the education and culture minister. The second son, Dou Yan, was conferred the title of Hall-of-Virtue Scholar and assigned to be an official in an important town of the country. The third son, Dou Kan, was assigned to be the official in charge of the daily life of the emperor. The fourth son, Dou Cheng, was promoted several times before being assigned to be the judge of the Supreme Court at Kaifeng. The fifth son, Dou Xi, was assigned to be the resident official in the imperial palace. The five sons were later referred to as "the five dragons of the Dou family" for their merit of all having passed the highest imperial examination.

Popular artists used to base their New Year's paintings on the five sons of the Dou family. They would send away their paintings as their New Year blessings for relatives and friends, wishing their children a successful career.

This painting depicts a playful scene of the five Dou brothers while they were still young.

五子夺魁说的是五代(公元 907－960 年)晚期渔阳窦禹钧五个儿子的事。窦禹钧在朝中为官,家境颇丰,但他从不娇惯孩子。他教子之方是刻苦加勤奋,请高师严加指点。窦家藏书万卷,五个儿子潜心阅读,个个知书达礼,知识渊博。

长子窦仪,中进士后,又入翰林,官至礼部尚书;次子窦俨,中进士后,加集贤殿学士,出使重镇为官;三子窦侃,应试及第,官拜起居郎;四子窦称,中进士后,几经升任,最后官拜开封府判官;五子窦喜,应试考中,官至左非阙。窦禹钧五子登科,被世人称为"窦氏五龙"。后来,民间艺人以窦氏五兄弟为题材画成年画,逢年过节赠友人,送亲戚,祝愿亲友的子弟们成才。这幅画中表现的是五兄弟小时候在一起玩耍的场面。

Zhao Yun Saves Young Master Single-Handedly　单骑救主

This is an episode from the novel *Three Kingdoms*. Though Liu Bei was outnumbered by Cao Cao's troops in the Xinye battle, Liu defeated Cao thanks to the smart tactic he had resorted to. Cao soon commanded an army of 500,000 to take his revenge. When Liu Bei and his force of 3,000 got to Dangyang County, they were stopped by Cao's troops. A bitter fight lasted until dawn and the Liu army narrowly managed to elude the chasing enemy.

As day broke, General Zhao Yun discovered that Liu Bei's wife and son were missing. Zhao was in charge of safeguarding Liu's family. Zhao gathered 30 troops and fought his way back onto the battlefield to look for Liu's wife, Madam Mi, and son, A Dou. With the help of a middle-aged woman, Zhao Yun found Madam Mi and A Dou by the side of a dry well behind a collapsed wall. Madam Mi said: "A Dou is safe now with you, General. I'd rather die than encumber you." When Zhao Yun was not looking her way, Madam Mi threw herself into the well. Suddenly, Cao troops came charging to-ward Zhao Yun. With tears in his eyes, Zhao Yun pushed down what remained of the collapsed wall to cover the dry well. He then held A Dou against his chest and rode his horse onward as he fought off attackers. It took Zhao Yun three rounds of combat to fight off the chasing enemy. At one point Zhao was engaged by General Zhang He and a unit of Cao's troops. Zhao and Zhang fought a dozen rounds and Zhao tried to break the siege. But Zhao Yun and his horse unexpectedly fell into a trap. Just as Zhang He charged to pierce Zhao Yun with his spear, Zhao's horse leapt out of the trap. Zhang He was taken aback by the sudden move and his horse backed off several gaits. Zhao Yun fought Cao's generals and troops single-handedly. No one could get close to him. Cao Cao, who was watching the battle from a nearby hilltop, ordered that Zhao Yun be captured alive. Zhao Yun made the most of Cao's no-kill order and broke through the siege in the end. When he returned to his camp, Zhao Yun handed the young master to Liu Bei.

《三国演义》中的故事。　新野一战,刘备以少胜多打败曹操,曹操引五十万大军前来报仇。刘备的三千人马走到当阳县,突然被曹兵截住,战到天明才摆脱曹兵的追赶,护卫刘备家小的赵云发现不见了刘备,走散了麋夫人母子,急集合三十骑,又杀回乱军中寻找。赵云在一位大嫂的指引下,在一截断墙后面的枯井旁找到麋夫人母子。麋夫人说:"见到将军阿斗有救了,……我死而无恨!"说完,趁赵云不注意跳井身亡。这时曹兵向这边杀来,赵云含泪推倒土墙掩埋了夫人,急忙抱起阿斗往外冲。曹将杀来,战三回合,被赵云杀死。没走多远,又碰上曹将张郃,战十余回合,赵云夺路而走,不料连人带马落入陷井。张郃挺枪来刺,忽然赵云的马平空一跃,跳出陷井,张郃吓得一个劲后退。赵云力战众将,威武勇猛。正在山上观战的曹操见赵云势不可挡,传令一定要活捉。赵云利用这个机会冲出包围,终于将阿斗交给了刘备。

This is an episode from the novel *A Dream of Red Mansions*. One day in late spring, Baoyu took a copy of the novel of *West Chamber* with him and walked into the garden. As he read there, he praised it as a good book. As the flowers were withering and falling onto the ground at that time of year, Daiyu came to the garden to bury the debris. When she saw Baoyu was reading, Daiyu asked to have a look at the book. Baoyu handed the book to Daiyu and said, "My good sister, never tell others you have read this book. If you have read it, you won't think of having your meals again."

Daiyu was soon enchanted by the book. As she was reading, she tried to remember the words from the book. Baoyu smiled and asked, "Is it a good book?" Daiyu nodded her head several times. Baoyu smiled again and said: "I am that body harassed by anxiety and ailment while you are that pretty face unparalleled in the whole country." Daiyu blushed at Baoyu's words. She put on an angry face. She pointed at Baoyu and said: "Damned you resort to those lewd lines of the book to bully me!" As soon as she uttered the word of "bully," tears gushed into her eyes. She turned to walk away.

Baoyu immediately caught up to her and blocked her way, imploring, "My good sister, please pardon me one more time. Rather than bully you, I'd prefer to fall into this pond and be eaten by a leprosy-headed tortoise and become a turtle myself. When you become the wife of a high-ranking official and then die of old age, I would come to your grave and carry your tombstone on my back for my whole life." Daiyu grinned at his words. Daiyu rubbed her eyes and said, "Look how frightened you are and what you have been talking about. It turns out that you are an impressive looking but useless person."

Daiyu and Baoyu thus became good brother and sister again.

《红楼梦》中的故事。 暮春季节,一天,宝玉拿一本《西厢记》独自来到花园读了起来。边读边夸是好文章。黛玉为葬花也来到这里,看见宝玉用心读书,想要过来瞧瞧,宝玉递过书说:"好妹妹,好歹看了别告诉别人。你要是看了,连饭都不想吃。"黛玉接过书来,越看越爱看,边看边出神,内心还默默地记诵着。宝玉笑着问:"你说好不好?"黛玉连连点头。宝玉笑说:"我就是'多愁多病的身',你就是那'倾国倾城的貌'。"黛玉听了,不觉满脸通红,桃腮带怒,指着宝玉说:"你这个该死的,又用这些淫词艳曲中的混帐话来欺负我。"说到"欺负"二字时,眼圈也红了,转身就走。宝玉急忙拦住央告说:"好妹妹,饶我这一回吧! 我要是存心欺负你,让我掉在这池子里,叫癞头龟吃了,变成个大王八,等以后你作了一品夫人,病老归西的时候,我就到你坟上,替你驮一辈子石碑!"直说得黛玉"扑嗤"一笑,一面揉眼一面说:"瞧你吓得那样子,还只管胡说,原来你也是个'银样蜡枪头'"。二人重归于好。

This is an episode from the novel *Strange Tales from Make-Do Studio.* An Daye turned out to be outstandingly clever while he was very young. He was also very handsome. His parents loved him very much and regarded him as a precious pearl on their palms. They hoped that their son would be successful in his career and thereby glorify his ancestors. Neighbors in the village vied each other to marry their daughters to An Daye. One night, Daye's mother had a dream which told her that a princess would marry her son. So, Daye's mother gratefully declined all marriage offers. Yet several years had passed and there was still not the marriage suggested by the dream. Daye's mother began to regret declining all the marriage offers by her neighbors.

One day while Daye was reading, a graceful young lady walked into his room accompanied by several maids. The young lady introduced herself as Princess Yunluo from the official residence of Shenghou. Daye was pleasantly surprised. Daye and the princess sat down to play a board game. The princess was so good that she defeated Daye several games in a row. After the game, the princess stood up and prepared to leave. Daye was reluctant to part with the princess. Princess Yunluo gave Daye 50 kilograms of gold and told him to build a new house with the money. She promised to come again after the house was built.

The princess came as she had promised. At night, Daye proposed to marry the princess. Princess Yunluo said: "I'll be with you for six years if we get married, but I'll be with you for 30 years if we remain as fellow players of the board game and fellow lovers of the cup." Daye said: "We might as well get married in the first place. Let the future take care of all other matters." The princess did not say anything. Daye and the princess got married that night.

Time elapsed quickly. Princess Yunluo gave birth to two baby boys for Daye. As she had warned, the princess left without saying good-bye at the end of the six years. Daye missed the princess so much that he swore not to marry again.

《聊斋志异》中的故事。 安大业从小聪明绝顶，俊美出群。父母爱他如掌上明珠，希望他将来能光宗耀祖，成一番大事业。长大后，村中人争着给他说媒。一天晚上，大业母亲突然做一梦，说大业将娶一位公主为妻，于是婉言谢绝了那些提亲的人。但梦过几年也不见公主到来，大业母亲后悔当初不该回绝别人的提亲。一天，大业正在房内读书，只见几个婢女拥着一个窈窕少女进屋。经问，说是圣后府上的云萝公主，大业惊喜万分。二人坐下对弈，精通棋道的大业连败。下完棋，公

主要走，大业不舍，公主拿出一千两黄金，要大业盖新房，等新房盖好后再相会。公主如约赶到，当晚大业向公主求婚，公主说："如我俩结为夫妻，我们只能在一起生活六年，我俩如果作为棋友、酒友，可生活三十年。"大业说："我俩还是先结婚吧，以后的事再说。"公主默默不语，当夜成婚。一晃六年过去，公主为大业生了两个男孩。公主按原先约定的时间不辞而别，大业日夜想念公主，暂不再娶。

After his beloved concubine Wu died, Emperor Xuan Zong (712-758) of the Tang Dynasty felt very unhappy. The emperor, who paid more attention to beautiful women than to state affairs, was later attracted by his daughter-in-law, Yang Yuhuan, who was very, very pretty. Regardless of ridicule from his subjects, the emperor vied with his son and took his daughter-in-law to be his own concubine.

After he succeeded in obtaining Yang Yuhuan, Emperor Xuan Zong conferred on her the title of highest-ranking imperial concubine. After Yang Yuhuan became his lover, the emperor seldom attended court affairs. He stayed in his imperial harem for days on end. Emperor Xuan Zong often took his beloved concubine to a hot spring at the foot of Mount Lishan that boasted fine quality water. Whenever Yang Yuhuan bathed in the water there, her skin would feel wonderously tender and smooth. She was as fresh and beautiful as a lotus blossoming in the water. It is said that after her baths, Yang Yuhuan could put on one hundred different faces of charm.

唐玄宗(公元712－756年在位)自武惠妃死后,成天闷闷不乐。这个重色轻国的君王被自己的儿媳杨玉环美丽绝世的容貌所吸引,他不顾国人耻笑,从儿子手中把儿媳夺过来占为己有。唐玄宗得到杨玉环后,封她为贵妃,从此他很少朝政,日日在后宫欢娱。在骊山脚下,有一温泉,水质纯净,唐玄宗经常带着杨贵妃去骊山宫华清池中沐浴。出浴的贵妃,皮肤细嫩柔滑,倩姿玉体,有如出水芙蓉,妩媚百生。有诗写道:春寒赐浴华清池,温泉水滑洗凝脂。侍儿扶起娇无力,始是新承恩泽时。"诗把杨贵妃出浴后的娇态描写得栩栩如生。

Zhang Liang Picks Up Shoes for an Old Man 张良进履

Zhang Liang was born in the Han Dynasty (206 B.C.-A.D.25). Both his grandfather and father served as the prime minister of the State of Han. After the State of Qin conquered the State of Han, Zhang Liang made up his mind to take revenge for his country. One morning while Zhang Liang was strolling near a bridge, he saw an old man sitting on the rails of the bridge and singing happily. As Zhang Liang approached, the old man kicked off his shoes and tossed them down the bridge. He said to Zhang Liang: "Young man, would you go under the bridge and pick up my shoes for me." Just as Zhang Liang was about to lose his temper, he saw that the old man's hair and brows were completely white. He calmed himself down and went under the bridge to pick up the shoes for the old man. As soon as he got back onto the bridge, the old man protruded his feet before Zhang Liang and said, "Put them on for me." Zhang Liang was shocked. But Zhang reasoned that the old man must be unusual to do that. He therefore knelt down and respect- fully put on the shoes for the old man. After Zhang Liang put the shoes on, the old man stood up and walked steadily down the bridge without saying thank you. Since Zhang Liang thought that the old man was unusual, he followed the old man down the bridge. Before long, the old man turned back and said, "You are a promising young man. I am willing to teach you something. Come here to see me in the morning in five days." Five days later, Zhang Liang came to the bridge in the morning, though he arrived a bit late. The old man said, "You have kept an old man waiting for a young man. Come again in another five days." Another five days passed but Zhang Liang was late again for the rendezvous. So he had to wait for five more days. For the third rendezvous, Zhang Liang got up at midnight of the fourth day and went to the bridge to wait for the old man. When the old man saw Zhang Liang waiting for him, he was so happy that he fished out a copy of the *Military Tactics of Taigong* and asked Zhang Liang to study it.

Zhang Liang studied day and night and came to really understand the essence of the book. He later helped Liu Bang to conquer the State of Qin.

汉朝(公元前 206 – 公元 25 年)的张良,其祖父和父亲均做过韩国的相国。秦灭韩后,张良决心替韩国报仇。一天早晨,张良来到一座桥边散步,见一老人坐在桥上晃着双腿唱歌。他见张良过来后,抬脚把鞋甩到桥下,说:"小伙子,你去桥下给我把鞋拾上来。"张良刚要发怒,但见这是一位白发白眉的长者,压着怒火下桥把鞋给他拾上来。刚上桥老人伸过脚来说:"给我把鞋穿上。"张良愣了一下,心想:此人绝非等闲之人,就跪在地上恭恭敬敬地给他穿上。穿好后,老人连个"谢"字都没说,就大摇大摆地走下桥去了。张良见老头非常奇特,也就紧跟着老人下桥去了。没走几步,老人转过身来说:"你这小伙子有出息,我愿教导教导你。五天后的早晨,你来这里见我。"五天后的清晨,张良来到桥边,老人说:"和老人相约,你让我等你,再过五天来吧!"又过五天,张良又来晚了,只好再等五天。第三次,张良半夜就到桥上等老人。老人见到张良,很高兴地拿出《太公兵法》让张良潜心学习。张良得到这部兵书,日夜攻读,苦心钻研,真正领会了其中精华。后来协助刘邦推翻了秦朝。

This is a story about the life experience of Han Xin while he was young. As a kid, Han Xin only knew how to study and practice martial arts. After his parents died, he could not make a living for himself. He had to go and share meals with his neighbors. Day in and day out, his neighbors mistook him for a lazy young man and began to dislike him. Sometimes Han Xin would go fishing by the riverside, but he had to go hungry if he could not catch anything. Living by the riverside was an old laundry woman who made her living by washing clothes for rich families. The old woman was known as Old Laundry Woman. She was honest and kindhearted. When she saw Han Xin was starved and pale, everyday the old woman split her meals with Han Xin. Han Xin once said to the old woman, "Granny, you're taking good care of me even though you yourself are poor. I will never forget your kindness and I'll repay you in the future." The old woman said angrily, "I have never counted on getting repaid by sharing my meals with you every day. A person will have no future if they do not aspire to do something unusual." Han Xin felt ashamed that an old woman knew more than he did. He uttered his agreement several times and left the old laundry woman immediately.

Later on during the conflict between the states of Chu and Han, Han Xin assisted Liu Bang to defeat Xiang Yu. After he was conferred the title of Marquis of Huaiyin, Han Xin sent someone to give the old laundry woman 50 kilograms of gold.

漂母分食待韩信(? —前 196 年),讲的是韩信小时候的一个故事。韩信小时,只会读书习武,丧父母后,他生活贫困潦倒,只能到别人家吃饭。久而久之大家认为他好吃懒做,都非常讨厌他。韩信只好去淮水边上甩竿钓鱼,如钓不到鱼便忍饥挨饿。在淮水边上,住着一位靠给有钱人家漂洗衣纱的老奶奶,大家都叫她"漂母"。老人家心地善良,她见韩信饿得面黄饥瘦,便十分可怜这个孩子,每次都把自己的饭分一半给韩信吃,天天如此,从来不间断。有一次,韩信对老奶奶说:"老奶奶,你生活这么困难,还待我这么好,使我终生难忘,将来我一定好好报答你对我的恩情。"老奶奶生气地说:"我每天分食给你,并不指望你来报答我。一个男子汉,如果不想干一番事业,那就太没出息了。"韩信觉得,一个老妪都懂得这个道理,我却不及,连声说:"是,是!"并马上走开了。后来,韩信在楚汉相争之时,帮助刘邦打败项羽,被刘邦封为"淮阴侯"后,他派人找到漂母,并以千金报答。

This is an episode from the novel *Three Kingdoms*. Cao Cao sent a letter to Zhou Yu to summon him to surrender. Zhou Yu tore Cao's letter to pieces. Zhou Yu's classmate, Jiang Gan, was working for Cao Cao as an adviser. Jiang offered to travel to Wu to persuade Zhou Yu to surrender. One day while Zhou Yu was discussing with his subordinates how to defeat Cao Cao, he was told that Jiang Gan had come to see him. Zhou immediately figured out that Jiang must have come to persuade him to surrender. Zhou Yu devised a clever plan to thwart his efforts and enlisted the help of his subordinate to carry it out. Then he went to meet Jiang Gan all smiles. Zhou Yu took Jiang Gan's hands and marshaled him into his tent and treated him to a banquet. When all his generals and subordinates came for dinner, Zhou Yu told those around the table: "This is an old friend of mine. Though he came from the Cao Cao camp, he did not come to persuade me to surrender. Please do not suspect him." After the banquet, Zhou Yu pretended that he had too much and invited Jiang Gan to his bedroom for a rest. Zhou Yu soon pretended to have fallen asleep. Jiang Gan took this chance to thumb through Zhou Yu's documents. He was shocked to find a letter from Cai Mao and Zhang Yun, two generals of the Cao camp, who had written Zhou Yu to surrender. Jiang hid the letter of surrender in his pocket and returned to the bed, pretending that he was still asleep.

After midnight, someone sneaked into Zhou Yu's tent and woke him up, telling him "A messenger came from the Cao camp to say that Cai Mao and Zhang Yun were not yet a position to carry out their plan." After he heard the news, Zhou Yu went back to sleep. Jiang Gan got up again silently and snuck out of Zhou Yu's camp. He crossed the river immediately and handed the letter of surrender to Cao Cao. Cao was enraged and he had Cai Mao and Zhang Yun executed.

When the news spread to Wu, Zhou Yu burst into laughter and said, "Cai Mao and Zhang Yun were the two generals I feared most. Now I fear no one." Before long, Cao Cao realized that he was cheated by Zhou Yu's stratagem of sowing distrust in Cao's camp.

《三国演义》中的故事。 曹操给周瑜下了一道降书,周瑜见书,撕得粉碎。周瑜的老同学蒋干在曹操手下当谋士,他自告奋勇去东吴劝降周瑜。这天,周瑜和部下商议破曹计策,有人报告蒋干来了。周瑜一听,就知道蒋干来作说客,眉头一皱,向部下说出了自己的妙计,然后笑着出帐迎客。周瑜挽着蒋干的手进帐,并设宴招待。待众将到齐后,周瑜对大家说:"这是我的老朋友,虽然从曹操那里来,但不是来当说客的,大家不要怀疑。"宴毕,周瑜假装喝醉,挽蒋干同榻休息,不一会,周瑜佯装睡着。蒋干轻轻起身,翻看周瑜的案卷,得知曹军中的蔡瑁、张允二将军给周瑜写了降书,大为吃惊,急忙藏起降书,轻轻躺回床上,假装睡着。后半夜,有人进帐叫醒周瑜说:"曹营有人来了,蔡瑁、张允说现在还不能下手……"周瑜听罢,躺下又睡。蒋干偷偷起来,径直出营,过江把信交给曹操。曹操大怒,杀了蔡瑁,张允。消息传到东吴,周瑜哈哈大笑说:"我所担心的就是这两个人,现在我什么都不怕了。"事后,曹操醒悟,知道中了周瑜的反间计。

This is an episode from the novel *Outlaws of the Marsh*. On his way to visit his brother, Wu Song was at a place called Mount Jingyang. Though a bit drunk, he began to climb the mountain. Before long he saw a sign posted on a tree: "Travelers are advised to group together to climb over the mountain since tigers have killed some singular travelers of late. Please do not risk your life." Wu Song reasoned that the sign must have been written by the inn keeper at the foot of the mountain for the sake of scaring travelers into spending the night in his inn. He did not pay attention to the sign and continued on his way.

At sunset he came to an old temple on top of the mountain. There Wu Song saw another official sign warning of tigers. He now believed that there were indeed tigers on the mountain. Still, he decided not to return to the inn at the foot of the mountain for fear that the owner would laugh at him. He felt too drunk to walk on, so he decided to lie down on a slab of gray stone. Just as he was about to fall asleep, he felt a gust of wind whistling around him: It was a mammoth tiger charging at him. Wu Song immediately turned his body and dodged the animal. The tiger leapt again, but Wu Song managed to evade it. The beast got so angry that it used its tail to sweep toward Wu Song. Wu Song jumped to dodge the attack. He lifted his cudgel to hit the tiger while it was turning around, but his cudgel caught the branches of a tree and broke in two. The tiger was annoyed and launched another assault. Wu Song threw away the remnant of his cudgel and jumped onto the back of the tiger. With his left hand, he grabbed the skin of the head of the tiger, and he used his other fist to hit the eyes, mouth, nose and ears of the tiger. Before long, the tiger was bleeding all over and lied on the ground motionless. Wu Song was afraid the tiger was pretending to be dead, so he wielded the broken cudgel to hit the tiger until he was sure the tiger was dead.

The incident on Mount Jingyang made Wu Song famous far and wide.

《水浒传》中的故事。 武松回家探望哥哥,途中路过景阳冈。在冈下酒店喝了很多酒,跟跄着向冈上走去。行不多时,只见一棵树上写着,"近因景阳冈大虫伤人,但有过冈客商,应结伙成队过冈,请勿自误。"武松认为,这是酒家写来吓人的,为的是让过客住他的店,竟不理它,继续往前走。

太阳快落山时,武松来到一破庙前,见庙门贴了一张官府告示,武松读后,方知山上真有虎,待要回去住店,怕店家笑话,又继续向前走。由于酒力发作,便找了一块大青石,仰身躺下,刚要入睡,忽听一阵狂风呼啸,一只斑斓猛虎朝武松扑了过来,武松急忙一闪身,躲在老虎背后。老虎一纵身,武松又躲了过去。老虎急了,大吼一声,用尾巴向武松打来,武松又急忙跳开,并趁猛虎转身的那一霎间,举起哨棒,运足力气,朝虎头猛打下去。只听"咔嚓"一声,哨棒打在树枝上。老虎兽性大发,又向武松扑过来,武松扔掉半截棒,顺势骑在虎背上,左手揪住老虎头上的皮,右手猛击虎头,没多久就把老虎打得眼、嘴、鼻、耳到处流血,趴在地上不能动弹。武松怕老虎装死,举起半截哨棒又打了一阵,见那老虎确实没气了,才住手。从此武松威名大震。

A Crane's Shadow Flits Across a Chilly Pool　寒塘鹤影

This is a story from the novel *A Dream of Red Mansions*. One Mid-Autumn Festival Lady Dowager and her relatives from the mansions of Rong and Ning were at the Convex Emerald Hall enjoying the bright full moon. Without the presence of Xue Baochai and her sister, who had gone home, and Li Wan and Wang Xifeng, who were ill, the old lady felt bored. As a result the party did not last as long as usual. After the party all of them went back to their rooms except Daiyu and Xiangyun who went to Concave Crystal Hall and sat under the bright moon. The scene was beautiful: the moon reflected in the water just like a round mirror. Daiyu and Xiangyun felt carefree and joyous. As they were enjoying themselves by jointly composing poems, Daiyu, pointing at the shadow in the pond, said with a start: "Look out at the pool. It looks as if a man in the dark. Could it be a ghost!" "I am not afraid of ghosts," said Xiangyun. "Let me hit it." As she was speaking, she picked up a stone and threw it into the pool. With a sound of chirping a white crane took off from the pond. Xiangyun, deeply touched by the scene, blurted out:

A crane's shadow flitting across the chilly pool.

Hearing the words Daiyu could not help shouting "excellent" repeatedly. Then she pondered for a while and said with a smile: "I have finished another one to match yours."

The poet's spirit is buried in the cold moonlight.

"What do you think about it?" Xiangyun clapped her hands and shouted "bravo!" Soon afterward, she sighed and said, "Your line is, of course, fresh and excellent, but it sounds too depressing. Since you are ill, so you should not make poetry as depressing as this." While they were absorbed in the discussion they suddenly heard someone cry out, "Excellent poem, excellent poem." It turned out that it was Miaoyu who had been listening to them from behind the hill. Miaoyu invited them to have a cup of tea in her Green Lattice Nunnery and asked them to write down all the lines of poetry they had made. Then Miaoyu continued to made up the rest part of the poem. They talked happily until daybreak. Then Daiyu and Xiangyun went back for a rest.

《红楼梦》中的故事。　有一年中秋节，贾母率荣宁两府的人在凸碧堂赏月。只因宝钗姐妹回家，李纨、凤姐得病，少了这四个人，贾母觉得冷清，热闹了一会，大家就散了。独黛玉和湘云没走，二人来到凹晶馆坐定。天上皓月当空，水中明月如镜，二人心旷神怡，联诗取乐。正在兴头，黛玉突然指了指池中黑影说："你看那河里，怎么像是个人到黑影里去了，敢是个鬼吧！"湘云说："我是不怕鬼的，等我打他一下。"说着捡起块石头扔了过去，只闻"嘎"的一声，池面飞起了一只白鹤。湘云见景生情，马上说出"寒塘渡鹤影"的佳句。黛玉连声叫好，琢磨了一会，笑着说："冷月葬花魂"。湘云一听，拍手叫绝。可又转念，叹了一口气说："诗固然新奇，只是太颓丧了些，你现在病着，不该作过于凄凉奇谲之语。"二人谈诗，正在兴头上，突然听山后有人叫："好诗，好诗！"原来是妙玉在山后偷听，她请黛玉、湘云去栊翠院喝茶，又让黛玉和湘云把刚才的联诗全部抄下来，而后，妙玉又续了半首。三个人高高兴兴地谈论到天快亮时，黛玉、湘云才回潇湘馆歇息去了。

This is a story from *Outlaws of the Marsh*. One day Li Kui and Yan Qing, two heroes in Liangshan Marsh, spent the night in the town of Jingmen, which is near to the Liangshan Marsh. In the manor the squire told them that Song Jiang, head of the Liangshan Marsh, had snatched his daughter away by force. Li Kui got so angry that he ignored the facts and Yan Qing's doubts and immediately went to Liangshan Marsh. He went directly to Loyalty Hall and without a word took his axes and cut down the apricot-yellow banner inscribed with "Act in Heaven's Behalf" and ripped it to shreds. Axes in hand, Li Kui charged across the hall towards Song Jiang. Some commanders in the hall hurriedly blocked him and asked him for reason. Li Kui told them what he had heard, which Song Jiang strongly denied. Seeing that Li Kui did not believe him, Song Jiang asked him to search his house. But Li Kui said it would be impossible to find the girl because every man in the fortress was under Song Jiang's command. Finally Song Jiang said, "The squire isn't dead yet. I'll go and confront him." In the manor, Li Kui discovered the truth: it was someone else who misbehaved in Song Jiang's name. He began to regret his impatient, hasty actions. He carried a thornstick on his bare back and asked Song Jiang to take the stick and beat him. Song Jiang said, "I'll forgive you if you capture the two impersonators and bring the girl home." After taking a great deal of bother Li Kui finally found the two perpetrators, Wang Jiang and Dong Hai. He killed them and saved the squire's daughter.

《水浒传》中的故事。 一天,梁山好汉李逵、燕青来到离梁山泊不远的荆门镇投宿。他们听庄主太公说他的女儿被梁山泊首领宋江抢走。李逵非常气愤,不问青红皂白,也不听燕青劝阻,赶回梁山直奔忠义堂,抢起两把大斧砍倒了堂前的旗杆,把"替天行道"的旗子扯得粉碎。接着又冲上堂去,举斧直奔宋江,在堂上议事的头领们急忙拉住李逵问原因,李逵把在荆门镇听到的事情说了一遍。宋江否定,李逵不信,宋江让他去搜,李逵说山上向着宋江的人多,搜不出来。宋江无奈说:"太公没死,我们前去对质。"宋江一行来到庄上后,李逵才知道有人冒名顶替,自己后悔莫及,便负荆请罪。宋江说:"你找到假宋江,救回姑娘,便可饶你。"李逵下山,几经周折,终于在牛头山找到了抢人的王江和董海两个草寇头目,杀死了强盗,救出了太公的女儿。

This is a story recorded in the book *Records of the Historian*. It is about how Zhuan Zhu assassinated King Wu.

The State of Wu had two princes. Prince Guang aspired to taking back the crown from his brother King Wu. Prince Guang befriended Zhuan Zhu and treated him favorably, just like one of his family members. The special treatment made Zhuan Zhu feel uneasy. He once told Prince Guang, "I am just an uneducated chap. I don't know how to repay your kindness. Tell me if ever you have difficulties and need my help. I wouldn't hesitate even to risk my life." Prince Guang cried and told Zhuan Zhu that he planned to kill his brother and snatch back the throne. He also told Zhuan Zhu that his brother, King Wu, liked to eat fish very much and that it was possible to get close to him at dinner time.

Then Zhuan Zhu learned cook fish in a restaurant. He soon became a good cook and was hired to cook meals for Prince Guang. One day, Prince Guang invited his brother to dinner at his home. King Wu was afraid of assassins, so he put on a suit of armor and was accompanied by more than 100 bodyguards. The guards would search the chefs before allowing them to serve the dishes to the host and guest. When Zhuan Zhu carried out a dish of fish, King Wu could not help but praise the chef for his skill. Just as King Wu uttered his praise, Zhuan Zhu pulled out a sword from inside of the fish and stabbed King Wu in the chest. The sword pierced through the armor and killed the king at once. Zhuan Zhu was immediately killed by the guards, but Prince Guang took back the crown title and the throne.

《史记》中记载的故事。吴国公子光,一心想从公子僚手中夺回本应属于他的王位。经人介绍,他认识了专诸,公子光给专诸优厚的待遇,对待专诸如同一家人,使专诸非常过意不去。一次,专诸对公子光说:"我是个粗人,你待我这么好,我不知道该怎么报答,你如果有为难之事,用得着我,我在所不辞。"公子光哭着把自己打算杀吴王僚夺回王位的事说了,并告诉专诸,吴王僚很喜欢吃鱼,只有送饭时才能靠近他。为此,专诸特意学习烧鱼。由于虚心求学,烹调技术小有名气,便给公子光当厨师。一天,公子光请吴王僚来家赴宴,僚怕人行刺,身穿铠甲,随身带了一百多名卫士,并对前来送菜的厨师都要上下搜遍,然后才能送菜上桌。当专诸端来一大盘鱼时,吴王僚连夸做得好。话音刚落,专诸突然从鱼腹中抽出一把利刃猛向吴王僚刺去,穿过铠甲,刺穿后背,吴王僚当场毙命。专诸也被卫士杀死。公子光夺回了王位。

This is an episode from the novel *Three Kingdoms.* Zhou Yu ordered Zhuge Liang to manufacture 100,000 arrows within ten days. Zhuge said, "Give me three days." He also signed a pledge placing himself liable for punishment should he fail to complete the order. Zhou Yu ridiculed that Zhuge Liang was looking for self-destruction. On the one hand, Zhou Yu ordered his troops not to provide Zhuge Liang with materials to make the arrows. He also sent Lu Su to spy on him to find out what was going on. In fact, Zhuge Liang had already realized that this was a plot by Zhou Yu to frame him up. As soon as Lu Su got into his room, Zhuge said to Lu Su, "Save me please." He asked Lu Su to lend him 20 boats, each lined with straw-made scarecrows and manned by 30 soldiers. He requested that Lu Su not tell Zhou Yu what was happening.

When Lu Su came again to see Zhuge Liang, he did not find anything unusual. Nothing happened on the second day either. In the small hours of the third day, Zhuge Liǎng invited Lu Su for a boat ride. The 20 boats were tied together with strong ropes. Zhuge's fleet sailed toward the camp of Cao Cao. A thick mist had spread over the surface of the river. People could hardly see each other on the river. When Zhuge's fleet got close to the Cao camp before dawn, Zhuge Liang ordered his soldiers to shout and beat drums to fake an attack. Zhuge and Lu Su simply sat inside one of the boats and drank wines to enjoy themselves.

As soon as the Cao camp heard the shouting and drum beating, they mistook it for a surprise attack by the Zhou Yu camp. Since they could see nobody on the river, they gathered 3,000 bow men and ordered them to shoot arrows towards where the shouting and drum beating came. The front of the scarecrows was quickly shot full of arrows. After a while, Zhuge Liang had his fleet turned around to expose the other side of the scarecrows. When this side was also shot full of arrows, the day broke. Zhuge Liang ordered his soldiers to return to their base port. The soldiers shouted, "Thank you, Cao Cao, for your arrows." After they got back to their camp, they collected more than 100,000 arrows from the scarecrows.

《三国演义》中的故事。 东吴与刘备联合抗曹,东吴大都督周瑜命诸葛亮十日内制作十万支箭。诸葛亮说:"只需三日。"并立下军令状。周瑜笑诸葛亮是自取灭亡。周瑜一边吩咐士兵不给诸葛亮准备制作箭的材料,一面让谋士鲁肃去探听虚实。其实诸葛亮早已知道,这是周瑜想借造箭一事加害于他。鲁肃刚进门,诸葛亮就说:"救救我吧!"他要鲁肃偷偷借给他二十条船,每船三十个军士,两边扎上稻草人,听候调用。又叮嘱鲁肃千万别告诉周瑜。鲁肃又来见诸葛亮,第一天不见动静,第二天也不动。第三天四更时分,诸葛亮密请鲁肃到船上。同时,把二十条船用绳索连好,向曹营进发。此时,江上大雾迷漫,对面看不见人。五更时分,船只接近曹营。诸葛亮让军士们在船上擂鼓呐喊,装作周瑜来偷袭。无奈江上雾大看不清楚,曹操只好调三千弓箭手向船上射箭。待草人身上密密地插满了箭,天已放亮,诸葛亮下令收船。军士们高喊着:"谢谢曹丞相的箭。"高高兴兴地往回走了。回营后,把箭取下,十万有余。

This is a story from the book *Strange Tales from Make-Do Studio*. There was an old man with the surname Feng, he had a son named Xiangru. Xiangru studied hard but failed several times in passing the imperial examination. One night when Xiangru was reading books in the courtyard, he was surprised to see a beautiful girl on the wall looking at him affectionately. Xiangru invited her to come down from the wall and knew that her name was Hong Yu. From then on, Hong Yu came to meet Xiangru every night and soon they fell in love. One night, Feng happened to run into Hong Yu at the door of Xiangru's room. Feng scolded Xiangru severely. Hong Yu slipped away and she never came there again. Later, Xiangru got married. His wife was called Wei and they had a boy named Lucky. Unfortunately, the bully in the village, Song, was moved by Wei's good looks and snatched her away. Feng was so indignant that finally he died. Another day, a brave man rushed into Xiangru's room and said, "Have you forgotten that your father has died and your wife was snatched away by Song?" Xiangru hurriedly told the man that he wanted revenge but had no way to achieve it. Then, Song was beheaded that same night. The county government suspected Xiangru and detained him. The evening that Xiangru was arrested, no sooner the governmental official lied down than he saw a knife stabbed on the head of the bed. He was scared and set Xiangru free the next day. One day at his home, Xiangru heard his child talking to somebody outside the door. He opened the door and was surprised and glad to see Hong Yu standing there with Lucky. Hong Yu smiled and said, "I am not a common girl, but a fox spirit. I know that you have been in trouble; I am secretly protecting you." Since then, Hong Yu stayed with Xiangru to manage the family affairs and teach the child.

《聊斋志异》中的故事。 冯翁年近六旬，膝下一子相如。他潜心读书，但运气不佳，屡考不中。一夜，相如在院中读书，忽然传来"索索"的声音。只见墙上一美丽少女，含情脉脉地看他读书。相如请她下来，问她姓名，方知叫红玉。从此红玉夜夜必到，二人互相爱慕，山盟海誓。一晚，冯翁从相如门口过，撞见红玉，责骂相如。红玉见状，悄悄溜走，从此再也没来。后来，相如娶妻卫氏，夫妻恩爱并生一男孩，名唤福儿。然而，乡里恶霸宋某见卫氏姿色好，带家奴抢走卫氏，气死冯翁。有一天，一位勇士撞进相如房内说："难道你忘了杀父抢妻之仇吗？"相如忙把想报仇，但无计策的心事告诉了那勇士。就在当晚霸宋某人头落地，县衙怀疑相如，派人捉拿归案。晚上，县令刚躺下，就见一把利刃扎在床头，县令害怕，放了相如。相如回到家后不久，听到门外有小孩说话声，开门见是红玉带着福儿进来。红玉笑着说："我不是凡人，是狐仙，知你必有大难，一直在暗中保护你。"从此，红玉再也未走，帮相如操持家务，教育孩子。

This is a story from the novel *A Dream of Red Mansions*. On a day in March, Lin Daiyu was on her way back home when she heard sweet fluting and singing over the wall of Pear Fragrance Court. She knew that this was the actresses' rehearsal of *Peony Pavilion*. At that moment, she heard two lines clearly:

What an enchanting sight on this fine morning,
But who is there that takes delight in the spring?

Daiyu nodded. "So there are fine lines in these operas," she thought. "What a pity that people just care for the spectacle without understanding the meaning." Then she listened the next lines:

For you are as fair as a flower
And youth is slipping away like flowing water.

The two lines affected her so much that she sank down on a rock to ponder the words. They reminded her of lines,

Water flows and flowers fall, knowing no pity,
Spring departs with the flowing water and fallen blossoms.

Her heart ached and tears coursed down her cheeks when she thought about herself: her parents had died and she had to live under her relative's roof, what's more, no one supported the love between her and Jia Baoyu.

《红楼梦》中的故事。　三月里的一日，黛玉葬完花回潇湘馆，走到梨香院墙外，听到墙内笛声悠扬，歌声婉转，知道是戏班正在演习《牡丹亭》。"良辰美景奈何天，赏心乐事谁家院……"黛玉听了这两句点头说："原来戏上也有好文章，可惜世人只知道看戏，未必领会到其中的趣味。"紧接着又传出"只为你如花美眷，似水流年……"。黛玉听到这里，不觉心动神摇，

站立不稳。坐在一块石头上，细嚼"如花美眷，似水流年"这八个字。她想起古人的"水流花谢两无情"、"落花流水春去也"等佳句；看到暮春时节，残红遍地，落花纷纷，随风而去；想到自己，父母双亡，过着寄人篱下的凄苦生活；她和宝玉的爱情，又找不到支持者。触景生情落下泪来。

During the reign of the Xiaowu Emperor of Jin (140-87 B.C.) a fisherman in Wuling, Hunan, sailed along a river fishing. He was so engrossed in his work that when he looked up, he saw he was in a strange place: peach trees in fine bloom flanked the river, flower petals drifted along, propelled by a gentle breeze. At the end of the river, there was a mountain, on which a cave was seen. He went up the mountain and into the cave. He couldn't believe his eyes when he saw another world inside: on a vast plain nice houses were built and vast fertile lands stretched far and wide. By the fields in which people were working, and by the houses, grew luxuriant mulberry trees and bamboos. The sounds of dogs barking and roosters crowing were heard occasion-ally. It was a picture of a peaceful life.

People were surprised to see him. Their ancestors, they said, had moved to this out-of-reach place to avoid wars during the Qin Dynasty. They knew nothing about the changes outside, about the downfall of Qin, nor the succeeding Han, Wei, and Jin dynasties. They listened with great interest when the fisherman described the outside world. After a couple of days the fisherman said farewell to them. Outside the cave he traced his way back. Back home he told this unique encounter to the local governor, who immediately sent men to have a look, but they failed to find the place. The story was recorded by Tao Yuanming, the famous literary man of the Jin, in "The Peach Flower Land," a prose piece.

在晋孝武帝(公元 373－396 年)时。湖南武陵有一位渔夫划船沿溪捕鱼,只顾劳作,不知走到了什么地方。只见两岸都是桃树,枝头桃花盛开,花瓣飞舞。渔夫顺流来到溪的源头,见有一座山,山上有个小洞,渔夫下船,信步走进洞内,只见这里房屋整齐,土地肥沃,许多男女在田里耕作。田边屋旁种满了桑树和翠竹,鸡鸣犬吠处处相闻,呈现出一派升平景象。洞里人看到渔夫,都很惊讶。主人告诉渔夫,他们的祖先为避秦朝的战乱,率妻带儿,扶老携幼,来到这个与外界隔绝的地方。他们既不知道有汉朝,也不知道有魏晋。渔夫把山外的事情讲给他们听,并在这里呆了几天,便和他们告别。沿来时的路回到了自己的家,把此事告诉了太守,太守立即派人按渔夫指出的路线去找,但没找到这个地方。此事被晋代文学家陶渊明写成散文《桃花源记》流传下来。

Two Yu's Listen to Music 双玉听琴

This is an episode from the novel *A Dream of Red Mansions*. As Xi Chun and Miao Yu were playing a board game, Bao Yu came to the Lufeng pavilion to look for Xi Chun. But Xi Chun and Miao Yu were not aware of Bao Yu's presence. Bao Yu laughed at Xi Chun and Miao Yu for their absorption in the game. The two maids were taken aback by Bao Yu's laughter. Before long, Miao Yu said that she would have to leave. Bao Yu said, "Let me show you the way." As they were passing by the Xiaoxiang Lodge, Miao Yu and Bao Yu heard a tune played on a stringed musical instrument. Bao Yu said, "It must be Sister Lin playing her *guqin*. Let's go and see her." Miao Yu reasoned, "Ever since ancient times, the *guqin* has been an instrument only to be listened to and not to be looked at." Miao Yu and Bao Yu sat down on a small mound of stones and quietly listened to Daiyu playing and singing along. The tune was sorrowful and desolate. So was Daiyu's song. Both the tune and song expressed the nostalgic feeling of Daiyu and her feelings about living away from home. Miao Yu, whose life experience was much like that of Daiyu, was deeply moved by the tune and song.

《红楼梦》中的故事。 惜春和妙玉正在下棋,宝玉来蓼风轩找惜春,两人竟一点也没发觉。宝玉对着棋兴正浓的惜春、妙玉哈哈大笑,把二人吓了一跳。一会,妙玉要走,宝玉说:"我给你带路。"他们路过潇湘馆时,忽然听有琴声。宝玉说:"定是林妹妹在弹琴,咱们去看她。"妙玉道:"自古以来只有听琴,没有看琴。"于是二人在山石上坐下来,静静听着黛玉边弹边吟。黛玉婉转低沉的琴声动人心弦;凄凉悲哀的歌声,感人肺腑。这琴声和歌声抒发了黛玉怀念故乡、不甘寄人篱下的心情,同时也感染了境遇相同的妙玉。

Kong Rong Offering the Pear to Others 孔融让梨

Kong Rong is a descendant of the great sage Confucius (551-479 B. C.) who lived at the end of Spring and Autumn Period. Kong Rong was killed by Cao Cao for his straight forwardness. This is an anecdote of young Kong Rong. There were seven children in Kong Rong's family and he was the sixth. When Kong Rong was four years old, his father bought some pears for them. Kong Rong's sisters and brothers asked him to choose first; they were surprised to see that Kong Rong selected the smallest one. When his father asked why, he said, "I am the youngest and should have the smallest pear." From then on, Kong Rong was famous for his modesty. Later on, the story of Kong Rong and the pears was edited into the enlightenment textbook *The Trimetrical Classic* which was very popular in old China.

孔融是春秋末期思想家、政治家、教育家孔子(前 551 – 前 479 年)的后代。他为人正直,敢于直言,终因得罪曹操而被杀害。孔融让梨写的是他小时的一个故事。孔融兄弟七人,他是老六。在孔融四岁那年,父亲买来一些梨,让他们分着吃,哥哥姐姐们让孔融先拿,结果他拿了其中最小的一个。大家都很惊奇,父亲问孔融为什么拿一个最小的,他说:"我年纪最小,应该吃小梨。"从此,孔融谦虚礼让的美德流传四方。后来,孔融让梨又被编入中国旧时流行的启蒙课本"三字经"中加以颂扬。

The unicorn is a mythical animal in China, symbolizing auspiciousness. It is said that Confucius was very modest and eager to learn but was quite worried for there were no books for him to learn from. One night, he saw a stream of red smoke while he was half asleep. He calculated that a sage was probably born where the red smoke was arising. He then called on his disciples Yan Hui and Zi Xia to come with him at once to search for such place. They walked till day break when they suddenly saw a child stoning a unicorn on the riverbank. Getting off the carriage, Confucius ran towards the riverbank in haste. When the child saw him coming, he hid the unicorn in a thick growth of grass. When Confucius finally found the unicorn, he took off his clothes to warm the unicorn and bound its wounds carefully. The unicorn looked at Confucius gratefully and licked his hand. Suddenly, the unicorn spat out three books, then turned away, jumped into the river and disappeared. Thus Confucius received three precious books. He studied these day and night and at last became a sage of great knowledge.

　　麒麟是传说中的一种神兽, 代表着吉祥。据传, 孔子当年虚心好学, 到处求教, 由于没有书, 学起来很困难, 他常为此而苦恼。一天夜里, 他在朦胧中看到一个地方升起一股紫红的烟气, 常聚不散, 他预测可能在紫气升起的地方有圣贤出世。于是, 马上叫醒弟子颜回和子夏, 驱车前去寻找。他们走到天亮, 忽然看到前边的河岸上, 有个小孩正用石头打一只麒麟, 孔子下车, 急忙向河岸跑去。小孩见有人来, 就把麒麟藏在草丛中。孔子扒开草丛, 看到麒麟被小孩打伤, 一边责备小孩, 一边脱下衣服给麒麟盖上, 又小心翼翼地给麒麟包扎伤口。麒麟用感激的目光看着孔子, 并用舌头舔他的手。突然, 麒麟从口中吐出三部书, 猛一回身, 跳到河中无影无踪了。孔子得到三部宝书, 日夜苦读, 终于成了知识渊博的圣人。

Rescues His Mother by Splitting the Mountain 劈山救母

This is a mythic story. Scholar Liu Yanchang was on his way back after taking an examination. When he passed Huashan Mountain in Shaanxi, he saw the statue of Sage Mother, which was so beautiful that he chanted a poem to express his love. Sage Mother was moved by Liu Yanchang's love, then, despite the rules of Heaven, descended to the world and married him. A year later, they had a boy Chen Xiang and lived a happy life. God Erlang, Sage Mother's brother, got so enraged at the news that his sister married a common person that he had Sage Mother pressed under Huashan Mountain. Chen Xiang missed his mother very much and cried all day long. God Thunderbolt was moved by his cry and decided to teach him martial arts in the mountain. Not until fifteen years later did God Thunderbolt tell Chen Xiang what had happened to his mother and give him a magical axe to rescue his mother. Chen Xiang asked his uncle, God Erlang, to set his mother free. However, God Erlang was so ironhearted that he disagreed and even wanted to kill Chen Xiang. Chen Xiang, at the end of his patience, began to fight with him. Four immortals who sympathized with Chen Xiang and helped him defeat God Erlang. Chen Xiang hurried to the foot of Huashan Mountain. Calling his mother, he split the mountain into two with the axe and helped her out.

　　神话故事。　书生刘彦昌赶考回来,路过华山(陕西境内),看到三圣母塑像美丽动人,不由得留诗一首,表达了对三圣母的爱慕之情。三圣母被刘彦昌的真情所感动,于是,冲破天上的禁令,下凡和刘彦昌结为夫妻,一年后,生子沉香。二郎神得知妹妹下嫁凡人的消息,非常气愤,他不顾骨肉之情,把三圣母压在华山脚下,生生拆散了这个温馨快乐的家庭。

　　沉香天天哭着要妈妈,哭声引起了霹雳大仙的同情,就把沉香带回山中,并天天教他武艺。十五年后,大仙把他母亲的遭遇告诉了沉香,并送给沉香一把开山神斧,让沉香去搭救被压在华山底下的母亲。沉香找到二郎神,求他放出母亲,铁石心肠的二郎神不但不放人,还要把沉香置于死地。沉香在忍无可忍的情况下,抢起神斧和二郎神厮杀起来。这时来了四位神仙,他们都很同情沉香,协助沉香打败了二郎神。沉香急忙来到华山脚下,高呼着母亲,举起神斧把华山劈开,救出了被压多年的母亲。

This picture was made according to Tao Yuanming's masterpiece *The Ballad of Returning Home*. Tao Yuanming, literary name Qian, is a native of Caisang in Xunyang (in today's Jiangxi Province) and is a renowned poet of the Eastern Jin Period (317-420). He had been an official several times and had the aim of saving people from suffering. But the corruption of society and the ugliness of reality hit him with one blow after another and in the end he was forced to resign his post. *The Ballad of Returning Home* was written after he resigned his post as a magistrate. It expresses his dissatisfaction with the society at that time. He wrote at the beginning of the poem that he had lost direction and suffered a lot during his thirteen years as an official. Then he quickly forgot his sufferings and had the excited feeling of "the boat tenderly sailing in far distance, wind gently blowing up my clothes." He was anxious to return to his home and when he arrived, "the servants are welcoming and the smallest child is waiting by the door." The whole family was elated to welcome him back. Tao Yuanming left the officialdom where everyone jockeys for position. He returned to nature and led a life of "pleased to hear the caring words of relatives, removing worriness by listening to music and reading books."

这幅画是根据陶渊明的名作《归去来辞》画的。陶渊明,名潜,字之亮浔阳柴桑(今江西境内)人,是东晋(公元 317 – 420 年)著名的诗人。《归去来辞》是他辞去县令后作的,通篇表达了作者对当时社会的不满。文章一开头就写到"归去来兮,田园将芜胡不归,既自以心为形役,奚惆怅而独悲。悟以往之不谏,知来者之可追。实迷途其未远,觉今是而昨非。"作者称自己十三年的官场生活是迷失了方向,内心是痛苦的。但很快能从痛苦中挣扎出来,表现出"舟摇摇以轻扬,风飘飘而吹衣"的兴奋心情。他归心似箭,日夜兼程往家奔。到家后是"僮仆欢迎,稚子候门"全家人都为他的到来惊喜若狂。作者离开勾心斗角的官场,回到悠然自得的田园,心情恬静而惬意,真正过上"悦亲戚之情话,乐琴书以消忧"的生活。

Liu Bei Crossed the River to Keep an Appointment   江东赴会

This is a story from *Three Kingdoms*. Zhou Yu of Wu Kingdom was a strategist but he was narrow-minded and jealous of people smarter than him. So he had always been thinking of killing Zhuge Liang and Liu Bei of Shu Kingdom. One day, he invited Liu Bei to cross the river, while did not let Zhuge Liang—who was then staying in Wu for help—know about it. Zhou Yu was very glad when he saw Liu Bei's coming. He had arranged an armed man to kill Liu Bei at the banquet when he threw a cup to the ground as the signal. Zhuge Liang was surprised when he discovered Liu Bei were meeting with Zhou Yu. Anxiously he went to the tent and relieved to see Liu Bei had Guan Yu standing behind to protect him. Then he went to a small boat by the river, waiting for them to come back. At the banquet, host and guest had savored several rounds of wine when Zhou Yu stood up, cup in hand. Observing Lord Guan, hand on sword, Zhou

Yu inquired who he was. "My younger brother, Guan Yunchang," replied Liu Bei. "Not the one who cut down generals Yan Liang and Wen Chou?" Zhou Yu asked nervously. "The same," Liu Bei answered. Zhou Yu, alarmed, broke out in a cold sweat. He poured a cup for Lord Guan and drank with him and said, "You are really famous for you have slain six generals and breached five passes!" When Liu Bei asked where Zhuge Liang was, Zhou Yu said he'd better meet him when Cao Cao was defeated. Lord Guan eyed Liu Bei, who sensed his brother's intent and rose to bid Zhou Yu farewell. Zhou Yu made no effort to detain his guests. When Liu Bei and Lord Guan reached the edge of the river, where they were happy to find Zhuge Liang in his boat. "My lord," said Zhuge Liang, "You were in more danger than you knew today. If not for Lord Guan, Zhou Yu would have killed you."

《三国演义》中的故事。　东吴的周瑜虽有计谋，但心胸狭窄妒贤嫉能，一心想害刘备和诸葛亮。一天，他瞒着正在东吴帮助决策的诸葛亮，请刘备过江，意欲杀害刘备。周瑜见到刘备后很高兴，以为计谋就要得逞，并安排好刀斧手，准备在宴席上摔杯为号把刘备杀掉。诸葛亮探得刘备过江，大吃一惊，急忙前去救主，走到帐外往里一看，原来刘备后面有关羽保护，随之放心而去，在江边一条小船上等候刘备的到来。酒过数巡，周瑜起身给刘备敬酒，见刘备身后站一员大将，威风凛凛，按剑而立，忙问是谁? 刘备说："这是我二弟关云长。"周瑜说："就是斩颜良，诛文丑的关云长吗？"刘备说："是。"周瑜惊得出了一身冷汗，马上给关羽斟酒恭维道："将军斩颜良、诛文丑，过五关斩六将，天下闻名啊！"刘备要见诸葛亮，周瑜说待破曹后才能见到。关羽给刘备使眼色，刘备会意，起身告辞。周瑜也不相留。行至江边见诸葛亮在船上等候，很高兴。诸葛亮说："你今天过江很危险，周瑜本意杀你，要不是云长在场，他就得逞了！"

This story is from the novel *Journey to the West.* One day, the Jade Emperor invited Monkey Sun, the Great Sage Equalling Heaven, to Heaven, and asked him to administer the Peach Orchard. The Great Sage was overjoyed because anyone who ate the ripened peaches became eternal, living as long as Heaven and Earth. Everyday he picked the best peaches to enjoy, and after he had his fill, he shrunk himself to only two inches long and slept on the branch of a tree. One day the Queen Mother arranged a banquet of peaches by the Jade Pool. When the fairies sent by her were picking peaches in the Peach Orchard, the Great Sage awoke and was annoyed to discover he was not invited to the feast. He spoke a magic spell which immobilized the fairies, then he went straight to the Jade Pool where he saw rare fruits and fine delicacies and smelt the fragrance of jade liquor. He performed a spell by pulling several hairs from his body and chewing them up, the hairs turned into sleep-inducing insects which then bit all the busy servants, causing them to fall asleep. Then the Great Sage ate rare delicacies and drank precious wines until he was completely full. He put the leftovers in a big bag for the small monkeys on the Mountain of Flowers and Fruit. After this, he went to the place where Lord Lao Zi kept the elixir. The Great Sage ate up all the golden pills of elixir in the precious gourd, then he rushed out of the Gate of Heaven and went straight down to the Mountain of Flowers and Fruit.

《西游记》中的故事。 玉皇大帝邀造反的孙猴子上天,给了他一个"齐天大圣"的官衔,指派看管桃园。孙大圣早就听说吃了这里的仙桃,不但能得道成仙,而且能与天地同寿,便欣然前去。他每天专拣最好的桃子吃,饱餐后,就变成二寸长的小人,躺在树梢上睡觉。一天,王母娘娘宴请四方众仙,在瑶池摆蟠桃盛会,派仙女去采摘仙桃时,惊动了正在睡觉的大圣,仙女们急忙讲明情况。当大圣得知这次宴会没有请他时,很是生气,用定身法定住仙女,直奔瑶池。来到瑶池后,只见这里奇果佳肴,无比鲜美;琼浆玉液,香气扑鼻。大圣拔下两根毫毛一吹,变作许多瞌睡虫,忙碌的仙女立即睡着了。大圣放开肚量,痛吃狂饮,待酒足饭饱后,把剩下的东西,满满装了一大袋,准备带回花果山给小猴们吃。之后,又来到太上老君炼丹的地方,把葫芦内金丹吃了个精光,这才混出天门,回花果山去了。

Jia Baoyu in Love 宝玉痴情

This story is selected from the novel *A Dream of Red Mansions*. Jia Yucun came to the Grand View Garden. Shi Xiangyun thought that Jia Baoyu should go to meet Jia Yucun to learn something about administration. Upon hearing her words, Baoyu was not happy because he was not interested in that kind of things and he thought that Miss Lin Daiyu would never forced him to study. Lin Daiyu, who was walking just outside the door, happened to hear what Baoyu said about her. The words surprised and delighted her but also grieved her. She was delighted to know she had not misjudged him, for he had now proved just as understanding as she had always thought. Surprised that he had been so indiscreet as to acknowledge his preference for her openly. Grieved because her parents had died, and there was no one to propose the match for her. Besides, she might not live long due to her sickness. These thoughts sent tears coursing down her cheeks. Instead of entering she turned away to walk back. When Baoyu came out of the door he saw Daiyu walking slowly ahead and wiping her tears. Baoyu took out his handkerchief to wipe away her tears. Knowing what she was thinking about, Baoyu said to her vaguely, "You mustn't worry about this." Daiyu said she didn't understand his words. "If you really don't understand," Baoyu said, "all my devotion's been wasted and even your feeling for me has been thrown away. If you'd take things less to heart, your illness wouldn't be getting worse every day...." His affectionate words moved Daiyu very much and she said, "You needn't say anything now, I understand."

《红楼梦》中的故事。　贾雨村来大观园，湘云让宝玉过去，并劝他应该多会会官，听听仕途经济。宝玉听后很不高兴，并说："林姑娘从来就不说这些混帐话。"宝玉的话恰被走到门外的黛玉听见，黛玉又惊又喜，又悲又叹。喜的是自己眼力不错，宝玉果真是自己的知己；惊的是宝玉在人前不避嫌，恐怕被人嫉妒中伤；悲的是父母早逝，婚姻大事无人诉说；再加上自己有病，恐怕不久于人世。边想边落泪，转身就往回走。宝玉出门见黛玉在前面边走边擦泪，忙追上去，掏出手绢给她擦泪。宝玉知道黛玉的心思，含含糊糊地对她说："你放心……"黛玉说听不懂他的话。宝玉又道："你不明白我的话，难道我素日在你身上的用心都错了，而且连你平日待我的心也都辜负了；你但且宽慰些，病也不会一日重似一日……"黛玉听了这番话深情地说："什么也别说了，你的话我明白了。"

This is a story from *Strange Tales from Make-Do Studio*.

As a child, Xiliu was smart and liked to read biographies of ancient sages. She decided to follow the examples of previous worthies and leave behind a reputation that would be noted for generations to come. At the age of nineteen she married Gao Sheng, who had just lost his wife and had a son named Changfu. A year later Xiliu gave birth to a boy and named him Changhu. Before long, Gao Sheng, still young, died of an illness, leaving Xiliu to care for her sons. Seeing Changfu was often truant in his studies, Xiliu sent him to work with the shepherd boys as punishment. Changfu could not endure the hardship. A few days later, he got down on his knees and asked his mother to allow him to return to school. Xiliu refused, and this provoked criticism from neighbors. Winter came and Changfu, like a beggar, huddled himself up with cold. A grandmother in the village interceded and took care of the boy. Xiliu told her, "If Changfu is ready to take a beating of 100 strokes, I'll take him back." Changfu decided that he would take the beating. Aware of Changfu's genuine repentance for his errors, Xiliu did not beat him and asked him to continue his studies.

Changhu was a slow-minded child, so Xiliu asked him to quit school and work in the fields. But Changhu was so lazy that he often neglected work. Xiliu then asked him to engage in trade, but he used up all his money in gambling. At last, Xiliu sent him to Luoyang to sell goods, where he was put into jail for using fake silver in a whorehouse. In jail he suffered a lot. One day Xiliu called Changfu in and said: "I gave the fake silver to your brother on purpose, intending to make him suffer. Now you go and get him out." Back home, Changhu knelt before his mother, bitterly remorseful. He finally gave up evil and returned to good. Fellow villagers then began to understand Xiliu. She loved her children by tempering them in sufferings.

《聊斋志异》中的故事。　细柳从小聪明，喜读圣人烈传，立志长大后效仿前贤，流芳百世。她十九岁嫁给丧偶不久的高生，前妻留一子名长福。一年后，细柳又生一子名长怙。高生命短，不久病故，细柳和两个儿子相依为命。大儿长福不用功读书，经常逃学，细柳让他和牧童一块干活。没几天，长福熬不住，跪求母亲让他再读书，细柳不允。乡亲邻居都责备细柳。冬天到了，长福冻得缩头缩脑如同乞丐，村中一老妇为孩子说情，细柳说："如果长福肯挨一百棍就来见我。"长福情愿挨打。

细柳见他悔过，没打他，让长福继续读书。长怙大脑迟钝，细柳让他弃文务农，但长怙懒惰经常逃工；细柳让他经商，长怙把本钱赌光。后来，细柳让长怙去洛阳贩货，他因用假银逛妓院而入狱，受尽磨难。一天，细柳把长福叫来说："你弟弟这次出去，是我有意给他假银，让他吃尽苦头，你现在去救他吧！"长怙回来后跪在母亲面前，悔恨交加，从此改邪归正。这时乡亲们才明白，细柳让孩子在磨难中锻炼，才是真正爱孩子。

Ehuang and Nüying　娥皇女英

Ehuang and Nüying, beautiful and bright, were daughters of the King Yao (a king in China 4,000 years ago), who, in his late years, wanted to leave his throne to a dependable young man. He chose Shun, who had both ability and virtue, to inherit the crown and married his two daughters to him, Ehuang as the queen, Nüying the concubine. Shun did not disappoint Yao. He sent Yu to regulate rivers and watercourses, so that people could live a stable life. Ehuang and Nüying also make efforts to help Shun do good to the common people. In Shun's later years, a chaotic war arose at Jiuyi Mountain. Shun told Ehuang and Nüying he wanted to go and see the real situation there. Worried about Shun's age and poor health, both ladies wanted to accompany him on his journey. Considering the high mountains, dense forests,

tortuous roads, and all the hardships, Shun did not want his wives to make the trip. Without informing his wives he left bringing just a couple of attendants with him. Ehuang and Nüying, hearing that Shun had left without them, immediately set out to pursue him. They met with a great storm at the Yangtze River and were sent by a fisherman to the Dongting Mountain, where they were informed that Shun had died and was buried at the foot of Jiuyi Mountain. Day by day, they looked far ahead in the direction of the Jiuyi Mountain and sobbed, laying hands on bamboos to support themselves. Their tears soaked the bamboos, which have been called the "Bamboos of the Xiang Ladies" by later generations. In the end, the two ladies threw themselves into the Xiangshui River and became the Goddesses of Xiangshui.

传说聪明美丽的娥皇和女英,是上古时部落酋长尧帝的两个女儿。尧帝晚年,想物色一个满意的继承人。他看到舜是个德才超群的大贤人,于是,就把帝位传给了舜,并让娥皇和女英作了舜的妻子。娥皇封为后,女英为妃。舜不负尧的信任,让禹治洪水,使人民过上了安定的生活,娥皇、女英也鼎力协助舜为百姓做好事。舜帝晚年时,九嶷山一带发生战乱,舜想到那里视察一下实情。舜把这想法告诉娥皇、女英,两位夫人想到

舜年老体衰,争着要和舜一块去。舜考虑到山高林密,道路曲折,于是,只带了几个随从,悄悄地离去。娥皇、女英知道舜已走的消息,立即起程。追到扬子江边遇到了大风,一位渔夫把她们送上洞庭山,后来,她俩得知舜帝已死,埋在九嶷山下便天天扶竹向九嶷山方向泣望,把这里的竹子染得泪迹斑斑。后来,她俩投湘水而亡,成了湘水之神。

Stories about the He and He Immortals are abundant in China. In old times, people often hung pictures of these two immortals in their houses or displayed them at wedding ceremonies. They are two smiling, messy-haired fellows, one holding a lotus (*he*) and the other a round box (*he*). Pronunciations of these two articles in Chinese remind people of a Chinese expression *he he mei mei*, meaning harmony and happiness. According to a popular legend, both immortals lived in a small village in the north when they were young. The elder is called Han Shan and the younger Shi De. The two were dearer to each other than blood brothers. Both young men loved the same girl without the other's knowledge. Only when Han Shan was about to marry the girl did he discover Shi De's affection for her. For Shi De's happiness, Han Shan left home for Fengqiao, a Suzhou suburb, shaved his head and became a monk. Learning this, Shi De said to the girl, "I can not marry you. I must go to look for my brother." Crossing over mountains and rivers, he searched for Han Shan high and low and finally found out where he lived. He went to see him with a blooming lotus in his hand as a present. Han Shan came out to receive him holding a dinner box. Seeing each other, the brothers danced for joy. They decided to build the Hanshan Temple and practice Buddhism together. To this day in the Hanshan Temple in Suzhou there remains a stone tablet on which the figures and names of the brothers are carved.

和合二仙在民间有很多种说法。旧时, 在家中或婚礼的场面常悬挂画有蓬头笑面的两个人, 一人持荷花, 一人捧圆盒, 是取汉语中和(荷)合(盒)两字的谐音, 意寓"和合美好"。还有传说, 和合二仙同时居住在北方的一个小村庄, 哥哥叫寒山, 弟弟叫拾得, 他俩虽不是一母所生, 但二人特别要好, 赛过亲兄弟。兄弟二人共爱着同一个姑娘, 但互相都不知对方爱其女。一直到哥哥将要结婚时, 才知道弟弟也爱这个姑娘。寒山为了弟弟的幸福, 远离了故乡, 来到苏州枫桥削发为僧。弟弟知道哥哥为了自己的幸福远离家乡, 就对姑娘说, 我不能娶你, 我要去找我哥哥。于是, 爬山涉水, 四处寻找, 最后打听到哥哥的住处。他折了一支盛开的荷花作为给哥哥的见面礼, 哥哥忙拿一个盛斋饭的盒出来迎接, 兄弟二人见面, 高兴得手舞足蹈。二人决定一起修行, 并共同开山立庙为寒山寺。现在, 在苏州的寒山寺内还保存着一块石碑, 碑上刻有兄弟二人的形象和寒山拾得的名字。

This is a story from *Three Kingdoms* that happened before the Battle of Chibi. One night, Zhou Yu was thinking hard in his tent about how to defeat Cao Cao's army, when Huang Gai came in. He suggested attacking with fire. "Well, it's exactly what I mean to do," said Zhou Yu. "That's why I'm keeping those two spies: to convey false information to Cao's camp. But I need a man to play the same game for us." Huang Gai said he was willing to do it. They decided to carry out the trick of being flogged to win the enemy's confidence.

The next day Zhou Yu convened a general assembly of his commanders outside his tent. He ordered the commanders to take three months's rations and prepare to defend their line. Huang Gai came forward and said: "We don't need three months. If we can beat them this month, then let's do it. If not, we'd better throw down our weapons and sue for peace."

Zhou Yu exploded in fury. "I bear our lord's mandate," he cried, "to lead our troops to destroy Cao Cao. How dare you weaken our morale? Remove him and execute him!"

Huang Gai said proudly, "I have served the Southland through three successive reigns. Where do the likes of you come from?"

The entire assembly got on their knees to intercede for Huang Gai. Zhou Yu said at last: "In consideration for the commanders' views, I shall not kill you. Give him one hundred strokes across the back!"

Huang Gai was forced facedown to the ground. Not yet at fifty blows of the rod, his skin was broken and his oozing flesh was crossed with welts. He fainted several times.

Zhou Yu let Kan Ze, Huang Gai's friend, to deliver the letter of surrender to Cao Cao, which Huang Gai had prepared. Before long, Cao Cao received a letter from the two spies, saying "Look for a boat with a blue-green flag at the bow. That will be Huang Gai." In Huang Gai's boat there were combustibles. In this way, Huang Gai was able to set fire to Cao Cao's camp. When the red current of fire passed through the surface of the river, Cao Cao's ships, linked with chains, turned into ashes.

《三国演义》中的故事。　赤壁大战之前，周瑜苦思破曹之计。一日深夜，老将黄盖来到帐中，商议破曹以火攻为好。周瑜说："我也这样想，所以才留下假投降的蔡氏兄弟，只是无人去曹营诈降。"黄盖自告奋勇，甘愿领此重任。当夜二人定下"苦肉计"。第二天，周瑜传各路将军帐下议事，命大将们各领三个月粮草，准备抗敌。黄盖反对说："不用三个月，如果这个月能破敌就破，不能破敌，早点投降！"周瑜听后大怒道："我奉命督军破敌，你敢动摇军心，推出去斩了。"黄盖骄傲地说："我是东吴三世重臣，南征北伐时，你还不知在哪呢？"在场的将领们跪下替黄盖求情。周瑜狠狠地说："看在众将面上，饶你不死，打一百军棍！"武士们把黄盖推倒在地，没打到五十下，已皮开肉绽，鲜血直流，几次晕死过去。黄盖的好友阚泽，根据周瑜的安排，带着黄盖早已写好的投降书前去诈降。不久，曹操又接到蔡氏兄弟的密信，说只要见到插有青牙旗的船只就是黄盖来投降了。结果在赤壁一战中，黄盖引火船冲入曹营，大江之上一片通红，把曹操用铁链连起来的几千条战船烧成灰烬。

This is a story from the novel *Journey to the West*. The Great Sage caused havoc in Heaven and the Jade Emperor ordered Heavenly soldiers and generals to punish him. But no one could manage to subdue him. Then the Lord Lao Zi threw his Diamond Jade bracelet at the Monkey King, who was then preoccupied with fighting the God Erlang, and it hit him neatly on the head. Thus the Great Sage was caught. The Jade Emperor wanted to execute him but failed to inflict a single wound on him by sabres, axes, fire and thunder. Then Lord Lao Zi put him into the Eight Trigrams Furnace, which is used for refining elixir, and wanted to burn him to ashes. The furnace was made up of Eight Trigrams--*qian, kan, gen, zhen, xun, li, kun* and *dui*--so he squeezed himself into the "Palace of *xun*," for *xun* was the wind, and where there was wind there could be no fire. All that happened was that the smoke made both his eyes red. After the fire burning forty-nine days, the Lord Lao Zi thought the Great Sage must be ashes so he opened the furnace. At the moment, the Great Sage leapt out of the furnace with his as-you-will cudgel, knocked all soldiers down and left. From then on, he had a pair of fire eyes with golden pupils.

《西游记》中的故事。 孙猴大闹天宫，玉皇大帝降旨严惩，无奈天兵天将都对付不了他。太上老君献计说他有法对付。在孙猴和二郎神打得难解难分之际，太上老君暗中把金钢琢扔在孙猴的天灵盖上，捉住了孙猴。玉皇想处死孙猴，但任凭刀砍斧劈，火烧雷击，都伤不到孙猴的一根毫毛。太上老君请令，把孙猴扔进炼金丹用的八卦炉，想用猛火把孙猴烧成灰。

八卦炉是按天、水、山、震、风、火、地、泽划分的，孙猴知道其中的奥妙，进去后便钻进"巽宫"位置上。巽是风，有风无火，烧不到他，只是烟熏红了他的一双眼睛。孙猴在八卦炉中，烧了七七四十九天，太上老君以为孙猴已化成灰烬，下命令开炉。谁知孙猴手提金箍棒一跃而起，打倒众天将而去。从此，孙猴更炼就一双"火眼金睛"。

Monkey Hit the Lady White Bone Thrice 三打白骨精

This is a story from *Journey to the West*. The Tang Priest (Sanzang) and his three disciples were on their way to the Western Heaven to obtain Buddhist scriptures. One day they were traveling in a high mountain. When Monkey (Wukong) saw it was cloudy and misting in the valley, he knew this mountain was bound to harbor fiends. He drew a magic circle with his cudgel on the ground to protect his master. He told Pig and Friar Sand to protect the Tang Priest and for the three of them not to leave the circle. He then went to have a look at the mountain and pick some fruit to bring back to eat. This mountain did indeed have a corpse fiend called Lady White Bone, who had been here for a thousand years. It had heard that anyone who ate a piece of the Tang Priest's flesh will live forever, so it tried three times to capture him. The first time it changed itself into a young, beautiful girl holding a basket of food. With her charming smile, she almost succeeded in talking the master and his two disciples into coming out of the circle. Just at the last moment, Monkey came. Realizing that she was an evil spirit, he raised his cudgel and hit her. The fiend changed into a gust of smoke and fled. The second time the fiend turned itself into an old woman, who walked towards them leaning on a stick with a crooked handle. Monkey recognized it and struck it again. Like the first time, the fiend fled. The third time it turned itself into an old man, sitting before a hut waiting for the Tang Priest to come. Monkey saw through the fiend's disguise, raised his cudgel and struck it down. The fiend this time left a piece of cloth from the cloud, saying: "If you're as kind as a Buddha, how can you kill? Keep Wukong with you and no scriptures will you get." Sanzang believed the writing. He blamed Wukong for killing three people one after another, and forced him to leave. Without Monkey, Lady White Bone captured the Tang Priest easily and invited its mother to eat Sanzang's flesh together with it. But, Wukong came just in time to save him. He killed the old fiend on the way to its daughters', impersonated it, then got into the cave and saved the Tang Priest.

《西游记》中的故事。 唐僧师徒去西天取经。一日，走到一座大山中，只见天色阴沉，谷中浓雾弥漫，悟空料定必有妖怪。他用金箍棒在地上划一圈，让八戒、沙僧保护师父在圈内休息，他去探听虚实，顺便采些鲜果来充饥。

这座山内有千年修行的白骨精，她听说吃了唐僧肉可长生不老，于是她三次设计捉拿唐僧。第一次，她变成一个美丽少女，手提一篮馒头，笑着想把师徒三人从圈内骗出，悟空赶到，举棒就打，女妖化一缕青烟跑掉。第二次，她变成老婆婆，拄一根拐杖从山后走来，悟空认出又是白骨精变的，举棒又打，白骨精故技重演，化烟脱逃。第三次变作一个老头，在一间茅屋前坐等唐僧的到来。悟空看见，上来就打，白骨精招架不住，便用计从云端扔下一黄绢，上写：佛心慈悲，切勿杀生；再留悟空，难取真经。唐僧信以为真，怪悟空连伤二命，逼悟空离开。悟空走后，白骨精顺利地捉了唐僧。在白骨精邀母亲来吃唐僧肉时，孙悟空赶到，并打死老妖，变成白骨精的母亲进洞救出了唐僧。

This is a well-known myth of ancient China. It was said that in Emperor Yao's reign, the God of Heaven could not control his ten sun sons who slipped out to play, drying all the crops and trees and burning the land. People could not live at all. Emperor Yao appealed loudly to the God of Heaven, describing the overwhelming disaster the ten suns had brought to his people. The God of Heaven then sent Hou Yi, an archer god, to settle the problem. Hou Yi, with his wife Chang'e, descended from the Heaven. He shot down nine of the ten suns and left one. The climate then became mild, plants began to grow, and people were able to live a good life again. The God of Heaven at first just wanted Hou Yi to give his sons a start, never expecting him to kill nine of them.

Bearing a grudge, the God of Heaven reduced Hou Yi and Chang'e to common people, never to return to Heaven. Feeling wronged, Chang'e was at odds with her husband every day. Hou Yi, unable to bear this, had to go to Mt. Kunlun to ask the West Mother Goddess for the elixir of life. The West Mother Goddess told him: "If two people eat it together, they will neither get old nor die. If one person eats it all, he will ascend to heaven and become an immortal." Hou Yi brought the elixir home and told all he had heard to Chang'e. One day when Hou Yi was absent, Chang'e secretly ate all the elixir herself. At once she felt her body become as light as a swallow, flying towards the moon. Later, Chang'e was confined in the palace of the moon, living a lonely life.

嫦娥奔月是著名的神话故事。相传尧在位的时候，天空有十个太阳，它们是天帝的儿子，十个儿子悄悄溜了出来，把大地烤焦，庄稼树木晒死，老百姓根本无法生活。尧帝向天帝大声疾呼，陈述十个太阳给人们带来的灭顶之灾，天帝便派了擅长射箭的天神羿下凡为民解难。羿带妻子嫦娥下凡来到了人间。经过一段时间，羿连射下九个太阳，只留下一个，从此以后，天气温和，地里万物滋生，老百姓又过上了好生活。当初天帝派羿下凡，只想让羿吓唬一下他的十个儿子，没想到羿不讲情面，

把九个儿子置于死地，天帝记恨在心，把羿和嫦娥贬为凡人，永不能上天。嫦娥感到自己受了丈夫的连累，于是天天和丈夫打架闹气。羿受不了嫦娥的吵闹，到昆仑山上向西王母讨长生不老药。西王母告诉他："这药二人吃了长生不老，一人吃了就会升天成仙。"羿把药拿回家，如实告诉嫦娥。有一天，嫦娥趁羿不在家，偷偷把药全吃了。只觉得身轻如燕，飞上天空，一直向月宫奔去。后来嫦娥被禁锢在月宫过着寂寞冷清的生活。

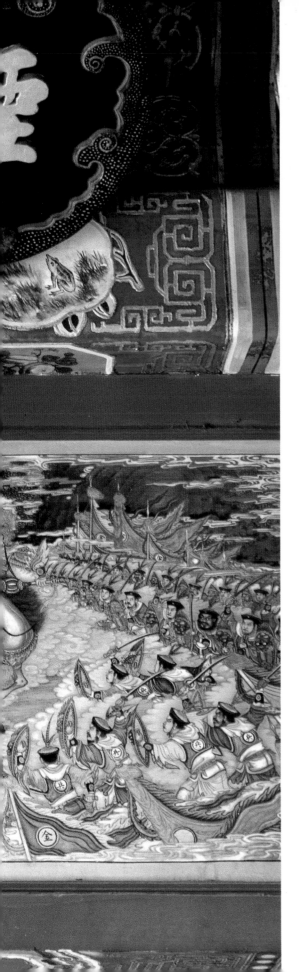

Battle in Zhuxianzhen 大闹朱仙镇

This is a story from *Complete Biography of Yue Fei*. Wuzhu, the commander of Jin gathered a 600,000-strong army at Zhuxianzhen, intending to invade Song. Yue Fei, together with three other supreme commanders, Han Shizhong, Zhang Jun and Liu Qi, also raised a 600,000 force at Zhuxianzhen to confront the Jin regime. After organizing a twisting golden dragon tail formation, Wuzhu delivered the letter of challenge to the Song army, asking for a decisive battle. Receiving the challenge, Yue Fei and Zhang Jun led their men to attack the formation from the left, Han Shizhong and Liu Qi from the right. Only when they got into the golden dragon formation, did they know the head and tail of the dragon can help each other according to the changing situation. Every time they beat back a crowd of Jin soldiers, there was another. When the Song and Jin armies were locked in the struggle, three young generals—Di Lei, Fan Cheng and Guan Ling came to help, frightening the Jin soldiers with their hammers, spears and swords. In the golden dragon formation, Yue Yun wielded a pair of silver hammers, Yan Chengfang wielded golden hammers, He Qingyuan wielded iron hammers and Di Lei wielded copper hammers. The eight hammers flew up and down, left and right, glittering coldly in the air. The twisting golden dragon tail formation was utterly routed. Numerous Jin soldiers died and their blood flew like a river. The Jin army abandoned their tents and deserted, and on their way were ambushed by Commander Liu Qi. Only five thousand Jin soldiers survived this attack. Wuzhu had no choice but to lead the remnants back to Jin.

《说岳全传》中的故事。 金兀术调集六十万兵马侵犯中原，来到朱仙镇附近。岳飞为了迎敌，会合了韩世忠、张俊、刘绮三位元帅起兵六十万也来到朱仙镇。金军在阵前摆出"金龙绞尾阵"之后下战书，要与宋军决一死战。宋军内，岳飞、张俊二元帅带兵打左边，韩世忠、刘绮二元帅带兵打右边。谁知"金龙绞尾阵"头尾互为照应，杀了一层，又是一层。正杀得难解难分时，狄雷、樊城、关铃三位小将拍马进阵，锤打枪挑、刀砍斧劈，杀得金兵不敢靠近。阵中岳云使一对银锤，严成方使一对金锤，何元庆使一对铁锤，狄雷使一对铜锤。只见八大锤上下飞舞，一起一落，金光银光互相交织，寒气逼人。只见金兵，尸体如山，血流成河。把个"金龙绞尾阵"打得七零八散，溃不成军。金兵弃阵而逃，又遭到刘绮元帅布下的埋伏，使金兀术的六十万兵马只剩下五千余人。金兀术只好收拾残兵悄悄地回金国去了。

A Trip of Xuan Zong to the Moon　玄宗游月宫

It is said that Luo Gongyuan, a Taoist priest in the Tang Dynasty, could practice supernatural Taoist magic, such as summoning wind and rain and flying in the air. Emperor Xuan Zong called him in the palace as his companion. One mid-autumn night, when Xuan Zong, accompanied by Luo Gongyuan, was watching the silver, round moon. He wished he could go there to see the beautiful Chang'e and have a taste of the sweet osmanthus wine on the moon! Observing this, Luo came up to Xuan Zong and said: "Your Majesty, do you want to go to the moon to have a look?" Thinking he was joking, Xuan Zong gave no answer, but only a smile. Luo continued: "If Your Majesty really wants to go, it is not difficult. Please follow me." He threw his horsetail whisk to the air, which immediately changed into a silver

bridge leading to the moon. Luo Gongyuan and Xuan Zong walked to the moon through the bridge. When they got there, Wu Gang, an immortal on the moon, holding the osmanthus wine in his hands, came out to receive them. Chang'e, together with dozens of fairy maidens, began to dance for them. Enchanted by the graceful dance and the beautiful music, Xuan Zong wanted to know what the music was. Luo Gongyuan told him it was called *Ni Shang Yu Yi Qu*. Xuan Zong remembered the melody by heart. Back at palace the next day he called in the palace musicians, who wrote down the tune according to his memory. He then revised it over and over again, and the beautiful music of heaven finally could be heard in the material world.

传说，唐朝道士罗公远，能呼风唤雨，遨游天空，道术很高明。唐玄宗把他召进宫中，陪伴自己。有一年中秋之夜，罗公远伴唐玄宗赏月。唐玄宗望着银色的月亮，恨不能亲登月宫目睹嫦娥的仙姿，品尝桂花仙酒。罗公远看出了唐玄宗的心事，他走到皇上面前说："陛下，你想不想到月宫里去逛逛？"唐玄宗以为他在说笑话，只是笑了笑，没有回答。罗公远又说："如果陛下想去，这也没什么难的，请你跟我来。"说完，把拂尘

往空中一掷，"唰"的变了一座银桥，罗公远和唐玄宗走上桥去，桥载着他们直奔月宫。来到月宫，只见吴刚捧着桂花酒前来迎接，嫦娥带领百十名仙女翩翩起舞。唐玄宗被美妙的舞姿和动人的乐曲所打动，急问曲名，罗公远说是《霓裳羽衣曲》，唐玄宗暗暗记下。

第二天，唐玄宗召集乐工，依自己的记忆作出曲调，经反复修改，把天堂美妙的《霓裳羽衣曲》移到凡间。

This is a story from *Three Kingdoms.* After suppressing the separatist forces in the north and taking control of the court, Cao Cao led his 830,000-strong army to the north bank of the Yangtze River, aiming to destroy Sun Quan and Liu Bei who were on the other side of the river. It was the thirteenth year of Jian An, the fifteenth day of the eleventh month. The weather was clear and bright, the wind calm, the waves still. Cao Cao ordered a feast and entertainment for the commanders that evening. The moon was bright and the Great River lay slack, like a belt of white silk unrolled. Aboard ship, all the attendants were in damask coats and embroidered jackets. Cao Cao spoke to the assembly: "We have raised this force to purge evil, dispel threats to the ruling family and to calm the empire. The Southland alone remains outside our sphere. Today I invite you to join me. When we have received the submission of the Southland and the empire is at peace, we shall share with you the enjoyments of wealth and glory." The audience rose as one to give Cao Cao thanks. Cao Cao was gratified and offered wine to the river. Then he quaffed three full goblets and, leveling his spear, said to his commanders, "Here is the weapon that broke the Yellow Scarves, took Lü Bu, eliminated

Yuan Shu, subdued Yuan Shao, penetrated beyond the northern frontier, and conquered the east as far as Liaodong. In the length and breadth of this land no man has withstood me. My ambitions have always been those of a man of action, a leader among men. And now the scene before us fills my soul with profound passion. I shall perform a song, and you must join me." Cao Cao recited:

Here before us, wine and song!
For man does not live long.
....
It southbound circles thrice a tree,
That offers him no haven.
The mountaintop no height eschews,
The sea eschews no deep.
And the Duke of Zhou spat out his meal,
An empire's trust to keep.

As Cao Cao finished, Liu Fu, an imperial inspector, pointed out ominous words in the ode. Cao Cao, already drunk at that time, pierced Liu Fu through with his spear, killing him. Liu Fu's words were proved later in the battle at Chibi, where Cao Cao almost lost his life.

《三国演义》中的故事。 曹操平定了北方割据势力,控制了朝政。他又亲率八十三万大军,直达长江北岸,准备渡江消灭孙权和刘备,进而统一全中国。建安十三年(公元208年),冬十一月十五日,天气晴朗,风平浪静,曹操下令:"今晚在大船上摆酒设乐,款待众将。"到了晚上,天空的月亮非常明亮,长江宛如横飘的一条素带。再看船上众将,个个锦衣绣袄,好不威风。曹操告诉众将官:我自起兵以来,为国除害,扫平四海,使天下太平。现在只有南方我还没得到,今天请你们来,为我统一中国同心协力,日后天下太平,我们共享荣华富贵。文武们

都站起来道谢,曹操非常高兴,先以酒奠长江,随后满饮三大杯。并横槊告诉众将说:我拿此槊破黄巾、擒吕布、灭袁术、收袁绍,深入塞北,直达辽东,纵横天下,颇不负大丈夫之志,在这良辰美景,我作歌,你们跟着和。接着,他唱曰:"对酒当歌,人生几何……绕树三匝,无树可依,山不厌高,水不厌深,周公吐哺,天下归心。"歌罢,刺史刘馥说,此歌不祥。曹操乘醉,将他用槊刺死。果不出所料,曹操乐极生悲。赤壁一战,险些丢了性命。

Fighting in the Bottomless Cave 闹无底洞

This is a story selected from *Journey to the West*. When Tang Priest and his three disciples come to Mount Pitfall there is a female mouse spirit there. As soon as she sees Tang Priest she falls in love with him. Since he is so handsome, she wants to marry him. The mouse spirit first changes herself into a pretty girl and then tied herself to a tree. Then she waits for the Tang Priest and his devotees to pass by. When they see her they save her. Then the evil mouse spirit asked them to take her with them by telling a fabricated story designed to win their sympathy. At night they stayed in a temple. The evil spirit took Tang Priest to her Bottomless Cave using an evil wind. When the three disciples couldn't find their master they followed them to the Bottomless Cave. Monkey changed himself into an insect to go inside the cave. He saw that the evil spirit was urging his master to drink wine so he would get drunk and agree to marry her. Then Monkey changed himself into an eagle to turn the table upside down. The evil spirit trembled with fear. Then Monkey changed himself into a fly and flew into the ear

of his master and said something. Tang Priest did what he said: He invited the evil spirit to take a walk with him in the garden. There he picked a big peach and offered it to her. She was very pleased and ate the fruit right away. After a moment, her stomach was in such pain that she couldn't bear it. Just then, Monkey shouted in her stomach: "Let my master go, otherwise I'll kill you!" It turned out that the peach was changed by Monkey. As soon as Tang Priest went out of the cave, Monkey jumped out from the stomach of the evil spirit. Monkey, Pig and Friar Sand had a fierce fight with the evil spirit and there was nobody to protect the Master. Tang Priest was again taken into the cave by the evil spirit. Monkey entered the cave and did not find his master but he saw the memorial tablets for Heavenly King Li and Nezha. Monkey went to the Jade Emperor with the tablets in his hands. The Jade Emperor ordered Heavenly King Li and Nezha to subdue the mouse spirit and get Tang Priest out of the cave. Then the master and three disciples went on their way to the West to find Buddhist scriptures.

《西游记》中的故事。 唐僧师徒四人，来到陷空山，山上有一个耗子精，她见唐僧仪表堂堂，便想拦来成婚。她先变成一个年轻美貌的姑娘，把自己绑在树上，待唐僧师徒救起，又编出一套谎言骗得唐僧同情，让带她一同前行。夜晚，耗子精用妖风把唐僧摄到住处无底洞。悟空三人发现没有了师父，便追到无底洞，悟空变作一只小虫飞往洞中，他见女妖正给唐僧劝酒，逼唐僧与她成婚，又忙变成一只老鹰，直扑过去，掀翻桌子，女妖吓得胆颤心惊。悟空又变成小蝇，飞到唐僧耳边，低声

说了几句。唐僧照计行事，请女妖来花园散步，唐僧从桃树上摘下一个大桃子递给女妖，女妖欢天喜地吞食下去。片刻，肚子疼痛难忍，悟空在肚子里高叫："快放我师父出去，饶你性命！"这只桃子正是悟空变的。女妖放出唐僧，刚到洞口，悟空从女妖口中跳出，悟空、八戒、沙僧大战女妖，唐僧无人保护，又被捉走。悟空二次进洞，没找到师父，却见到李天王和哪吒牌位。悟空捧牌位找玉帝，玉帝命李靖父子收服耗子精，放出唐僧。师徒四人继续西行取经。

This is a classic Chinese fairy tale. It was said that there is a kind of poisonous grass that causes people to die after eating it. People said that people who died of eating this grass would become ghosts. They could reincarnate only by finding a person who had also died by eating the poisonous grass. A young man, named Zhu Sheng, went to visit his friend. It was the middle of summer and he was very thirsty. He still had half of his journey ahead of him. Then he spotted a tea house along the road and stopped in for a cup of tea. He eagerly drank the tea that the teahouse owner Ms. Kou brought for him. As soon as he got home he felt a pain in his stomach. He realized that Ms. Kou had given him a cup of tea made with the poisonous grass to benefit her reincarnation. The young man hated her and vowed to get revenge. After his death, he took Ms. Kou back to the nether world. There the two of them got married in the nether world. The young man's mother cried all day long because she missed her son very much. One day, the young man heard the crying of his mother and persuaded his wife to go back to the human world to take care of his mother. The couple worked hard and was comforted and helped the old woman. Though their life was getting better and better, the old woman still did not feel at ease because she knew that her son and daughter-in-law were ghosts. So she pleaded with them to find their replacements. But the young man said: "I won't do things offensive to God and reason. My only hope is to take good care of you and let you live a happy life." So the couple did their best for the old woman until she died. God was moved by the couple's deeds and then God sent a fairy cart to bring them to heaven. They finally became immortals.

《聊斋志异》中的故事。 水莽草是一种毒草,人误食会死。有人说吃水莽草死的人会变成水莽鬼,只有找到同样死的人才可脱生。少年祝生,到朋友家作客。时至仲夏,走在半路上口干舌燥,见一茶棚,饮了寇三娘端来的水莽草茶。走到家中,顿感腹中痛疼难忍,深恨寇三娘为脱生而害自己,并发誓说:"我死后也不让她脱生。"祝生死后,把已去投胎的寇三娘揪了回来,二人结为阴间夫妻。祝母因思念儿子,日夜哭泣。一天,祝生听到母亲的哭声,说服寇三娘一同回人间服侍老母。夫妻二人勤劳孝顺,家里日子一天比一天好。祝母知道儿子、儿媳是鬼,心里总不踏实,劝他俩再找替身。祝生说:"我不愿作那伤天害理的事,唯一希望就是把你服侍好,让你过上好日子。"就这样,祝生夫妻对母亲尽忠尽孝,直到母亲寿终归西。祝生夫妇的品格感动了天帝,天帝派一辆神车,把他夫妻二人接到天上,做了神仙。

Pointing at Xinghuacun in the Distance 遥指杏花村

The picture of "Pointing at Xinghuacun in the Distance" painted based on the poem of "Pure Brightness" written by Du Mu, a man of letters of the Tang Dynasty (618-907).

The poem is:

It is rainy in Pure Brightness;
People walking on the road look sad.
They try to find a restaurant;
And the shepherd boy points at Xinghuacuan in the distance.

Du Mu was a man who was upright, outspoken, knowledgeable and resourceful. He dared to criticize current social malpractice, but his way being an official was not smooth. His poems and proses could compare favorably with Du Fu's. At that time, Du Mu and Li Shangyin enjoyed a good reputation in literary circles after Li Bai and Du Fu, two renowned poets of the Tang Dynasty. Du Mu's lyric poetry and poems which describe scenery are vivid, lucid and elegant and move people deeply. "Pure Brightness" gives people a fresh and natural feeling and makes people feel as though they are in a landscape painting: in the early spring days of Pure Brightness people went to the suburbs for outings and to pay respects at the tombs of the dead. A cool shower soaks the tourists' clothes and dampens their spirits. Hoping to warm up by drinking wine, they started to search for a tavern. A shepherd boy told them that there was a wineshop in the deep apricot forest. As hearing that they saw the shop sign was swaying with the breeze. A pleasant and beautiful rural scenery appeared in front their eyes.

牧童遥指杏花村这幅画是根据杜牧《清明》这首诗的内容画的。诗内写到:"清明时节雨纷纷,行人路上欲断魂。借问酒家何处有,牧童遥指杏花村。"杜牧,唐代文学家。他性格刚直不阿,有见识,有胆量,敢于批评社会弊病,但仕途不顺。他的诗、赋可与杜甫比美,被人称为"小杜"。当时他和李商隐名噪文坛,被世人称为是继李白、杜甫之后又一对"李杜"。他的写景抒情诗,清丽生动,感人肺腑。《清明》这首诗,以清新自然之感,把人带入画境:初春的清明节,郊游、扫墓的人络绎不绝,略带寒意的细雨淅淅沥沥地扬洒下来,打湿了游兴正浓的人们的衣衫,想寻个酒店借酒驱寒,牧童告诉大家,在那杏林深处就有卖酒人家。经牧童一说,人们仿佛看见了那高高挂起的酒幌子在微风中摇动。

This is a fairy tale. The goddess of Luoshui, named Mifei, was a daughter of Fuxi, a legendary ancient emperor. Mifei became the goddess of Luoshui after she fell into the Luoshui River and drowned while she was crossing the river in a ferry boat.

The goddess of Luoshui was a beautiful and lovely girl. After her drowning she married Hebo, the god of the Yellow River. He was romantic, unconventional, unrestrained and did not care about her. Everyday he loafed about idling away his time seeking pleasure. Mifei did not know what to do with her husband and became depressed and worried all day long. At that time she met Houyi, the god of shooting, who was also disappointed with his marriage. They sympathized with each other and soon fell in love. After that the goddess of Luoshui started a new life. Not long afterward Hebo came to hear of their romance. He turned himself into a white dragon and went to look for Houyi to make him pay for his transgressions. Unfortunately, one of Hebo's eyes was shot out in his fight with Houyi and he became blind. When Mifei see what had happened to her husband all because of her and the endless quarreling between Houyi and his wife Chang'e because of Houyi and Mifei's romance, she cut off her contact with Houyi. The beautiful goddess of Luoshui has been praised by poets through the ages. "The Goddess of Luoshui," a descriptive prose piece interspersed with verse, written by Cao Zhi, a poet during the Three Kingdoms, describes the graceful and beautiful goddess of Luoshui with lovely and vivid words. It imagines that the poet and the goddess fall in love at first sight and that they pour out their hearts and are reluctant to part from each other. The piece reveals the poet's regret that they are living in the two different worlds.

这是一个神话故事。洛神,原名叫宓妃,她是上古帝王伏羲的女儿,是个美丽动人的女子,一次游渡洛水时,不幸淹死,成为洛水女神。

宓妃落水后,嫁给了黄河神河伯为妻。河伯是一个风流、放荡的人,根本没把宓妃放在眼里,宓妃整天生活在忧郁之中。就在这时,她碰上了失意的射神后羿,两人很快相怜相爱了,从此洛神开始了新生。这件事被河伯知道了,他变成一条白龙去找后羿算帐,结果被后羿射瞎了一只眼睛。善良的宓妃看到因为自己使丈夫受到了伤害,还引起了后羿和妻子嫦娥无休止地争吵,于是,她就和后羿割断了这段情缘。美丽的洛神被历代诗人所称颂。曹植写的洛神赋更是把娇艳的洛神描写得维妙维肖。赋中写作者和洛神一见钟情,互诉衷肠,但因人神殊途,只得恋恋不舍地分离。

Lu Ji Conceals Oranges in His Clothes　陆绩怀桔

Since early childhood Lu Ji was a dutiful son. It is said that when he was six, his father brought Lu Ji with him to visit Yuan Shu, a rich and powerful man in Jiujiang, who welcomed them warmly. Touched by the boy's wit, politeness and knowledge, Yuan Shu liked the boy and let his man serve him with oranges. Lu Ji picked a small one and ate it. Tasting how sweet and flavorful they were, he furtively snatched three big oranges and stuffed them into his clothes. At the sunset when he bowed down to say good-bye to the host, the three oranges came spilling out of the chest pocket where he had stowed them, and fell to the ground. When Yuan Shu saw what had happened, he was disappointed with the boy and said in angry tone, "Little boy, as a guest, why do you try to take oranges away without asking permission?"

Lu Ji kneed down at once and said, "I tasted a small orange and know that they are flavorful. My mother likes oranges very much, so I wanted to ask for some for my mother, but I didn't know how to ask it out. As these oranges were offered to me, I thought I wouldn't eat them and might take some for my mother. Please excuse me for what I have done and don't think I was trying to steal your oranges." Yuan Shu and the guests present were moved after hearing what Lu Ji had said and praised him as a dutiful son. After he grew up Lu Ji became an erudite scholar. His highest official position was prefecture magistrate.

陆绩从小就是个很有名的孝子。据说，在陆绩六岁时，他和父亲一块去九江大富豪袁术家作客，袁术热情接待父子二人。袁术看到陆绩聪明伶俐，知书达礼，非常惹人喜爱，就让家人拿出新鲜桔子给他吃。陆绩先拣了一个小的尝了尝，觉得甘甜味美，便又拿了三个大的鲜桔放入怀中。傍晚，当陆绩向主人鞠躬告辞时，三个桔子从怀中掉出，一齐滚到袁术的脚下。袁术见此情景，感到失望并生气地说："你这小孩，在我家作客，为何又私自拿走我家的桔子？"陆绩，连忙跪地说："我尝了一个小的，知道你家的桔子很好吃。我妈妈很喜欢吃桔子，我想要几个给妈妈吃，但又不好开口。这些桔子既然是你送给我吃的，我不吃，可以拿回去给我妈妈尝尝，请你原谅我吧，不要认为我偷了你的桔子。"袁术和在座的客人听后均受感动，连声称赞陆绩是孝子。陆绩长大后，博学多识，官至太守。

Three Travel-Stained Chivalries refers to Li Jing, Hongfu (red horsetail whisk), and Qiu Ranke (a man with curly sideburns) in the Sui Dynasty (581-618). Li Jing was very ambitious and far surpassed the others in ability and wisdom. One day, he came to the house of Governor Yang Su. A singing girl with a red horsetail whisk saw him and fell in love with him because she thought he was not an ordinary man. Without anyone's knowledge, she came up and asked Li's address. Li told her. The next morning, hearing knocking at the door, Li opened it and saw the singing girl with the red horsetail whisk. She said her name was Zhang Hongfu. "I think Yang Su is fierce and cruel, and even among his followers, he has enemies. I think the Sui Dynasty will soon fall. I only met you yesterday, but I believe you are a hero. Therefore, I came to join you." she said. Impressed by Hongfu's boldness and affection, Li Jing married her immediately. Together they packed their things and ran away to Taiyuan. On their way to Taiyuan when Hongfu was combing her hair one morning, a man with red curly sideburns laid down nearby looking at Hongfu. Li Jing was about to get angry when Hongfu stopped him. His name was Qiu Ranke and they invited him to breakfast. Qiu told them that Li Shimin was preparing to overthrow the Sui Dynasty and asked them to help him. After they met Li Shimin, Qiu Ranke gave all his jewelry and property to Li Jing and Hongfu and asked them to support Li Shimin in overthrowing the Sui Dynasty. Later, Li Shimin was successful in overthrowing the Sui Dynasty and became the Emperor of the Tang Dynasty. Li Jing was appointed prime minister.

　　风尘三侠指的是隋朝(公元 581 – 618 年)的李靖、红拂和虬髯客三人。李靖,心怀大志,才智超群。一天他来到杨素府中,有一歌女手持红拂尘,她见李靖相貌非凡,便生爱慕之心。趁人不备,上前问李靖住址,李靖如实告知。次日凌晨,李靖听到叩门声,开门一看,竟是持红拂尘的少女。少女自称姓张名红拂。并说:"我看到杨素为人凶残,众叛亲离,隋朝很快就会灭亡。昨天见到你,知道你是英雄豪杰,所以来投奔你。"李靖见红拂豪爽泼辣,美丽多情,当下娶她为妻,并一起逃往太原。途中结交大侠虬髯客。虬髯客告诉他们,李世民准备反隋,约他共事,说完便告辞先行。到了太原,三人又会面,一起见到李世民,虬髯客把家中珠宝财产全部给李靖夫妇,让他们好好辅佐李世民推翻隋朝。后来,李世民果然推翻隋朝,成为大唐皇帝。李靖作了宰相。

This story is from the novel *Three Kingdoms.* Cao Cao's troops had suffered heavy casualties in the Chibi Campaign and there were only 300 troops left. Cao Cao led these troops to Huarongdao in retreat. While marching on, Cao Cao, riding horseback, pointed his whip and laughed loudly, saying, "People say Zhuge Liang is wise and full of clever stratagems, but it seems to me he is as · incapable as the average general. If he had an army waiting in ambush over there, I would have no way out." Before he could finish his words, the thunder of cannons was heard and an army headed by Guan Yu stormed out of hiding to block their way. At the sight of Guan Yu's mighty force, the hopeless and disappointed Cao Cao had to beg Guan Yu for a way out. "Now I am pressed in the corner. Please take mercy on me for our past friendship and let me go." "I have already repaid you for your kindness," replied General Guan. "Today I can't do anything harmful to the nation." "Do you remember your killing my six generals while you passed through the five passes?" Cao Cao reminded Guan Yu. In his mind, Guan Yu admitted that if Cao Cao did not ordered his men to let Guan Yu pass through, he would not have gotten through the five passes alive. Guan Yu, a man who valued loyalty highly, ordered his men to make a way and gestured Cao Cao to pass through. Thus, Cao Cao made it through alive.

《三国演义》中的故事。 赤壁之战曹军大败, 所剩三百人马, 跟随曹操向华容道退去。正走间, 曹操突然在马背上扬鞭大笑说:"别人都说诸葛亮足智多谋, 我看也是无能之辈, 如果他在这里埋伏一支队伍, 今天我们只有死路一条了。"曹操的话音刚落, 只听一声炮响, 关羽领一支人马拦住去路。曹操见了, 丢魂丧胆, 只得央求关羽说:"我今天无路可走了, 望将军看在我们往日的情份上, 给我留一条活路!"关羽说:"你的恩情我已报答, 今天不能为私情误了国家大事。"曹操说:"将军还记得过五关斩六将吗?"关羽听了, 心中暗想, 如果不是曹操关照, 我闯过五关也保不住性命。关羽是个重义之人, 忙叫士兵闪开一条路, 摆手让曹操他们过去, 曹操终于保住了性命。

This story is taken from *Journey to the West*. Red Boy, the Bull Demon King and Princess Iron Fan's son, had cultivated his physical and mental capacities and possessed magic abilities. With powerful magics he always had the idea of eating the meat of Sanzang, the Tang Priest (whose meat could make creatures live longer) to lengthen his life. One day while he was watching in the sky, he saw Sanzang and his disciples coming from afar. He knew that the disciples had excellent fighting skills, so he planned to capture Sanzang by making use of the priest's kindness and muddled mind, rather than use force. At a spot just ahead of where Sanzang and his group were, Red Boy turned himself into a boy of seven and hung himself on the top of a tree with his hands and feet tied with a rope and cried for help. The Tang Priest heard the boy's cries and asked Monkey to release him. Monkey, seeing that the boy was actually a demon in disguise, told his master not to bother. Sanzang got angry, and he asked Pig   to bring the boy down from the tree; he ordered Monkey to carry the boy on his back. As they started to go, Red Boy jumped into mid-air, leaving behind a false Red Boy for Monkey to carry. To kidnap Sanzang, Red Boy hurled a whirl of wind at him. Sanzang disappeared.

Monkey knew this was done by the demon and he asked Pig and Friar Sand to look after the luggage and he hurried to the Huofang Cave in the Withered Pine Valley to look for his master. A fierce battle ensued between Monkey and Red Boy. Knowing it is impossible to defeat Monkey, Red Boy spurted three types of flames which were so powerful even the Dragon King could not put out. Monkey, knowing he could not win, jumped out of the sea of fire and went to the South Sea to ask the Goddess Guanyin for help. The goddess vanquished Red Boy and brought him to the South Sea. Monkey saved Sanzang and Sanzang and his disciples continued their journey to the West in search of Buddhist scriptures.

《西游记》中的故事。 牛魔王和铁扇公主的孩子红孩儿，修炼得道，神通广大，为益寿延年，他一心想吃唐僧肉。一天，他正在空中了望，看见唐僧师徒远远地走来，他知道唐僧的徒弟武艺高强，硬拼怕不能取胜；于是，他想利用唐僧不辨真伪，心慈面软的特点来智取。他把自己变成七岁的孩童，用绳捆住手脚，高高地吊在树枝上喊"救人"。唐僧听到喊声，让悟空去解救。悟空认出那是妖怪变的，叫师父少管闲事。唐僧动怒，又要八戒将红孩儿救下。当唐僧让悟空背上红孩儿走时，悟空

背的只是个假的，红孩儿真身早已跳到九霄云外，并刮起一阵旋风，趁机劫走了唐僧。风停后，唐僧没有了，悟空知道是妖怪捣的鬼。他让八戒和沙和尚看好行李，自己赶忙来到枯松涧火方洞找师父。悟空和红孩儿一场恶战，红孩儿斗不过悟空，便喷出龙王也不能熄灭的三味真火，悟空急忙跳出火阵，见不能取胜，便到南海请观音菩萨。菩萨降服了红孩儿，把他带回南海。悟空救出了唐僧，师徒四人继续往西天取经。

This is a story from the *Outlaws of the Marsh*. The armored cavalry deployed by Huyan Zhuo could not be destroyed unless barbed lances were used. Tang Long presented a drawing of such a lance and lances could be made according to the drawing. However no one was able to use them. Tang Long suggested: "My cousin Xu Ning, an arms instructor in the capital, knows how to use barbed lances. The art has been handed down from generation to generation. We can bring him to the mountain." Everyone began to think how to lure Xu Ning to the mountain. Tang Long had a plan: "Xu Ning has a suit of goose-feather armor hooped in metal. It is a matchless ancestral treasure. Xu Ning cherishes it like his life. He keeps it in a leather box that hangs from the central beam in his bedroom. If we can get hold of that armor, he'll have to come here whether he wants to or not." Then he whispered his stratagem to Song Jiang. Military councilor Wu Yong sent Shi Qian to attend to this matter. Shi Qian, whose body was as light as a swallow, excelled at leaping onto roofs and vaulting over walls. Soon he arrived in the capital. Shi Qian inquired of Xu Ning's residence, studied the surrounding area and located where the metal-bound goose feather armor was placed. Finally, he learnt that Xu Ning would be on guard duty the next day at the fifth watch. At the fifth watch, Shi Qian stole into the kitchen when Xu Ning was having something to eat. As soon as Xu Ning had left, Shi Qian went upstairs to Xu Ning's bedroom. Xu Ning's wife, who heard sounds coming from the beam, asked her maid what it was. Shi Qian promptly squeaked like a rat. Thinking that it was only rats fighting, Xu Ning's wife went to sleep. Seizing this opportunity, Shi Qian snatched the armor. Xu Ning returned home and heard that his metal-bound goose feather armor had been stolen. Guided by Tang Long, Xu Ning ran after Shi Qian and ended up at Liangshan Marsh. Convinced by the gathered leaders, Xu Ning joined the forces in the stronghold. Later Xu Ning destroyed Huyan Zhuo's armored cavalry with his barbed lances.

《水浒传》中的故事。 呼延灼的连环甲马,必须用钩镰枪才能破。汤隆献出祖传的钩镰枪图样,可以照图打造,但无人会使用也是枉然。汤隆说:"我表哥徐宁,现在京城做金枪班教师,他家祖传使用钩镰枪,专破连环甲马。我们可以请他上山。"如何能让他上山,大家开始想计策。汤隆又说:"他家有一副雁翎锁子甲,是传家之宝,徐宁非常珍惜它,总是吊在他卧室的梁上,如能盗来,我可用计引他上山。"于是把计策低声告诉宋江。军师吴用派时迁前去。时迁身轻如燕,专能飞檐走壁。时迁来到京城,先打听到徐宁的住地,又查看了周围的情况,观察了放甲的地方,得知徐宁早晨五更入班的消息。于是,五更天,在徐宁用饭时,时迁趁机潜入厨房,待徐宁走后,他又摸上楼。徐宁的妻子听到梁上有声音,急忙问丫头,时迁赶紧学鼠叫,大家以为老鼠打架,没有理睬。时迁借机把甲偷走。徐宁回到家中,见雁翎锁子甲被盗,在汤隆的指引下,一路追赶时迁来到梁山,在众首领的劝说下也入了伙。后来,徐宁的钩镰枪破了呼延灼的连环甲马。

This is a story from *A Dream of Red Mansions*. Jia Baoyu refused his feudal family's arrangement for his official career, so he was often sternly scolded by his family. Love between Baoyu and Daiyu was also opposed by the family because of Daiyu's rebellious spirit. To marry Baochai to Baoyu, they held back the facts to Baoyu, telling Baoyu that he would marry Daiyu. One day Daiyu found a maid crying behind the rocks. She went up and asked: "Why are you so sad?" The maid replied, weeping: "My name is Numskull. I work for the old lady. I just made a slip of the tongue and sister slapped me." Daiyu asked: "What did you say wrong?" Numskull said: "Something about the marriage of our Master Bao to Miss Baochai." Daiyu felt thunderstruck.

Her heart beat wildly. Composing herself a little, Daiyu let Numskull tell her in detail. Numskull said: "I don't know how they settled it. They only let us prepare for the wedding of Baoyu and Baochai, but they don't allow anybody to talk about it. All I did was to remark: 'Things are going to be livelier here with Miss Baochai becoming Second Mistress Bao—how ought we to address her?' Yet sister slapped my face, saying she would throw me out." She started sobbing again. With a heart filled with despair, Daiyu walked back to Bamboo Lodge. Upon entering the room she spat blood and collapsed on her bed. When the wedding ceremony for Baoyu and Baochai was being held, Daiyu died quietly with grief and indignation.

《红楼梦》中的故事。 贾宝玉拒绝封建家庭为他安排的功名仕进之路，因而经常遭到他们严厉地斥责。宝玉和黛玉之间的爱情也因黛玉性格中的叛逆精神遭到家庭的反对。为了将薛宝钗嫁给宝玉，对宝玉隐瞒了真相，采取"只说娶林姑娘"的掉包计。一天，黛玉在大观园中看见一个丫头在哭，上前问道："你为什么伤心？"丫头流着泪说："我叫傻大姐，是老太太屋里的丫头。我说错了一句话，他们就打我。"黛玉问："你说错什么话了。"傻大姐说："还不是因为宝玉娶宝钗的事。"黛玉一

听这话，心里乱跳，又问她事情的经过。傻大姐说："我不知道他们怎么商量的，只让我们给宝玉宝钗准备婚事，还不让我们说，我只说了一句："以后对宝钗叫宝姑娘呢还是叫宝二奶奶呢？就为这个打我嘴巴，还要把我赶出去。"说着又哭了起来。黛玉听后，昏昏沉沉地走回潇湘馆，一进屋，口吐鲜血，晕倒在床。几天后，就在宝玉和宝钗成亲之时，她带着满腔的悲愤，悄悄地离开了人间。

This is a story from *Strange Tales from Make-Do Studio*. The Ans had two sons. The elder son An Dacheng married Chen Shanhu. Shanhu was a kind woman with a sweet temper. Dacheng's mother, Shen Shi, was irritable and fierce. She often beat and cursed Shanhu. Shanhu never uttered a word of complaint. Later, Shen Shi went so far as to force Dacheng to divorce his wife. After Shanhu had left, Shen Shi tried to make Dacheng remarry. However no one dared to marry Dacheng because of his notorious mother. Later Shen Shi's younger son, Ercheng, married Zanggu, who was more fierce than Shen Shi. Every day, Shen Shi adjusted her behavior to Zanggu's expression. Even so, Shen Shi was often scolded and cursed by Zanggu. Ercheng, a weak man, dared not to stop his wife. Finally Shen Shi was sick due to overworking. Shen Shi had to ask her elder sister to wait on her. Every day, a person from her sister's home sent delicious food to Shen Shi. Shen Shi sighed: "I would be happy if I had a good daughter-in-law like my sister's." After she recovered, Shen Shi went to stay at her sister's home. She often admired her sister for her daughter-in-law. Her sister said: "Shanhu is a good woman, but you often beat and cursed her. To tell you the truth, the delicious food you ate when you were sick was made by Shanhu. Shanhu made money by spinning yarn and prepared food for you. Where else can you find such a good daughter-in-law?" Upon hearing it, Shen Shi felt ashamed. She said while crying: "It's my fault!" At this moment, Shanhu ran out from the rear room and knelt down in front of her mother-in-law. Shen Shi regretted her actions, beating her breast and stamping her feet. Then Dacheng and Shanhu got remarried. Later after many hardships, Shanhu educated Zanggu, who was determined to thoroughly rectify her errors. Then all five members in the Ans lived a happy life.

《聊斋志异》中的故事。   安家两兄弟中安大成娶陈珊瑚为妻。珊瑚人品出众,性情娴淑。大成母沈氏性格暴燥,为人凶狠,对珊瑚非打即骂。珊瑚忍气吞声,从无怨言。后来,婆婆竟逼大成休掉珊瑚。珊瑚走后,沈氏想给大成另娶,因大成母恶名远扬,无人敢嫁。后来,沈氏给二成娶妻臧姑。她比沈氏更加凶悍。沈氏每每看臧姑的脸色办事,稍不小心,沈氏便会遭到臧姑的责骂。二成天生懦弱,也不敢管,致使沈氏操劳过度成疾,只好请来姐姐服侍自己。沈氏见每天都有姐姐家人送好饭菜来给自己吃,叹道:"我要有姐姐这样的好儿媳就好了!"沈氏病好之后,住在姐姐家,总夸姐姐的儿媳妇好。后来姐姐说:"珊瑚对你多好,你总打骂她。告诉你吧,你病中吃的好东西,都是珊瑚纺线赚钱买来做给你吃的。这样的好媳妇,你到哪去找呀!"沈氏听了后,倍觉羞愧,边哭边说:"是我对不起珊瑚呀!"这时,珊瑚从后边屋里跑出来,跪在婆婆面前。沈氏非常后悔,捶胸顿足。后来,历经磨难,二成的媳妇也痛改前非,全家五口,又和和美美地生活在一起了。

Su Xiaomei was a younger sister of Su Dongpo, a famous poet of the Song Dynasty. From her early childhood, she was very intelligent and good at writing poems and articles. Her father loved her very much. As time went by, Su Xiaomei grew up and many young men came to the Su's household to make offers of marriage. However Su Dongpo and his father favored none of them. Finally they decided that the young man who wrote the best article would be Su Xiaomei's fiance. Qin Shaoyou's article was the best. But Su Xiaomei said that she would not marry Qin Shaoyou until he passed the government examination. Soon Qin Shaoyou succeeded in passing the government examination and came to the Su residence to marry his fiancee. A double blessing had descended upon him. Qin Shaoyou was very pleased with himself. When he was about to enter the bridal chamber, he was stopped by a maid, who said, "Under my lady's orders, you may not enter the bridal chamber until you pass three tests."

The first test was to write a *jueju* (a poem of four lines). Qin Shaoyou picked up a brush and finished writing at one go. The second test was to solve a riddle. Qin Shaoyou solved it right away. The third test was to write the second line of a couplet. The first line read: "Closing the door to find the moon over the window." At the first sight, Shaoyou thought it was easy to write the second line. However, after he thought for a while, he found it difficult. He thought hard, but could not get the right line. Anxiously, he walked back and forth in the courtyard, murmuring the first line. Upon seeing his brother-in-law in trouble, Su Dongpo attempted to help him. When Shaoyou stopped by a water jar, thinking, Dongpo threw a small stone into the water. Shaoyou suddenly woke up to reality, and wrote the second line immediately: "Throwing a stone into the water to break a world at the bottom." At this moment, the door was open. Su Xiaomei was waiting for her bridegroom.

　　苏小妹是苏东坡的胞妹，从小聪明过人，能诗善文，很得父亲的宠爱。小妹长大后，上门求婚的人很多，但都没被苏氏父子看上。于是，他们想出一个以文求婚的办法。秦少游的文章，被小妹看中。小妹说：待到金榜题名时才能完婚。秦少游一举考中，来到苏府成亲。他双喜临门，心中非常得意，待要进新房时，却被丫环拦住说："奉小姐之命，在此等候，再三试俱中，才能进洞房。"秦少游笑着打开第一试题，是和一首绝句，秦少游大笔一挥即成。第二题是猜谜题，他又毫不费力的猜中

了。打开第三题，是一个对子，上联是"闭门推出窗前月"七个字。少游初看，觉得很容易，但仔细一想，又觉得很奇巧。左思右想，不得下联，心里着急，嘴里叨咕着"闭门推出窗前月"这七个字，在院中徘徊。东坡来看妹夫，见此情景有心想帮助他，见少游在缸边沉思，东坡灵机一动，便投一小石入水。少游猛然醒悟，马上写出"投石冲开水底天"。只见门"吱"一声开了，小妹在内迎候。

Zhou Dunyi Loves Lotus Flowers   敦颐爱莲

Zhou Dunyi was born in the mid Northern Song Dynasty (960-1127). Later he served as an official. He was deeply loved by common people because he was fair and just in handling affairs and was not afraid of big-wigs. When he served as roving judge in Guangdong, he went everywhere to inspect common people's life. In addition, he interrogated criminals in person, corrected wrong cases, and redressed wrongs for folks. Hence he was regarded as an honest and upright official by people. Later he was sick and went to live at the foot of Mount Lushan. The scenery around his house was beautiful, with lotus ponds linked together, and beautiful mountains and rivers. Lotuses in the ponds stood upright and lotus leaves looked proud and aloof. He wrote an essay "Love for Lotus Flowers." It says: "A large number of without creeping vines and branches. Their faint scent goes far. Slim and graceful, they can be appreciated in a distance without being desecrated." This essay indicated that he remained undefiled in spite of general corruption in official circles and would not go along with corrupt and dark forces in their evil deeds. As an upright man, he was likened to lotus flowers. Zhou Dunyi's love for lotus flowers was spoken highly of by the people then. flowers growing on the land and in the water are lovely. Tao Yuanming of the Jin Dynasty (265-420) was keen on chrysanthemums. After the Tang Dynasty (618-907), the people loved peonies very much. I myself have a special love for lotus flowers, because they come out of the dirty mud unsoiled. They have hollowed and straight roots

周敦颐(公元 1107－1073 年)北宋哲学家,曾在朝中为官。他办事公平,不惧权贵,深得老百姓爱戴。他任广东转运判官时,不辞辛苦,四方体察民情,亲自提点刑狱,改判错误案例,为黎民百性洗冤,被百姓誉为清官。后来他积劳成疾,晚年辞官,在庐山脚下养病。在他住的周围,荷塘相连,他写下了著名的《爱莲说》。文中说:"水陆草木之花,可爱者甚蕃。晋陶渊明独爱菊;自李唐来,世人甚爱牡丹;予独爱莲之出淤泥而不染,濯清涟而不妖,中通外直,不蔓不枝,香远益清,亭亭净植,可远观而不可亵玩焉。"周敦颐以莲花的"出淤泥而不染,濯清涟而不妖",表达自己虽被官场陋俗熏染,但能保持洁身自好的品德。以"中通外直,不蔓不枝,香远益清,亭亭净植"的句子,表达自己一生不甘和腐败、黑暗的势力同流合污。周敦颐爱莲,成为古今的美谈。

This is a story from *Three Kingdoms*. Tricked by Zhou Yu, Liu Bei married Sun Shangxiang, Sun Quan's younger sister. After the wedding ceremony, Liu Bei stayed in the state of Wu. In light of Zhuge Liang's plan, Zhao Yun made a false report to Liu Bei before his departure, saying that Cao Cao was attacking Jingzhou. He urged Liu Bei to go back. Believing it was true, Liu Bei discussed the matter with his wife and decided that they would pretend to offer sacrifice to the ancestors at the river and would leave the Southland under the escort of Zhao Yun without announcing it. The day came and Liu Bei and his wife headed to the river. Suddenly, generals and soldiers sent by Zhou Yu arrived. Liu Bei was frightened. He rushed to the front of Lady Sun's carriage and appealed tearfully to her: "When your elder brother and Zhou Yu conspired to call me to the Southland to marry you, they did not do so for your sake. All they wanted was to confine me so that they could retake Jingzhou, and after that to kill me. But I came, because I admire you. Today, no one but you can save me. If you are not willing, I prefer to die here before your eyes." Upon hearing this, Lady Sun rolled up the front curtain of her carriage, and shouted to the generals from the state of Wu: "Are you in revolt? Zhou Yu! The renegade,

the traitor!" she cried. "What injury has the Sun family ever done you? Liu Bei is my husband. Both my mother and my brother were informed that I would return to Jingzhou. Does this blockage mean you're going to plunder our goods?" She denounced Zhou Yu loudly and then ordered her carriage moved forward. The carriage had hardly advanced five or six *li* when the second pair of commanders sent by Sun Quan arrived. Lady Sun let Liu Bei proceed. She herself and Zhao Yun held the rear. Lady Sun regarded the two commanders sternly and spoke reproachfully: "You have come between my brother and me. My mother has sanctioned our trip back to Jingzhou. Even my brother has to conform to what ritual enjoins. Do these weapons mean you want to murder me?" The commanders stared at one another helplessly. Though Liu Bei was nowhere to be seen, Zhao Yun was right there, ready for bloody combat, eyes angry and wide-staring. At last, the generals had to withdraw. Later when another two generals arrived with Sun Quan's sword, Liu Bei and Lady Sun were already on one of the boats led by Zhuge Liang, heading for Jingzhou. Later the people said: Trapped a second time in his own tricks, Zhou Yu tasted humiliation added to rage.

《三国演义》中的故事。 周瑜设计,让刘备和孙权的妹妹孙尚香成亲。婚后,刘备一直住在东吴。赵云按临行前诸葛亮设的计策:假称曹操攻打荆州,催刘备回去。刘备信以为真,和夫人合计,谎称去江边祭祖,让赵云保护着悄悄离去。正行走,周瑜派追兵赶来,刘备十分惊慌,于是来到车前泣告孙夫人说:"你哥哥和周瑜合谋将你嫁给我,是想用美人计杀我,再夺回荆州。我冒死前来,是敬慕夫人的名声,今天只有夫人出面才能解救,如夫人不出面,我只有一死。"孙夫人一听,立即卷起车帘,大声对追兵说:"你们想造反吗? 周瑜这个贼子,我东吴不

曾亏待于他。刘备是我的丈夫,我母亲和我哥哥知道我要回荆州,难道你们是来抢我们的财物吗?"孙夫人一面大骂周瑜,一面让人推车前进。又走了不到五、六里,孙权派兵将赶来。孙夫人让刘备先走,自己和赵云在后,并叱喝来人说:"你们专门挑拨我兄妹不合,我奉母命回荆州,便是我哥哥来了也得以礼送行,难道你们想害我吗?"来将不敢说话,一看又无刘备,只有赵云怒目而视。只得回营禀报。待追兵再带孙权宝剑赶到江边时,诸葛亮已亲自带船接应,把刘备和孙夫人接回荆州。

Monkey Makes Three Attempts to Borrow the Plantain Fan 三借芭蕉扇

This is a story from *Journey to the West*. The Tang Priest and his three disciples, Monkey (Wukong), Pig and Friar Sand, were heading towards the Western Heaven. Gradually they began to feel hotter and hotter in the warm air. It was very strange, because it was autumn. Later they learnt that the Fiery Mountains were just ahead of them. The mountains had a circumference of 800 *li*, on which not a blade of grass could grow. A young man selling cakes told them that it was not possible to cross the mountains without a special plantain fan which could only be borrowed from Princess Iron Fan. After having made arrangements for his master, Monkey left for the Plantain Cave to see Princess Iron Fan. The princess was the wife of the Bull Demon King and the Red Boy's mother. Some time ago, Red Boy had tried to eat the Tang Priest and Monkey had subdued him. Hence Princess Iron Fan hated Monkey and refused to lend the fan to him. Instead she blew Monkey right out of sight with a single wave of her plantain fan. Bodhisattva Lingji

heard about this and gave Monkey a Wind-Fixing Pill. Monkey came to borrow the magic fan for the second time. With the Wind-Fixing Pill in his mouth, Monkey could not be moved no matter how hard the princess waved the fan. The princess hurried back to the cave and had the doors closed tightly. However, Monkey turned himself into an insect and got into the princess' belly when she was drinking tea. The princess could not stand the pain, so that she agreed to lend the fan to Monkey, but she actually gave him a false one. The third time Monkey came for the fan he decided to turn himself into the Bull Demon King. He got the fan. Upon hearing of this trickery, the Bull Demon King came hurriedly chasing after Monkey. They engaged in a fierce struggle. Soon Pig and Friar Sand came to Monkey's help and forced the Bull Demon King to show his true colors. With the plantain fan, Monkey put out the fire. The master and his three disciples continued their journey to the West to fetch scriptures.

《西游记》中的故事。　唐僧师徒四人,一路风尘仆仆朝西行去。走着走着,渐渐觉得热气袭人,难以忍受。此时正值秋天,大家感到很奇怪。一打听才知道前方有座火焰山,方圆八百里寸草不生。又从卖糕少年嘴里听说,要想过山,只有向铁扇公主借芭蕉扇扇灭火后才能通过。悟空把师父安排好,前往芭蕉洞找铁扇公主。铁扇公主是牛魔王的妻子,红孩儿之母。因上次红孩儿想吃唐僧肉与悟空结下了冤仇,铁扇公主哪里肯借。悟空初次借扇,被铁扇公主用芭蕉扇扇得无踪无影。灵吉

菩萨得知实情,给他一粒"定风丹"让悟空再去借扇。悟空二次来借扇,公主又用扇扇他,悟空口含定风丹,一动不动。公主急忙回洞,闭门不出。悟空变作一只小虫,乘公主喝茶之际进入铁扇公主腹中。公主腹疼难忍,答应借扇,但给的是一把假扇。第三次,悟空变成牛魔王模样,骗得真扇。牛魔王到家得知真相后急忙追赶,悟空与牛魔王大战。八戒、沙僧上前助战,最后把牛魔王打得现出原形。悟空用芭蕉扇扇灭山火,师徒四人继续西行取经。

The West Chamber tells a story about the love between Zhang Sheng and Yingying. Zhang Sheng, a young scholar of the Tang Dynasty (618-907), was on his way to Chang'an (present-day Xi'an) to take part in the government examination. One day, he went to the Pujiu Temple for a visit, and there he ran into a beautiful girl. At the first sight of her, he fell into love. Later he learnt that she was Cui Yingying, the daughter of the former prime minister. Her father had died. She and her mother escorted her father's bier to their hometown. As the road ahead was blocked, they had to live at the Pujiu Temple for the time being.

After having seen Yingying, Zhang Sheng did not want to go to the capital for his official career. He decided to live in a small house in the temple. A few days later, Zhang Feihu, a bandit's chieftain, surrounded the Pujiu Temple with his troops, saying he would take Yingying as his wife. At this moment, Yingying's mother promised that she would marry Yingying to the man who could rescue them. Zhang Sheng wrote a letter to ask General Bai for help. General Bai came, captured Zhang Feihu alive, and rescued the mother and daughter from the siege. When Zhang Sheng was ready to marry Yingying, the old lady went back on her word. Zhang Sheng was so sad that he became sick. Yingying loved this young distinguished man deeply and was also disheartened. One day, Hong Niang, Yingying's maid, delivered a letter from Zhang Sheng. Yingying was very happy. She immediately wrote a letter to Zhang Sheng, including a short poem. She had Hong Niang send the letter to Zhang Sheng. With the help of Hong Niang, Zhang Sheng and Yingying broke through feudal rituals to find their own happiness.

《西厢记》，描写唐代书生张珙赴长安(今西安)赶考，一天他来到幽雅清静的普救寺游览，无意中遇到一位美丽佳人，顿生爱慕之情。后来他知道这位年轻女子是相国之女崔莺莺，因父病故，陪母扶柩回家安葬，因路途遇阻，寄居普救寺。张生见到莺莺，便不想求取功名，在普救寺借一小屋住下。刚住几天，乱贼张飞虎带兵围困普救寺，声称要娶莺莺作压寨夫人。老夫人以许配莺莺为条件请人解救，张生修书请来好友白马将军生擒张飞虎，解了重围。在张生与莺莺准备结婚时，没想到老夫人赖婚，害得张生一病不起。莺莺很爱这位年轻风流的张生，使女红娘为他们传书送柬并帮助这一对青年男女冲破了封建礼教，去追求自己的幸福。

Han Kang Sells Medicinal Herbs 韩康卖药

Han Kang, a native of the Eastern Han Dynasty (25-220), often went deep into the mountains to pick medicinal herbs and sold them on the market in Chang'an (present-day Xi'an). The herbs he sold were high in quality and he refused to bargain on prices, promising that his prices would remain unchanged for 30 years. Hence he was well known in the capital. To keep his identity hidden, Han Kang never sold medicines at a fixed spot. So people could not easily find him. One day, a woman came to Han Kang's stand, selected some herbs, and began to bargain. Han Kang refused to lower his prices. The woman said angrily: "You don't bargain on prices. You're Han Kang, aren't you? His prices remain 30 years unchanged." Upon hearing this, Han Kang thought his identity was exposed. He picked up all his belongings and went to Baling Mountains to live in seclusion. Later Emperor Huan of the Han Dynasty heard about Han Kang. The emperor thought that this must be a special man, that Han Kang must have unique views. He sent people time and again to invite Han Kang to the court. At last Han Kang had to agree. However, on the way to the capital, Han Kang suddenly changed his mind and returned to the mountains again because he really did not want to face people. After that, he lived in the deep mountains until his death. The characters "Han Kang, a Hermit" often seen on the pillars of some drugstores, refer to this story.

韩康,东汉人。他常到名山大川去采药,然后拿到长安市上去卖。他采的药货真质好;他卖的药,一是从来不言二价,二是药价三十年不变,名噪京城。后来,韩康为了隐姓埋名,卖药从不在一个地方,人们很难找到他。一天,韩康在一处设摊卖药,突然有一女子前来买药,她看好药后,百般讨价还价,但韩康就是不言二价。气得那女子说:"你卖药也不言二价,难道你就是三十年从不言二价的韩康吗?"韩康听到小女子这样一说,以为自己的身份已经暴露,就收拾起东西,到霸陵山过起了隐居的生活。汉桓帝听说了韩康的事情,觉得这个人很有性格,对事物有不同于常人的见解,几次派人请他出山作官,韩康推脱不过,只好答应了。但走到半路,因实在不愿在世人面前露面,就又返回深山,一直到死。后代,在一些药店楹联中,出现的"市隐韩康"之句,说的就是这个故事。

During the Southern and Northern Dynasties (420-581), famous painter Zhang Sengyou excelled at drawing human figures and animals, especially dragons. One year, he was invited to draw four dragons on the walls of the Anle Temple in Jinling (present-day Nanjing). People gasped with admiration at the vivid and true-to-life dragons he painted, but wondered why the dragons did not have pupils in their eyes. Many people asked Zhang Sengyou why this was so. Zhang replied: "If I add pupils to their eyes, they will fly away from the walls, then you wouldn't be able to look at them." Many thought he had cracked a joke, others asserted that Zhang had lied, and others believed he was just bragging.

Because of the controversy, he became notorious. One day, Zhang came to the murals in the Anle Temple, and added pupils to the dragons' eyes. As soon as Zhang Sengyou had finished drawing the pupils on two dragons' eyes, a violent storm arose: Lightning accompanied by peals of thunder. At this moment, the two dragons on which Zhang had just drew pupils jumped up and flew to the sky. Everyone was dumbstruck. Afterwards, only the two dragons that Zhang hadn't drawn pupils on were left on the walls. Later an idiom based on this story came into popular usage: "Bringing the painted dragon to life by drawing in the pupils of its eyes."

南北朝(公元 420－581 年)时,大画家张僧繇擅长画人物、动物,更以画龙出名。一年,有人请他在金陵(今南京市)安乐寺的墙上画了四条龙,龙的神态极为生动,形象逼真,令人赞叹不已。这四条栩栩如生的龙,都有眼无珠。很多人看了都问张僧繇为什么不给龙画上眼睛。张回答说:"我如果给它们画上眼睛,它们就会从墙上飞走,你们就见不到它们了。"大家听后,都认为他在说大话。为了挽回名声,他来到安乐寺壁画前,当许多人的面给两条龙点上了眼睛,张僧繇刚一收笔,天空顿时风雨大作,雷电破壁,点上眼睛的两条巨龙,腾空驾云而去,在场的人个个目瞪口呆。云雾过后,墙上只剩两条没点睛的龙。后来,这个故事被世人演化成成语"画龙点睛"。

Zhuge Liang Pays a Mourning Call 诸葛亮吊孝

This is a story from *Three Kingdoms*. Zhou Yu, chief commander of Wu, was talented and proficient in strategies and tactics but was narrow-minded and intolerant of others. He discussed with Zhuge Liang plans to conquer Cao Cao while simultaneously pondering how to murder Zhuge Liang. Zhou Yu had been wounded by a poisonous arrow when he was attacking Nanjun. Zhou's wound burst when he learned that Zhuge Liang had already taken over Nanjun, Jingzhou and Xiangyang. Zhou Yu, with a healing wound, racked his brains for ways to capture Jingzhou. His strategies, however, were all seen through by Zhuge Liang who even sent him a mocking message. Zhou Yu was vexed again. "Since *You*

(the Heaven) made me, Zhou Yu, why did *You* make Zhuge Liang too?" Zhou Yu grudgingly asked before he took his last breath.

Learning of Zhou Yu's demise, Zhuge Liang decided to go to pay respects. Fearing that Zhuge Liang might be murdered, Liu Bei send Zhao Yun with 500 warriors to protect him. Before Zhou Yu's coffin, Zhuge Liang personally offered libation, kneeled on the ground, and read his eulogy. Tears of grief gushed forth from Zhuge Liang. All the generals from Wu were moved. When Lu Su saw Zhuge Liang was in such grievance, he said to himself, "Zhou Yu was narrow-minded and he brought on his own death."

《三国演义》中的故事。 东吴大都督周瑜,精通兵法,才智超群,只是肚量狭小,不能容人。他和诸葛亮共商破曹大计,可又想加害诸葛亮。周瑜攻打南郡时,曾身中毒箭。当诸葛亮趁乱用计先取南郡、荆州、襄阳后,周瑜一气之下箭伤复发。病中的周瑜仍想智取荆州,均被诸葛亮识破。周瑜一气再气,在"既生瑜,何生亮"的怨恨声中死去。

诸葛亮得知周瑜的死讯,决定前去吊唁。刘备怕诸葛亮被害,派赵云带五百军士保护。在周瑜枢前,诸葛亮亲自奠酒,跪在地上读祭文,泪如泉涌,悲痛不已,众将均被感动。鲁萧见诸葛亮如此悲痛,自言自语地说:"周瑜肚量狭小,自取灭亡。"

This is a story from *Journey to the West*. Tang Priest and his three disciples traveled westward. One night, they arrived at the Tongtian River, which was 800 kilometers wide with torrential waters. They had to put up for the night in a nearby village because they had no way to cross the river. They came to a house in which lived a man named Chen Cheng and his family. The whole family was crying. The group soon learned that in the Tongtian River there was a spirit who asked the village to send him a virgin girl and a virgin boy every year as a sacrifice. And this year was Chen Cheng's turn. Learning this, Monkey King consoled the Chens, and promised them that he and Pig would act as the boy and girl to wait for the spirit in the temple. At midnight, the spirit came to the temple to reach for the girl. Pig, the pretended girl, in a hurry swirled his rake at the spirit. The spirit fled into the river. The next morning, Tang Priest and his disciples woke up and found the 800-kilometer-wide river frozen. San Zang urged his disciples to cross the river over the ice. When they reached the middle of the river, the ice cracked and the river swallowed Tang Priest who was then captured by the spirit. The three disciples ran after the spirit who knew he was no match for them and did not come out. Monkey King had to seek help from Guanyin (a Bodhisattva). It turned out that the spirit was a big goldfish in the South Sea lotus pond. The fish escaped from the Buddha to hurt people. So the Buddha was asked to retrieve the fish spirit. Later, the four were worrying about how to cross the river. Suddenly, there came an old turtle, who said," I used to live in the river. Now that you have chased away the spirit, I am back. Let me help you get across the river." So the four jumped over the turtle's back and the turtle took them to the other side of the river.

《西游记》中的故事。　唐僧师徒四人,一路往西行,傍晚来到了通天河。只见河宽八百里,水势汹猛,无法渡过,只好在附近村子借宿一夜。他们来到一户叫陈澄的家中,见全家人正痛哭流涕。经询问才知道通天河有一妖怪,要村里人每年送一对童男童女给它吃,今年正好轮到陈澄家送人。悟空听了,安慰陈家人不要怕,他和八戒扮作童男童女到庙中等妖怪。半夜妖怪闯进庙中,刚伸手抓女孩,扮女孩的八戒心慌,抡起钉钯就打,妖怪一溜烟地跑回河中。第二天清晨,唐僧师徒醒来,见八百里河面冻得明镜一般,唐僧急催徒弟们踏冰过河。走到河的中心,只听"咔嚓"一声,河面裂开一个大口,唐僧落到河里被妖怪捉去。三个徒弟追到河底,妖怪自知不是对手,闭门不出。悟空没办法,只好去求观音菩萨。原来这妖怪正是南海莲池中一条大金鱼,乘菩萨不备,跑出害人,于是菩萨收回这条鱼精。师徒四人正愁无法过河时,游过来一只老龟,老龟说:"我原住在河中,你们打走妖怪,我又回来了,我送你们过河吧!",于是师徒四人跳上龟背向河对岸漂去。

This is a story from *Strange Tales from Make-Do Studio*. Chang Dayong of Luoyang loved peonies very much. He went to Caozhou when he learned that the peonies there were the best of all. He resided in a big garden to wait for the peonies to blossom. When the peonies were budding and ready to blossom, he was already broke, so he pawned all his valuables to wait to see the peonies blossom. One day, Dayong saw a beautiful girl and they fell in love at first sight. The girl followed Dayong to Luoyang and married him. She was Gejin. Later, her younger sister, Yuban, married to Daqi, Dayong's younger brother. One year later, both of them gave birth to boys. The sisters never talked about their family background. When asked time and again about their father's family, they said, "His family name is Wei and his mother was named Lady Cao." Dayong felt strange at the word because there was no Wei family in Caozhou and moreover, how could such a distinguished family not send people out to find their missing daughters. With these questions in mind, Dayong went to Caozhou again to see the owner of the big garden. He asked the owner whether there was a Lady Cao in the vicinity. The owner took him to a big peony plant and said, "This is Lady Cao." At the word, Dayong began to realize that his wife and her sister were peony flower goddesses. When he returned home, Gejin said to him, "Three years ago, when I saw you loved peonies so much that I was moved and turned into a girl to marry you. Now that you know everything, I have to go." Saying this, she and Yuban, putting the children on the ground, disappeared. A few days later, two peony plants grew out of the place where the two boys had been put. They bore plate-size beautiful flowers, one in purple and the other in white. That is how the two famous peonies, Purple Gejin and White Yuban took their names.

《聊斋志异》中的故事。 洛阳常大用酷爱牡丹。听说曹州牡丹天下第一,他就跑到曹州,住在一个大花园内,天天等着牡丹开放。待牡丹含苞欲放时,大用已身无分文了,他将值钱的东西和衣服典卖,仍等着看花。一天,大用碰到一艳丽女子,二人一见钟情,那女子跟着大用回到洛阳,嫁给大用,她就是葛巾。后来,葛巾又把妹妹玉版嫁给了大用弟弟大器。一年后各生一子。二位女郎从不说自己的身世,在大用兄弟再三追问下她们才说:自己姓魏,母亲被封为曹夫人。大用听了更是奇怪。一是曹州没有魏姓,二是这样大的家族丢两个女儿怎么没人找。带着这两个谜,大用又来到曹州,找到那座花园的主人,问起当地可有曹夫人。主人领他到一株大牡丹前说:"这就是曹夫人。"大用这才知道自己的妻子和弟妹都是牡丹花神变的。大用回到家后,葛巾告之:"三年前,看到你对牡丹情深,很感动,便变为女子嫁你,现在你知道真情,我要走了。"说完和玉版把孩子往地上一放,就无影无踪了。几天后,在放儿子的地方长出两株牡丹,一紫一白,花朵像盘子大,花色艳丽。后人将这两种名花叫"葛巾紫"、"玉版白"。

This is a story from Buddhist Scriptures. One day, the Buddha was preaching on the lotus seat when he saw a propitious cloud coming from the east. He determined that Vimalakirti, one of his disciples, fell ill, so he sent his disciples to visit him. According to Vimalakirti's usual practice, Tathagata knew that he would avail himself of this opportunity to preach the dharma. So he sent celestial maids to check their self-cultivation. The celestial maids in colorful clothes with flower baskets in hands rode steadily through the sky on auspicious clouds. When they got to where Vimalakirti was preaching, they lowered down their heads and saw Vimalakirti giving a lecture. They raised the flower baskets and scattered the delicate flowers down. The flowers and their fragrance scattered everywhere. Flowers fell onto the ground by-passing every disciple except Sariputra whose body was covered with flowers. Vimalakirti said, "Flowers stick on the ones who have not realized the Way but do not stay on those who have achieved it." Hearing this, Sariputra knew that he had a long way to go, so he doubled his efforts in practicing Buddhism.

这是佛经里的一个典故。有一次,如来佛正在莲花宝座上讲经解法,忽见一片瑞云从东边而来,如来定眼一看,知道是弟子维摩诘患病,便令诸天菩萨和众弟子前去问候。根据维摩诘一贯作法,如来断定他必会借此说佛法。便派天女前去,检查众弟子修行的程度。天女身着彩衣,手提花篮,踏着祥云,舒展广袖,从长空冉冉而来。到维摩诘讲经的地方,低头一看,见维摩诘端坐,闭目合什,正与众人演说佛法,天女便轻举花篮,将娇艳的花朵散落下去。顿时鲜花四散,万里飘香。花落在每个菩萨身上都不能停留,纷纷落地,唯有舍利弗身上沾满鲜花。维摩诘说:"结习未尽,鲜花着身,结习尽者,鲜花不着。"舍利弗听后,自知修行甚远,便倍加努力精修起来。

In the period under the reign of Emperor Zhengde (1506-1521) of the Ming Dynasty, Wang Jinlong, the third son of the minister of rites, made an acquaintance with Su San, a famous concubine. They fell in love and pledged to get married. Wang Jinlong played ducks and drakes with money at the brothel. He was driven out into the street after he spent all his money. Su San missed him day and night. One day, when she learned the whereabouts of Wang Jinlong, she sent all her savings and treasures to him and asked him to go back home and assiduously study and strive for a good result in the imperial examination. From then on, Su San was determined to wait for Wang Jinlong and refused to receive guests. Seeing that she could no longer make money, the brothel sold her to Shen Yanlin, a rich businessman from Shanxi, as his mistress. On her way to Shanxi, Su San pretended to be sick to avoid humiliation from Shen Yanlin. Miss Pi, Shen's wife, was very angry to see Shen take Su San home, so she put poison in a dish to murder Su San, but, mistakenly, Shen was poisoned to death. Pi bought over officials to sentence Su San to death on the account of murdering her husband. Wang Jinlong did very well in the imperial examination and was promoted to governor for eight prefectures. Looking through cases, he noticed the name of Su San, so he ordered to bring Su San from Hongdong County to Taiyuan. By making secret investigations, he discovered what really happened and started the re-trial. At the trial, Wang Jinlong finally saw Su San, and he was overwhelmed by feelings of love for her. In the end, Su San was cleared of criminal charges and two lovers of the past soon got married.

明朝正德(公元 1506－1521 年)年间，礼部尚书的三公子王金龙结识了名妓苏三，二人一见钟情，发誓要结为夫妻。王金龙在妓院挥金如土，银子用完了，王被赶出妓院，流落街头。苏三日夜思念王金龙。一日，忽然打听到了公子的下落，派人送去自己的积蓄和金银首饰，并劝公子速速回家，发奋读书，争取早日考取功名。从此，苏三立志为公子守节，拒绝接客。妓院鸨母见她不再挣钱，便把她卖给山西富商沈燕林为妾。沈妻皮氏，见沈带苏三回家很气愤，便在饭中下毒想害死苏三，没想到毒死了沈燕林。皮氏买通官府，说苏三害死丈夫，定苏三死罪。王金龙科举中榜，升为八府巡按，在审理案卷中发现苏三的名字，命差官把犯人由洪洞县押到太原。他暗访案情，弄清事情的真相后升堂复审。大堂上，王金龙见到自己昼思夜想的苏三，再也无法控制自己的感情。二位陪审官也看出了其中的奥妙，帮助这一对昔日的情人破镜重圆，结为夫妻。

In Shanxi there is a county named "Jiexiu," which is said to mean the place where Jie Zitui rested. During the Warring States period (475-221 B.C.), Chong Er, after being in exile for 19 years, returned to Jin to succeed as Duke Wen of Jin. He wanted to reward those who helped him reinstate his dukedom by saying, "The awards may be divided into three grades: the first grade award goes to those followed me in exile; the second grade award goes to those who donated money; and the third grade goes to those who welcomed the return of my dukedom." He also announced a decree, "those who have supported me in other ways, but have not been rewarded, may report their names for awards." Jie Zitui had followed Duke Wen of Jin into exile. During the time of famine, Jie had cut off his flesh to be served as a meal for the duke. Jie was sick when the Duke issued the decree for awards. The duke even had forgotten him. Jie Zitui's neighbors felt that it was unfair when they saw that Jie was not awarded, so they went to him about it. Jie said: "That Chong Er became the duke is the will of heaven. It is a shame that all the officials and officers contended for merits. I would rather be poor for my whole life than seek any award." When Jie's mother saw his son with such noble quality, she asked him to leave the city with her. Jie Zitui carried his mother on his back to a mountain to live in solitude. Some people still thought the treatment of Jie Zitui was unfair, so they wrote a letter in his name and posted it on the city gate. When Duke Wen read the letter, he felt that he did not give Jie Zitui proper recognition and thanks, so he sent people to look for him in the mountain. They looked for the mother and son for days on end, but could not find them in the thick mountainous forests. They thought that if the forests were set on fire, Jie, being a filial son, would carry his mother out. The forests were set a fire for three days and three nights but Jie Zitui never came out. When the fire was dead, people found Jie and his mother holding each other burned to death under a withered willow tree. Everybody was moved at the scene. Later, the Shanxi county was named "Jiexiu" ("xiu" means *rest*) after him.

山西省有个介休县,据说"介休"二字意为介子推休息的地方。战国(公元前 475－前 221 年)时,晋公子重耳在逃亡十九年后回国继位,史称晋文公。他即位后对从亡者和有功之臣行赏,并发布"如有立下功劳没赏者,可以自己上报"的诏令。介子推跟随晋文公逃亡,饥饿时曾割下自己的肉给晋文公吃。这次行赏,他在家养病,晋文公竟然把他忘了。介子推的邻居,见介子推无赏,心中不平,特意上门告诉介子推。介子推说:"文公当国君是天意,大臣们争相居功,我真为他们感到耻辱。我宁愿终身贫困,也不去争功。"老母亲见儿子有这样的志气,劝儿子和自己一块离开闹市。介子推便背上母亲隐居起来。有人着实为介子推鸣不平,便假冒介子推写了一封信挂在城门上。晋文公看后,觉得很对不住介子推,就到山中去找。草深林密,晋文公带人找了好几天仍不见介子推母子的踪影。他想:介子推是个孝子,如果把山林点燃,他一定会背着母亲出来。熊熊烈火,烧了三天三夜,介子推始终没出来。火后人们才见介子推和老母相抱,烧死在枯柳下。众人看后,非常感动,以后,这里修城建县以"介休"为名。

The Cowherd and the Girl Weaver　牛郎织女

This is a fairy tale. It was said that the Girl Weaver, a granddaughter of the Celestial Goddess, often took bath in the Milky Way. The Cowherd, a poor orphan, was mistreated by his elder brother and sister-in-law. Later, his brother gave him an old cow as his only inhesitance and drove him out of the house. One day, the cow suddenly said to him: "You can marry the Girl Weaver if you are able to steal her clothes while she is taking a bath in the Milky Way." The Cowherd followed the old cow's words and quietly took her clothes away. When the fairy girls saw a stranger in the galaxy, they panicked and ran away. Only the Girl Weaver stayed in the water because she was shy and had no clothes. The Cowherd said to the girl that if she promised to be his wife he would return her clothes to her. The girl knew he was a kind and diligent boy, so she immediately agreed

to marry him. After they were married, they had a boy and a girl. They lived a happy and sweet life. When the Celestial Goddess found out, she sent the Celestial Army to catch the Girl Weaver. When the Cowherd returned from the field, he saw his wife being taken to the Celestial Palace. Grieved as he was, he put the two children into baskets and chased after his wife. The Celestial Goddess drew a line in the Celestial River and high waves rose from the water. The husband and wife could only weep and cry from opposite sides of the river. Later, the Celestial Goddess allowed the Cowherd and the Girl Weaver to meet once a year on the 7th day of the 7th month. That is why there is a saying that the rain on the 7th day of the 7th month is the tears shed by the Cowherd and Girl Weaver when they meet.

这是一则神话故事。　传说,天上的织女是王母娘娘的外孙女,常和诸仙女在银河里洗澡。牛郎则是人间的一贫苦孤儿,常受兄嫂的虐待。后来,狠心的兄嫂不给他任何财产,只给他一条老黄牛并把他撵出家门。一天夜里,老牛突然对他说:"织女要到银河里洗澡,如果你能拿到织女的衣服,就能娶织女为妻。"牛郎按老牛的话,悄悄地拿了织女的衣裳。众仙女看到有生人来到天河,惊得四处逃散。只有织女因无衣可穿,仍然羞愧地躲在水里。牛郎对织女说,要是能答应做我的妻子,就

把衣服还给你。其实织女早就知道这个勤劳善良的小伙子,马上就答应了他的要求。结婚后,他俩生了一双儿女,生活非常温馨甜美。后来,此事被王母娘娘发现,便派天兵天将把织女捉拿上天。牛郎从田间回来,看到织女正被押回天宫,十分悲痛,忙用箩筐担上两个孩子去追赶,眼看就要追上了,狠心的王母娘娘在天河中一划,天河立刻波涛汹涌,夫妻俩只好隔河相泣。后来王母娘娘只许牛郎和织女每年七月七日见一面。所以,在民间有七月七日下雨是牛朗织女见面时落的眼泪之说。

In the late Eastern Han Dynasty (200 A.D.), there was a famous calligrapher named Wang Xizhi, who loved geese all his life. Even nowadays, in many places there are still stone tablets with his inscriptions of "goose pond." One day, Wang Xizhi learned that an old granny kept a big white goose that sang like a flowing river, or sometimes like a fiddle. Wang Xizhi decided to go for a visit. When the old granny got the word, she thought that Wang preferred to eat goose meat. So she killed the goose and cooked a goose feast to entertain Wang Xizhi. Wang, deeply troubled by this, could not help sighing for days on end. Wang Xizhi's servants often went on secret expeditions in search of geese for their master. When they learned that a Taoist kept a flock of geese in his monastery in Yinshan Mountain, they told Wang. Wang Xizhi was especially pleased and got on a cart to see them. Seeing visitors, the geese danced and sang in high tunes. Wang wanted to buy some geese from the Taoist, who said, "I know you are the Calligrapher Saint. If you could write Taoist scriptures for the monastery, I would give you all the geese." Wang agreed. After taking a bath, Wang started to write. His brushes touched the paper like a flying dragon, a walking phoenix and floating clouds. After finishing the writing, Wang immediately ordered his men to get a big wooden cage for the geese, which were put on a cart to be taken back. The story of Wang Xizhi's love of geese has been passed on by many generations of Chinese people.

著名的书法家王羲之(公元 321－379 年, 一作 303－361 年), 一生爱鹅, 现在不少地方有他书写的"鹅池"石碑。有一次, 王羲之听说有一老太太, 家中养了一只大白鹅, 叫声有时似高山流水, 有时如古琴低奏, 王羲之便准备亲自乘车去观赏。老太太得知后, 以为王羲之爱吃鹅肉, 急忙把鹅杀掉, 款待王羲之。羲之见后, 非常婉惜, 不禁长叹数日。王羲之手下的人见他特别喜欢鹅, 便常常四处暗暗查访。他们探听到阴山有一位老道士, 在观中养了很多鹅, 急报羲之。王羲之大喜, 急忙乘马前往观看。鹅看到有人来便争着引颈长鸣。羲之恳请道士卖给他几只。道士说:"早就听说你是'书圣', 如能为我这小观写一篇《道德经》, 我便把这所有的鹅送给你。"羲之听后, 满口答应。羲之沐浴完毕, 很快来到桌前, 只见他飞龙走凤, 笔势飘若浮云。写完之后, 王羲之急忙命从人取来一个很大的木笼, 把道观中的鹅全部装入笼, 车载而归。羲之之爱鹅, 一直流传为佳话。

This is a story from *Strange Tales from Make-Do Studio*. Mr. Sun of Luoyang married the daughter of a magistrate. About twenty days after the wedding, his wife died of illness. Sun was extremely sad. One rainy day, an average-looking girl came to his house and said: "My name is Lü Wubing. I see how sad you feel about losing your wife at such a young age; I admire you for your courage at this difficult time. I come to offer help; I am willing to be your maid." Mr. Sun saw that she was simple, generous, diligent, kind and able to read and write, so he accepted her as his concubine, rather than as a maid. He later married a woman named Xu. A year later, Xu bore him a boy named Ahjian. Lü Wubing loved and treated the boy as her own child. Ahjian loved Lü Wubin more than his mother. When Ahjian was three years old, Xu fell seriously ill, and she told Sun, "Wubing loves Ahjian. Please let Wubing be the wife after I die." In tears, Sun promised he would do so. Nevertheless, he could not follow through on his promise because his family did not give its permission. His family elders dictated that Sun marry a woman named Wang, the daughter of an official. Wang, short-tempered, often beat and scolded Wubing and Ahjian. There the whole family was neither in harmony nor tranquil. Sun went far away from home to avoid the shrewish woman. After a while, Wubing could bear it no longer. She took Ahjian and escaped. She entrusted a friend to take care of Ahjian. She traveled around and tried to find Sun. When she found him, she told him about what had happened in the family and his son's whereabouts. While telling the story, she was weeping and crying and then suddenly she fainted, falling on the ground. Sun rushed to help her, only to find her clothes on the ground. She had disappeared. By then, Sun realized that Lü Wubing was the incarnation of a ghost. In memory of Lü Wubing, Sun set up a tombstone with the epitaph: "Tomb of Lü Wubing, my ghost wife."

《聊斋志异》中的故事。　洛阳孙公子，娶太守女儿为妻。婚后二十天妻子得一场大病去世，公子十分悲伤。一天下大雨，有一相貌平平的女子挑帘进来说："我叫吕无病，见公子青春丧偶，又屡屡悲伤，我慕公子才华，特来投奔，愿作使女。"公子见他朴素大方，殷勤温柔，又识文断字，便收为妾。孙公子又娶许小姐为妻，一年后生一子名叫阿坚。吕无病如同自己孩子一样爱惜，阿坚对吕无病比亲母还亲。阿坚三岁时，许小姐得重病，她叮嘱公子说："无病爱阿坚，我死后把无病扶正。"公子含泪答应，无奈家族不许，又娶王天官女儿为妻。王女性格暴躁，对无病、阿坚打骂为常事，吵得全家不得安定。公子为避恶妇远离家乡。后来，无病看到在这个家实在无法呆下去了，就带上阿坚逃跑了。她把阿坚寄托在熟人家中，自己千方百计去打听公子的下落。寻到公子后，告诉阿坚住的地方，又泪流满面的诉说家中发生的情况。边说边哭，昏倒在地。孙公子要去扶她，只见衣服在地上，人早没影了。孙公子这才明白，吕无病原是鬼变的。公子为纪念吕无病，专为她立了一块石碑，上刻：鬼妻吕无病之墓。

This is a legendary story. After failing to pass the imperial examination, Pei Hang took a boat to go back home. On his way, he ran into a boat. It was said that Lady Fan, an extremely beautiful woman, sat in the other boat. He wanted to talk with her, so he wrote a poem and sent it over to her. Pei Hang got aboard the boat and saw that Lady Fan had charming eyes like a nymph. When he returned to his boat, he received Lady Fan's poem:

A drink of crystal water starts everything.
After the herbal medicine is pounded,
Yunying will be seen.
Lanqiao is the goddess den,
Why go through twists and turns for jade crystal.

Pei Hang could not understand the poem. One day, Pei Hang felt thirsty at a place called Lanqiao. He asked an old lady for water. The old lady sized up Pei Hang and said, "Yunying, get some water here right now." At the word, a girl came out from the house. A charming and beautiful girl was in front of Pei Hang, who suddenly came to understand Lady Fan's poem. He was eager to marry Yunying. The old lady said, "I am old and sick. Yesterday, a goddess sent me some medicine. If you grind medicine with a jade pestle and mortar for a hundred days, I will let you marry Yunying." Pei Hang was very glad to hear this. He immediately went to town to buy a jade pestle and mortar in a drug store. He wasted no time and spared no efforts in pounding the medicine. One night, he heard a grinding noise. Investigating, he found a celestial rabbit grinding medicine for him. Pei Hang's loyalty to love had moved the celestial rabbit to help. One hundred days after Pei pounded the medicine, the old lady, keeping her word, allowed Pei Hang to marry Yunying. On the wedding day, Lady Fan, Yunying's sister, also came. The sisters were both goddesses. Lady Fan had seen that Pei Hang was kind and wrote good poems, so she had written suggestive poems to help her sister get married to him.

这是个神话故事。秀才裴航进京赶考不中,乘船回家。途中遇一船,船上有个美貌超群的樊夫人,很想与之交谈。于是,写诗一首,让人送去。裴航来到樊夫人船上,只见夫人俊眉修目,顾盼神飞,宛如天仙一般。刚回到自己船上,他便接到樊夫人回诗一首:一饮琼浆百生态,玄霜捣尽见云英;蓝桥便是神仙窟,何必崎岖上玉清。裴航看后,百思不解。有一天,裴航经过一个叫蓝桥的地方,觉得口干舌燥,向一位老妇要水喝,老人打量裴航一下说:"云英,快拿些水来。"随后,一女子从屋内出来,裴航见她容貌绝世,又想到樊夫人诗中提到的蓝桥和云英,裴航顿悟,便想娶云英为妻。老太太说:"我年老有病,昨天有神仙送药来,你若能用玉杵臼替我捣一百天药,就把云英嫁你。"裴航听后很高兴,急忙到城中药店买回了玉杵臼,每天捣药,从不怠慢。有一天夜里,裴航听到叮咚的捣药声,他出去一看,见一玉兔帮他捣药,原来他对爱情忠贞不渝的精神感动了玉兔。裴航捣药一百天,老妇不失前言,把云英嫁给他。迎亲那天,云英的姐姐樊夫人也来了,原来她俩都是神仙。樊夫人见裴航人好,诗好,所以才写诗指点,把妹妹嫁给他。

This is a story from *A Dream of Red Mansions*. After hearing Folly Sister say that Baoyu had married Baochai, Lin Daiyu felt her life's dream burst like a bubble. She returned to Xiaoxiang Lodge and vomited fresh blood. She felt that her days were numbered. Daiyu, pointing to her suitcase, asked Xueyan to get out her poem notebooks and handkerchiefs. Zijuan was very clear that Daiyu had written quite a number of poems on these handkerchiefs given to her by Baoyu. These poems fully expressed Daiyu's love toward Baoyu and her own sorrowful past. Seeing the poems on the handkerchiefs at this moment, she felt strong feelings welling up, grief mingling with sorrow. She used all her strength trying to tear the handkerchiefs but she was too weak to do it. Then she asked Xueyan to light the fire basin at once. Zijuan and Xueyan thought she felt cold and hurriedly moved the fire basin to her. Before they noticed, she had already thrown the handkerchiefs and poem notebooks into the fire and burned them into ashes. Completely cutting off her devoted love for years, she left the world with hatred against feudal society.

Note: Xueyan and Zijuan were Daiyu's two maids.

《红楼梦》中的故事。 林黛玉听傻大姐说宝玉已娶宝钗的事后,回到潇湘馆,口吐鲜血,自料难久于人世。黛玉叫丫环拿出诗本和当年宝玉所赠的手绢。手绢上有黛玉的题诗,这些诗充分表达了黛玉对宝玉的无限爱恋和对自己身世的伤感。

此时此刻,黛玉百感交集,悲愤交加,便用力撕扯手绢,但因身体过于虚弱,撕不动。然后,把手绢和诗本扔进火盆,断了多年来的这段痴情,含怨离开了这个世界。

Daiyu Burns Her Manuscripts 黛玉焚稿

This is a story from *Three Kingdoms*. Zhang Lu ordered Ma Chao to attack Jiameng Pass. Learning this, Liu Bei immediately went to his military advisor Zhuge Liang for ideas. Zhuge Liang said, "Mao Chao is so brave that only Zhang Fei and Zhao Yun can match him. But Zhao Yun is not available; only Zhang Fei is around at the moment."

Knowing that Ma Chao was attacking the pass, Zhang Fei came to ask for a fight against him. Pretending not to hear, Zhuge Liang said to Liu Bei, "Ma Chao is attacking, and only Zhao Yun can defeat him." Feeling snubbed, Zhang Fei noted his past merits and shouted, "If I can not defeat Ma Chao, I am willing to be punished according the rule." Only then did Zhuge Liang nod his agreement. Liu Bei himself acted as the chief commander and ordered Zhang Fei to fight in the vanguard. Liu Bei led the army to the pass. Time and again Ma Chao challenged them to fight. At every challenge, Zhang Fei wanted to engage him, but was stopped by Liu Bei. When Liu Bei saw Ma Chao and his army became fatigued, he ordered Zhang Fei to take on the challenge. Zhang Fei and Ma Chao fought one hundred rounds with an even hand. When Liu Bei saw that it was turning dark, he asked Zhang Fei to come back for a fight tomorrow. But Zhang Fei became infuriated and shouted, "Light more torches and get ready for a night fight. I will not return to the pass without defeating Ma Chao!" Ma Chao also pledged that he would not return to his camp without winning over Zhang Fei. Each of them mounted fresh horses to start the night fight. After another twenty rounds, Ma Chao saw that he could not win by force, so he had an idea. He pretended to flee. At the moment, Zhuge Liang arrived. He analyzed Ma Chao's situation and laid a trap for him. With Ma Chao in a fight spot, Zhuge Liang sent someone who succeeded in persuading him to fight for Liu Bei.

Note: Zhang Lu was the Magistrate of Hanning. Ma Chao was a general in Xiliang (nowaday Gansu Province) under Zhang Lu.

《三国演义》中的故事。 汉宁太守张鲁命马超攻葭萌关。刘备得知,忙找军师诸葛亮商议,军师说:"马超英勇无比,若要除他,只有张飞和赵云二人!"但赵云在外,只有张飞在此。张飞见马超攻关,大叫着请战。诸葛亮假装没听见,对刘备说:"马超来侵犯,唯有云长才能得胜。"张飞闻言不高兴,历述自己以前的战绩后说:"我若不胜马超,甘愿军令处罚。"诸葛亮这才答应。让刘备亲自带兵,命张飞为先锋。刘备领兵来到关上,马超三番五次叫阵。张飞屡欲下关迎战,均被刘备阻拦。后来,刘备见马超人马疲乏,令张飞下关克敌。张飞、马超大战一百回合,不分胜败。这时天色已晚,刘备劝张飞回关,明日再战。张飞却大叫:"多点火把,安排夜战,不胜马超,暂不回关!"马超也发誓:"不胜张飞,暂不回寨!"二人各换一匹马,开始了挑灯夜战。又战二十回合,马超见不能取胜张飞,佯装败走。此时,诸葛亮赶到,略施小计,使马超陷于困境,然后投降。

121

This is a story from *Three Kingdoms.* Huang Zhong, a veteran in the army of Shu, was one of its top five generals. Zhang He under Cao Cao had suffered one defeat after another. Cao Hong gave him a 5,000-strong army to attack Jiameng Pass. When Liu Bei learned this, he consulted with Zhuge Liang, his military advisor. Zhuge Liang said: "Zhang He is a distinguished general of Cao Cao. Only Zhang Fei could defeat him." This irritated veteran Huang Zhong. Huang shouted: "Advisor has looked down upon me. I will get his head off and offer it to you." Zhuge Liang prodded Huang again by saying, "Though you are valiant, I am afraid you are not Zhang He's match because you are too old." When Huang Zhong heard this, his gray hair angrily stood on end. He said, "Old as I am, I am able to open two bows and am full of vitality." Huang went down and got a big sword off the rack and performed with it. He took two hard bows off the wall and pulled them broken. Then Zhuge Liang said: "If you go, whom would you like to be your assistant?" Huang Zhong replied, "Veteran Yan Yan. If the two of us can not defeat Zhang He, my gray-haired head is yours." Liu Bei and Zhuge Liang were very pleased. The veteran generals were ordered to fight Zhang He. When Huang Zhong and Yan Yan got to Jiameng Pass, they laid a trap to defeat Zhang He. Then they used skillful tactics to take over Tiandang Mountain, the granary of Cao Cao's army. Later, they captured Dingjun Mountain. They reported back to Liu Bei and Zhuge Liang declaring a complete victory.

《三国演义》中的故事。 黄忠是蜀军中有名的老将。曹将张郃在连吃败仗的情况下,曹洪又给他五千人马叫他攻打葭萌关。刘备得知,与军师集众商议对策。诸葛亮说:"张郃是曹操手下名将,要想取胜只有张飞才行。"诸葛亮一句话,激怒了老将黄忠,只见他大声喊道:"军师太小看人了,我黄忠愿取张郃首级,献于军师帐下。"诸葛亮再激道:"你虽然很勇敢,但年纪太大了,恐怕不是张郃的对手。"黄忠听了,气的白发倒竖说:"我虽然老了,但两臂能开三石之弓,浑身还有千斤之力。"只见黄忠大步走下堂,取下架上大刀,舞动如飞,拿下墙上硬弓,一连拉断两张。诸葛亮说:"将军要去,谁做你的副将。"黄忠说:"老将严颜。如果我俩不能取胜,我愿献上这颗白头。"刘备、诸葛亮大喜。命二人带兵与张郃交战。黄忠、严颜到了葭萌关,先用计打败张郃,又用智夺取了曹操的屯粮重地天荡山。而后又攻下定军山,果然大获全胜而归。

This is a story from *Three Kingdoms*. Cao Cao appointed Yu Jin as the chief commander in charge of the southern expedition, together with Pang De in the vanguard. They led seven armies to rescue Fancheng City. When Guan Yu of Shu learned this, he led his army to take them on. Guan and Pang fought over one hundred rounds with neither gaining an advantage. The fight continued on the second day without an exchange of words. After another 50 rounds, Pang rode his horse to flee and Guan rode after him. Pang shot an arrow at Guan who was unable to dodge it. The wounded Guan went back to his camp for recuperation. Ten days later, Guan's wound got healed. Guan Yu learned from Guan Ping that Cao Cao's army had moved to the north of the city. Guan Yu went to a nearby hilltop to look at the terrain. He saw the enemy's troops in the northern mountain valley; also, he noticed that the Xiangjiang River was unusually swift. He hit on the idea of flooding the

seven armies. He ordered his army to get boats and rainwear ready. He had his men dam up several points in the river so as to flood Cao Cao's army. Pang De talked with his generals of moving out of the valley onto higher ground the next day. That night, wind blew fiercely and rain came down heavily. Pang De, sitting in his tent, heard the restless movements of the horses and the sound of battle drums. Alarmed, he went outside to look. From all sides, floodwaters were rushing in; the seven armies, thrown into a panic, had already lost untold numbers in the tide. The water reached a depth of over three meters. With their soldiers, Yu Jin and Pang De climbed to higher ground. Guan Yu urged his forces to strike. Yu Jin and Pang De's armies, seeing no way out, surrendered. Pang De, who had gotten hold of a boat, tried to escape westward. The boat, however, was knocked down by Zhou Cang's raft and Pang De was captured alive.

《三国演义》中的故事。 曹操命大将于禁为南征将军,庞德为先锋,统帅七路大军,星夜去救樊城。关羽得信,亲自披挂前去迎敌。关羽、庞德大战百余回合,不分胜负。第二日交战,二将齐出,并不答话,拍马交锋五十回合,庞德拨马逃走,关羽紧追不舍。庞德取箭,关羽躲闪不及中箭,回营养伤。十日后,箭伤愈合。又听关平说曹兵移到城北驻扎。关羽不知何意,骑马登高观望,看到北山谷内人马很多,又见襄江水势汹猛,水淹七军之计,油然而生。遂急命部下准备船筏,收拾雨具,又派人

堵住各处水口。庞德与众将商议,山谷不易久留,准备明日将军士移入高地。就在这天夜里,风雨大作,庞德在帐中,只听万马奔腾,喊声震天。出帐一看,大水从四面急剧涌来。七军兵士随波逐浪,淹死很多。于禁、庞德率将士登上小土山躲避,关羽带大军冲杀而来,于禁见四下无路,投降关羽。庞德和身无盔甲的残兵败将,被关羽的兵马团团围住,战不多时,众将全都投降。只有庞德夺一小船,想顺流西去,却被周仓的大筏撞到水中,后被生擒。

Boya Broke the Fiddle　伯牙摔琴

"Boya was good at playing the fiddle and Ziqi was fond of enjoying it." The two were regarded as bosom friends. Yu Boya, a man in the Spring and Autumn Period (770-476 B.C.), played the fiddle with superb expertise, but very few could understand it. Boya felt that it was a pity for him not to have someone to appreciate his music. One mid-autumn night, he got to Hanjiang River Port by boat. Under the clear autumn sky and the bright moon, Boya excitedly played the fiddle. He was very much absorbed in playing when one of the strings suddenly broke. At this moment, a man came and said: "When I passed by, the playing of the fiddle arrested me. I never expected to disturb you." Hearing this, Boya knew he was an extraordinary man, so he invited him to have a talk on the boat. The man was named Zhong Ziqi. The two chatted about the fiddle and music and soon developed mutual admiration. Ziqi could explain the meaning and the style of every song

that Boya played. The two got to know each other very well through music and became sworn brothers. The next day, they parted and promised to meet again at the same time and place next year. The following year's mid-autumn night, Boya returned. He took the fiddle out and started to play with the expectation that Ziqi would soon arrive. He waited for several days, but Ziqi did not arrive. Boya went ashore to look for him. He ran into Ziqi's father who told him that Ziqi had passed away several months before. Before taking his last breath, Ziqi had asked his family to bury him at the river bank so that his soul would come for his appointment with Boya. Boya went to Ziqi's grave. While playing the fiddle, he cried, "Ziqi is gone while Boya is waiting, with a broken heart and pointless music of high mountain and floating water." He broke the fiddle at the gravesite to thank his understanding friend.

"伯牙善鼓琴,子期善听琴,"视为知音。俞伯牙,相传春秋时人,弹奏古琴,技术非凡。但能听懂的人很少,伯牙也为难寻到知音而婉惜。有一年中秋之夜,他乘船来到汉江口。秋高气爽,明月当空,他琴兴大发,取琴弹奏起来。正在兴浓之际,一弦忽然崩断。此时,岸上有一人走过来说:"我在此路过,这琴声使我心旷神怡,谁知却惊动了大人。"伯牙听后,感到此人非同一般,忙请上船来叙话。这人就是钟子期。二人谈琴论乐,甚为投机。伯牙每弹一曲,子期都能讲出曲子的含义和其

独特的风格。两人通过音乐,互诉衷肠,遂结为兄弟。次日,二人惜别,约定来年此时,在此重会。第二年中秋之夜,伯牙又来到此地弹奏。但等了几天,不见钟子期到来。伯牙上岸去寻找,碰到钟子期的父亲,他告诉伯牙,子期在几个月之前,已经离开了人世,他死前告诉家人,将他葬在岸边听琴的地方,他要用灵魂来赴前约。伯牙到子期坟前,边弹边哭诉:子期不在伯牙望,高山流水痛断肠! 曲终摔琴,以谢知音。

Zhang Chang came from Pingyang of Hedong (in today's Shanxi). His family had been officials for generations. Zhang Chang was honest, frank, scrupulous, just, fair and selfless. After he was transferred to the capital, he saw that the social order in Chang'an, the capital, was in chaos. Emperor Jing (156-141 B.C.) of the Han Dynasty had changed several mayors but to no avail. When Emperor Jing was in a dilemma, Zhang Chang volunteered to take the post. The first thing he did after taking office was deal with theft and robbery. He laid down a trap by disseminating the word that Zhang Chang would hold a banquet for all the chieftains of thieves and robbers, who thought that Zhang was afraid of them. So they came to the banquet. When they got drunk, Zhang Chang ordered the ambushed officers to take action. All the thieves and robbers were captured. The second thing he did was handle those evil-doers who were relatives or family members of high officials. They saw Zhang Chang was different from his predecessors. Fearing that he would fix them, they tried everything to find out Zhang Chang's shortcomings. When they learned that Zhang Chang did mascara for his wife every day, they accused him of being frivolous and disgraceful as a high official. When asked about this by Emperor Jing, Zhang Chang uprightly answered: "Is whether or not a husband applies mascara for his wife a question that should concern the emperor?" Seeing there was something in what Zhang said, and noting his merits and achievements in putting Chang'an in order (which had won popularity among the people) Emperor Jing just smiled and let it go.

张敞,河东(今山西境内)平阳人。他家世代在朝为官。张敞为人耿直,为官清政廉洁,以公正无私著称。调任京官后,他看到当时长安的社会情况非常混乱,汉景帝(公元前156 – 141年在位)连换几任京兆均不奏效,张敞遂自荐。张敞到任后,第一步先整治小偷强盗。他设下一计,让人四处宣扬说,张敞要宴请盗贼头目。盗贼听后,都误认为张敞怕他们,于是,众盗贼纷纷前来赴宴。待到一个个烂醉如泥时,张敞大喝一声,四面埋伏下的刀斧手把这些盗贼一网打尽。第二步,整治那些为非作歹的皇亲国戚。这些人看到张敞不同于前几任京兆,怕整到自己的头上,就到处搜集张敞的短处。他们听说张敞每天为妻子画眉,便告他行为轻浮,有失大臣体统。汉景帝查问此事时,张敞理直气壮地回答:"夫妻之间,比画眉还风流的事多着哪,难道皇上你都一一查问吗?"皇上见他言之有理,又见他治理长安成绩显著,深得老百姓爱戴,只是一笑了之。

This is a story from *Three Kingdoms*. Guan Yu was hit by a poisonous arrow in the right arm while attacking Fancheng City. When his men took the arrowhead out, they found that the poison had already seeped into the bone, so they persuaded him to go to Jingzhou for treatment. Determined to take over Fancheng City, Guan refused to retreat. Seeing Guan's wound getting worse day by day, they sent out scouts to look for famous doctors. One day, a man named Hua Tuo came by boat to the camp especially to cure Guan Yu. Guan asked him about how he would heal the wound. Hua said: "I am afraid that you will be scared, so I suggest that we set up a post with a loop to tie down your arm with rope. Then, when your eyes are covered, I will start the operation."

Guan laughingly said, "That's necessary." Then he gave orders to hold a dinner for Hua Tuo. After drinking several glasses of wine, Guan started to play chess. At the same time, he reached out his right arm to Hua Tuo and said, "It is at your disposal. I have no fear." Hua cut the skin and flesh open and scraped the bone with scalpel. Everyone present covered his eyes while Guan continued drinking and playing chess. In a moment, the blood filled a basin. When the poison was scraped off the bone, Guan stood up and smilingly said, "Now my arm can move freely just like before. Mr. Hua Tuo, you are a magic doctor!" Hua said, "Since I started medical practice, I have not seen anyone like you. You are a magic general."

《三国演义》中的故事。　关羽攻打樊城时，被毒箭射中右臂。将士们取出箭头一看，毒已渗入骨头，劝关羽回荆州治疗。关羽决心攻下樊城，不肯退。将士们见关羽箭伤逐渐加重，便派人四处打听名医。一天，有人从江上驾小舟来到寨前，自报姓华名佗，特来给关羽治伤。关羽问华佗怎样治法？华佗说："我怕你害怕，立一柱子，柱子上吊一环，把你的胳膊套入环中，用绳子捆紧，再盖住你的眼睛，给你开刀治疗。"关羽笑着说："不用捆。"然后吩咐设宴招待华佗。关羽喝了几杯酒就与人下棋，同时把右臂伸给华佗，并说："随你治吧，我不害怕。"华佗切开肉皮，用刀刮骨。在场的人吓得用手捂着眼。再看关羽，一边喝酒，一边下棋。过了一会，血流了一盆，骨上的毒刮完，关羽笑着站起来对众将说："我的胳膊伸弯自如，好像从前一样。华佗先生，你真是神医呀！"华佗说："我行医以来，从没见像你这样了不起的人，将军乃神人也。"

This story took place in the late Song Dynasty (1200 A.D.) and it has long been passed on among Chinese people. One day, Xiao En, honest and forthright, and a master of martial arts, was fishing in a river with his daughter, Xiao Guiying. When his friends Li Jun and Ni Rong called him from ashore, he collected the fishnet and went ashore. He treated his friends with the fish he had just caught. Asked about things going on recently, Xiao sighed, "The weather is dry and water shallow, so the fish do not run into the net. Life is hard with debts of fishing taxes." At this moment, cohorts of Ding Zixie, a despot, came to collect taxes. Xiao told them that he did not have any money at the moment and would send it a few days later. On the second day, before Xiao got up, Ding's cohorts again came for the taxes and started to beat Xiao when he didn't pay up. Xiao went to court to sue them because they bullied so much. The unfair magistrate also had Xiao En beaten. Xiao Guiying felt uneasy after his father had gone. At midnight, she heard her father knocking at the door. When she opened the door, she was frightened to see her father's face and body were covered with blood and wounds. Xiao En told her, "The Ding family and the court are one of a kind. At the court I was given 40 floggings and was ordered to go across the river to apologize to the Ding's." Preparing to go to Ding's house, Xiao En asked Xiao Guiying to take her Qingding Pearl, her betrothal gift, with her. With swords hidden, they crossed the river that night. Ding Zixie was very pleased to see Xiao En and his daughter who carried the valuable Qingding Pearl. He took over the "gift" to have a careful look at it—suddenly Xiao En and his daughter took out their swords and killed the despot who had committed so many evils.

这件事发生在北宋末年,在民间广为流传。性格豪爽,为人正直,武艺高强的萧恩,有一天和女儿萧桂英在江中撒网打渔,听到岸上有好友李俊和倪荣向他们打招呼,连忙收网靠岸,并把打到的鱼做熟招待好友。朋友问萧恩的近况,他叹道:"天旱水浅,鱼不上网,欠渔税很多,生活艰难。"正说着,恶霸丁子燮的家奴前来催税,萧恩说现在没有,改日送到家去。第二天,萧恩还没起床,丁家又催渔税,还动手打了萧恩。萧恩见丁家欺人太甚,便告到县衙。官府不能公断,反而把萧恩痛打一顿。

萧桂英自父亲走后坐卧不安。深夜,听到父亲的叫门声,开门一看,只见父亲满脸是血,浑身是伤。萧恩告诉女儿说:"丁家和衙门串通一气,上堂不问青红皂白,把我打了四十大板,还逼着我连夜过江,去向丁家赔礼。"官逼民反。萧恩让女儿带上婆家的聘礼"庆顶珠",父女二人随身暗藏戒刀利刃,趁月色渡过江去。丁子燮见萧恩父女连夜过江,又献上宝贝"庆顶珠",心中大喜。当他接过"礼品"细看时,萧恩父女拔出短刀,杀死了这个作恶多端的恶霸。

Wenji Pays Homage at Her Father's Grave 文姬谒墓

Cai Wenji was the daughter of Cai Yong, a calligrapher and writer of the late Eastern Han Dynasty (200 B.C.). She was a smart girl, good at musics and poems, but had a miserable fate. Her father had offended the powerful Wang Run and was persecuted to death. And her husband had died only two years after they were married. When the Huns (Xiongnu) invaded the central plain, Cai Wenji was taken away and forced to be the wife of one of the Hun's kings. Wenjin missed her homeland very much. During the time of her captivity, Cao Cao became the prime minister and he put down the rebellion of Wuheng to stabilize the northern frontier. He implemented a united and friendly policy toward the Huns and other minorities in the north. Cao Cao respected and admired Cai Yong for his works and knew Cai Wenji was a woman of letters. He wanted to have Cai Wenji back to sort out Cai Yong's manuscripts. There-

fore, he sent Dong Si, a relative of Cai Wenji, as an envoy to the Huns. He brought with him a large quantity of gold and silver and was successful in winning Cai Wenji's ransom. During the 12 years of her captivity, Cai Wenji had thought of her homeland day and night. Now she was on her way back to the homeland for the sake of her father's unfinished work. She was happy, although she had made the miserable and heart-breaking decision to leave her son behind. When she got to the outskirts of Chang'an, she came to her father's grave. She recalled her father's sad death and her uneven path of life with great sorrow. She sighed and played the *hujia* (a reed instrument) in front of her father's grave to express her feelings of her tragic life and deep mourning. The picture illustrates the scene when Cai Wenji passes the gravesite of Cai Yong.

蔡文姬是东汉末年人、大文学家、书法家蔡邕的女儿。她自幼聪明伶俐,擅长诗歌音律,但命运很悲惨。父亲因得罪权贵,被司徒王允所害。她出嫁后,只两年丈夫就死去了。在匈奴入侵中原时,蔡文姬被掠走,逼作了匈奴左贤王的妻子。在匈奴生活的十二年中,文姬时时思念故乡。曹操当汉朝承相后,他平定了乌桓之乱,稳定了北方边疆,对北部匈奴等少数民族实行团结友善政策。曹操敬慕蔡邕的才华,又知道蔡文姬是

个才女,很想让蔡文姬整理蔡邕的文稿,于是,就派蔡文姬的亲戚董祀,带了大量金银财宝出使匈奴,把蔡文姬赎回来。蔡文姬日夜思念故乡,这次为了父亲未尽之事,她忍痛抛下亲生儿子,踏上了回故乡的路。在经过长安郊外时,她来到父亲墓前,思绪万千,想到父亲的惨死,想到自己坎坷的人生,心中非常悲痛。她仰天长叹,并在她父亲坟上弹吟《胡茄十八拍》借以来抒发自己悲凉的人生和无限的哀思。

Mi Fu was a famous calligrapher and painter in the Northern Song Dynasty (960-1127). He was odd and unrestrained. Apart from his calligraphy and paintings, he was also crazy about stones. When he served as an official, he was honest and upright. He could not get along well with the county magistrate Mai, who was called "incompetent mouse" by the people. On odd-numbered days of the month, when the county had a meeting, Mi Fu had to make a courtesy call to the county magistrate in an official uniform. This made him even more annoyed. He thought of an idea: He asked his servant to move the old stones out from the house and displayed them every morning of the odd-numbered days. Then he put on his official uniform and prostrated himself before these stones as if he was before his superior. He said as he bowed: "I would rather bow to the innocent and clean stones than to you educated but dirty incompetent mouse." When the prostrations were over, he went to the county court for his regular courtesy call. Once he saw a huge stone of grotesque shape as he strolled in the open country. He was wild with joy. Then he straightened out his cloth and cap, bowed deeply and mumbled himself, "Brother stone, please accept my respect!" Later, Mi Fu did not want to work together with the corrupt officials. He wrote a letter of resignation, had it sent to the county government, and left his post.

米芾,是北宋有名的大书画家。他性情古怪,放荡不羁。除书画之外,他还爱石成癖。米芾当官时,清政廉洁,与当时被世人称为"面老鼠"的麦知府非常合不来。每月逢单日州衙议事,朝服参拜麦知府,更使米芾恼火。于是,他想出一个主意。他吩咐家人,每单日清晨把家中的古石摆出来,自己穿好朝服,像参拜上司一样拜这些石头。边拜边说:我愿拜无知的干净石头,也不拜你肮脏的"面老鼠"。拜过石头后,他再去州衙参拜议事。有一次,米芾到野外游玩,见到一块形状极为奇特的巨石,欣喜若狂,随即整理衣冠,伏首大拜。口中还念念有词地说:"石兄,请受我一拜!"后来,米芾不愿和脏官一起共事,便辞官而去。

Winning Over Jiang Wei by a Clever Stratagem　计收姜维

This is a story from the novel *Three Kingdoms*. Jiang Wei was adept with both pen and sword. He was not only a man of intelligence and bravery, but also a man of resources and astuteness. Zhuge Liang wanted to win Jiang Wei over to be his assistant. When he learned that Jiang Wei was a filial son whose mother was living in Jicheng City, he devised a plan to win him over. He ordered Wei Yan to attack Jicheng City by bluffing and blustering. As soon as Jiang Wei heard the news, he immediately led the troops to Jicheng City to save his mother. Zhuge Liang sent captured-general Xiahou Mao to Jicheng City to persuade Jiang Wei to surrender. When Xiahou Mao was only halfway there, he was told by people that Jiang Wei had already surrendered to the Shu State. Therefore Xiahou Mao had to go to Tianshuiguan. He came to the city and told the officers and soldiers protecting the city of Tianshuiguan about Jiang Wei's surrender. In the middle of the night, Zhuge Liang asked somebody to dress up as Jiang Wei and attack Tianshuiguan. This made the officers and soldiers in the city really believe that Jiang Wei's surrender to Shu State was true.

Jiang Wei tried every possible means to protect Jicheng City, although he lacked the necessary army provisions. One day Jiang Wei led his soldiers to seize army provisions. The soldiers of the Shu State took advantage of this and seized the city. Since Jiang Wei had lost the city, he could only run to Tianshuiguan. The generals and soldiers wouldn't let him into the city, because they mistakenly believed that he surrendered to the enemy. Jiang Wei had to go off into the wilderness. He went less than a few kilometers before Zhuge Liang came along in a carriage and his troops encircled Jiang Wei. Realizing he was trapped, he surrendered to Zhuge Liang.

《三国演义》中的故事。守卫天水郡的魏国大将姜维，文武双全，有智有勇有谋。诸葛亮想收姜维为自己的助手。他得知姜维是个孝子，其母住在冀城，便想出一条计策：命魏延虚张声势打冀城，姜维得知消息，便请兵杀回冀城救母。诸葛亮又派俘将夏侯楙带兵前往冀城劝姜维投降。夏侯楙走到半路，听老百姓说姜维已献城降蜀，他只好往天水郡来。夏侯楙进城，把姜维已投降蜀兵的消息告诉了天水郡守城官兵。深夜，诸葛亮让人假扮姜维打天水郡。守城官兵更认定姜维降蜀是事实了。

姜维苦守冀城，粮草缺乏。一日带兵劫粮，蜀兵乘虚取冀城。姜维失城只好向天水郡逃去。天水郡众将，误认姜维已经投降，不准他进城。姜维无奈落荒而去。走不到数里，诸葛亮乘车而出，姜维见自己陷入重重包围之中，便下马投降了诸葛亮。

The Four Venerable Elders from Shangshan Mountains refers to the story of the four well-known scholars who lived from the end of Qin Dynasty to the beginning of Han Dynasty (about 200 B.C.), namely: Dong Yuangong, Lu Li, Qi Liji and Xia Huanggong. They were not interested in becoming officials and hid themselves in the Shangshan Mountains for a long time. When they were appointed as officials, they were already in their 80s with white hair and eyebrows. Therefore they were called "The Four Venerable Elders from Shangshan Mountains." Liu Bang heard about these four well-known people long ago, and had many times invited them to be government officials. The Four Venerable Elders flatly refused. After Liu Bang became emperor, he made his eldest son Liu Ying crown prince and named his second son to be the king of Zhao State. Later when he found that Liu Ying lacked inherent talent and that his second son Ru Yi was quite intelligent and possessed outstanding knowledge, he wanted to dethrone Liu Ying and make Ru Yi crown prince. Upon hearing this news, Liu Ying's mother Empress Lü was rather worried. She asked the Four Venerable Elders to help her son by taking the advice of Zhang Liang, a general who founded the state. One day when Liu Bang had a dinner with the crown prince, he noticed the four elder men with white hair standing behind crown prince. He soon discovered that they were the Four Venerable Elders from Shangshan Mountains. The four elders bowed to the emperor and said: "We are told that the crown prince is a filial son with lofty ideals and he respects the lower ranking officials. So we came to be his guests." Liu Bang knew that everybody showed sympathy and the support for the crown prince. Therefore, he changed his mind about making Ru Yi the crown prince. Later, Liu Ying succeeded the emperor and became emperor of Xiao Hui.

商山四皓,指的是秦末汉初(公元前 200 年左右)的东园公、角里、绮里季和夏黄公四位著名学者。他们不愿意当官,长期隐藏在商山,出山时都八十有余,眉皓发白,故被称为"商山四皓"。刘邦久闻四皓的大名,曾请他们出山为官,而被拒绝。刘邦登基后,立长子刘盈为太子,封次子如意为赵王。后来,见刘盈天生懦弱,才华平庸,而次子如意却聪明过人,才学出众,有意废刘盈而立如意。刘盈的母亲吕后闻听,非常着急,便遵照开国大臣张良的主意,聘请商山四皓。有一天,刘邦与太子一起饮宴,他见太子背后有四位白发苍苍的老人。问后才知是商山四皓。四皓上前谢罪道:"我们听说太子是个仁人之士,又有孝心,礼贤下士,我们就一齐来作太子的宾客。刘邦知道大家很同情太子,又见太子有四位大贤辅佐,消除了改立赵王如意为太子的念头。刘盈后来继位为惠帝。

This painting is based on a poem: "Looking for a Recluse in Vain" by Jia Dao. Jia Dao was a famous poet in the Tang Dynasty (618-907). When he was a small child, he declared his intention to renounce his family and become a monk. He became a monk, but later he resumed secular life. He had high aspirations but did not achieve his ambitions. His poems were quaint and elegant with rare words, paying much attention to choosing the perfect words. He took a serious attitude in writing the poem "Looking for a Recluse in Vain," which reads:

Asking a child about a recluse under the tree,
The child said his master went to collect medicinal herbs.
He is surely in these mountains,
But can't be found because of the thick clouds.

The verse is not written with beautiful lines, but the simple and light language made people feel most delightful. By one question and three answers, the poem not only depicts the beautiful picture with towering old trees, the thickly forest mountains with sea clouds, but also implied a quiet and beautiful life of the recluse. The poet, with only 20 words, vividly described the events, people and environment. Therefore, it frequently aroused the interests of painters in drawing pictures.

这幅画是根据贾岛的五言绝句《寻隐者不遇》为题材画的。诗中写到："松下问童子，言师采药去。只在此山中，云深不知处。"贾岛(公元779－843年)是唐代著名的诗人。幼年曾出家当过和尚，后来还俗。他的诗清奇苦僻，十分注重词句的锤炼，

此诗虽无惊人佳句，但以朴素清淡的语言使人进入佳境；诗中一问三答，不但写出了古树参天，深山云海的美景，还内含了归隐于山林，恬静、清幽的生活。仅二十个字就把事、人、景写得出神入化。所以常常引起画家们挥笔。

This is a true story. Intellectual Xue Yan was quite knowledgeable, but he frequently failed his examinations. One day, as he thought of going to Kaifeng to get himself an official post, he called his three wives together and said: "This time I'm leaving you. I'm uncertain about my future. What will you do if anything happens to me?" The first wife and the second wife vowed solemnly and said: "No matter what happens, we will both maintain our chastity." But the third wife named Wang Chun'e neither vowed nor swore. She only said that she would do what she should do. Xue was not satisfied with her.

Xue Yan made a living by practicing medicine in Kaifeng and lost touch with his family. Several years later, the family heard that Xue Yan was dead. Soon, the first wife and the second wife, one after another, married to others. Only the third wife Chun'e stayed at Xue's home with his son Qi Ge born by his second wife. They depended on each other for survival. As a matter of fact Xue Yan was not dead at all. The emperor had made him a minister responsible for military affairs, for he had gained favor with the emperor by escorting him. On his way home to see his wives and children, he thought: "I will only be met by my first and second wives. My third wife has probably already married somebody else." Unexpectedly, when Xue Yan arrived back home, only the third wife came out to welcome him. Xue Yan expressed his thanks to the third wife for keeping her chastity and showed her his official uniform which was granted by the emperor. Just at that moment, Qi Ge, who had just received the title of Number One Scholar from the imperial examination came home too. He also brought his uniform to show to his third mother. After having gone through so much hardship and suffering, the third wife finally came to enjoy happiness.

这是一个真实的故事。 书生薛衍,颇有学问,但屡考不中。有一天,他想去开封求官,把三位夫人叫到一起说:"我这次出去,前途未卜,你们怎么办?"大娘、二娘信誓旦旦,都说:"无论遇到什么情况,我们都会守节。"三娘王春娥,不赌咒发誓,只说按自己该做的去做。薛衍心中很不满意三娘。薛衍在开封靠行医维持生活并与家人断了书信往来,几年后,家人们听说薛衍死了。于是,大娘、二娘先后改嫁。只有三娘春娥带着二娘生的绮哥留在薛家,教其苦读圣书,生活上细心关照,母子相依度日。其实薛衍并没有死,后因护驾有功,皇帝封他做了兵部尚书。他在回家探望妻儿们的路上寻思:这次只能见到大娘、二娘了,三娘可能已经改嫁他人了。没想到,当薛衍回到这个破家后,只有三娘迎接他。薛衍感激三娘,把诰命官服给了她。此时,中了状元的绮哥也回来了,也把自己的诰命官服送到三娘面前。于是,三娘苦尽甜来。

This is a popular Chinese fairy tale. According to legend, beautiful and kindhearted Ma Gu was originally from Jianchang. She cultivated herself according to religious doctrine in Guyu mountains southeast of Mouzhou and became immortal after mastering the religious doctrine and practices. Kindhearted Ma Gu was able to turn grains of rice into pearls, thus providing relief to poor people. No matter when people saw her, she was always as young as a lady of 18 or 19 years old. She set her hair in a bun and let the rest of the hair fall down to her waist. She wore clothes made of luxurious cloth and looked very beautiful. When people asked her how old she was, she said she had seen seas change into mulberry fields three times. She went on to say that the water in Penglai was shallower than before, so the seas were soon going to became mulberry fields again. Therefore people often regarded Ma Gu as a symbol of longevity. According to the legend, March 3rd is the birthday of the Queen Mother of the West. On that day, the Queen Mother of the West invites immortals from all directions to attend her magic peach birthday party. Once the four flower fairies, lily, peony, herbaceous peony, and Chinese flowering crabapple, collected different kinds of brightly-colored and beautiful flowers to bring to the Queen Mother. They also invited Ma Gu to attend the birthday party. Ma Gu made magic fungus immortal wine and offered it as a birthday present to the Queen Mother of the West. Traditionally, when Ma Gu was pictured presenting gifts at females' birthdays, it meant longevity.

是一个神话故事。 相传美丽善良的麻姑原是建昌人,修道于牟州东南姑余山,后得道成仙。善良的麻姑能掷米成珠,救济广大穷苦百姓。人们无论什么时候见到麻姑,她始终如十八、九的姑娘一样年轻。她发顶作髻,余发散落至腰间,锦衣绣服,相貌美丽,当人们问她年岁有多大时,她讲已经见过沧海三次变为桑田了。并说蓬莱那个地方水比过去浅了,沧海又要变桑田了。所以人们常用麻姑象征长寿。又相传每年的三月初三,是西王母的寿辰,四面八方的神仙都来为她贺寿。每当这天,西王母要设蟠桃会宴请众仙。有一次,百花、牡丹、芍药、海棠四位花仙采集各种艳丽的花,邀请麻姑一同去祝寿。麻姑用绛珠河畔的灵芝酿成仙酒,为西王母祝寿。故旧时祝女寿者多绘麻姑像赠送,意寓长寿。

This is a story from the novel *Three Kingdoms*. Zhuge Liang led 300,000 Shu State troops in a march towards Chencang, the vital communication stronghold of the Wei State. It was his second expedition against the Wei State. Hao Zhao, the general guarding the city dug the trenches deep and built the fortress strong. He waited for the attack. Everyday, Zhuge Liang sent soldiers to challenge the Wei army in battle, but the Wei troops held fast to their position and refused to come out. One day, a scout came back to report that Hao Zhao was seriously ill. Zhuge Liang thought that the chance had come at last. He ordered Wei Yan and Jiang Wei to take 5,000 troops and surround Chencang in three days. They were to attack the city when they saw a fire inside the city. After that, he gave Guan Xing and Zhang Bao secret instructions. As the health of the Wei State general Hao Zhao was deteriorating, suddenly it was reported to Hao Zhao that the troops from Shu State had arrived outside the city. Hao Zhao hurriedly ordered officers and soldiers to defend the city in their position. Unexpectedly,

a fire broke out on each of the city's towers. There was chaos inside the city. Hao Zhao was frightened to death. The troops of the Shu State smashed all enemy resistance and advanced into the city. Three days later when Wei Yan and Jiang Wei led their troops to the gate of the city, they heard somebody shouting from the top of the city wall, "You have come too late!" The two generals fixed their eyes upon the person. It was the Prime Minister of the Shu State, Zhuge Liang. The two generals got down from their horses hastily and saluted. Zhuge Liang said, "The reason that I asked you to attack the city in three days is to keep the soldiers calm. In fact, I had already sent Guan Xing and Zhang Bao to secretly leave the center area of Han the same night as I ordered you. By disguising myself, I hid among the soldiers and set out for Chencang by starlight. We gave the enemy a surprise attack. The fire was set on at my instruction and it threw the city into confusion. This is called "taking the enemy by surprise and striking when it is unprepared."

《三国演义》中的故事。 诸葛亮带领三十万大军再度伐魏,直奔交通要塞陈仓而来。守将郝昭在这里挖深沟筑堡垒,以守待攻。诸葛亮每天派人叫阵,魏军坚守不出。有一天,派出去的探子回来报告,说陈仓守将郝昭病重。诸葛亮觉得时机已到,马上叫魏延、姜维三天之后带五千人马围住陈仓,待见到城中起火,协同攻城。然后又唤关兴、张苞附耳暗授机密。魏将郝昭病势严重,忽然接到报告,说蜀军已到城下,急命将士上城把守。此时各城楼突然大火四起,城中顿时大乱。郝昭当即

吓死。蜀兵势如破竹,直入城中。三天后,魏延、姜维领兵来到陈仓城下,见城上有人大喊:"你二位来迟了!"二人定眼一看,不是别人,正是丞相诸葛亮。二人急忙下马行礼。诸葛亮说:"我叫你二人三天后领兵攻城。是为了稳住军心,其实我已叫关兴、张苞连夜暗出汉中,我化装藏在军中,星夜赶奔陈仓,让敌人一点准备都没有。那些城内放火的人是我早就安排好的。一着火,城内必然不战自乱,这叫'出其不意,攻其不备'。"

This is a story from *Complete Biography of Yue Fei*. One year, the imperial court had a martial arts competition. Xiaoliang Prince and Yue Fei fought for the top martial arts ranking. Xiaoliang Prince, named Chai Gui, descendant of Chai Shizong, an influential official, bribed all the chief examiners except marshal Zong Ze.

First was the literary talent exam. Yue Fei wrote an article "On the Spear." He finished the piece of writing at one go and it was full of wit and humor. Xiaoliang Prince wrote an article "On the Sword." He was afraid and nervous and did not know how to write.

Second was the archery test. When Yue Fei shot, the target was moved by Zhang Bangchang, a treacherous court official. But Yue Fei was cool and calm and all nine arrows hit the center of the target. He won cheers from the audience. Xiaoliang Prince was so intimidated that he was afraid to shoot his arrows.

Third was the martial arts test. Yue Fei was afraid of hurting the prince because he did not want to face the consequences of such an event. So he dared not to fully display his skill and merely dodged the prince's attacks. After several rounds, Yue Fei jumped out of the court and went up to the examiners. He asked them to write a "life-and-death document," otherwise he could not go on competing with the prince. The treacherous court official Zhang thought Yue Fei could not possibly win. He was so sure that the prince would win the competition. That he wrote out the requested document.

Throwing Xiaoliang Prince Down from His Horse 枪挑小梁王

When they started again Yue Fei was in high spirits and met the prince's attacks calmly. At one point in the match, Yue Fei made a feint attack and then threw the prince down from his horse. The prince died instantly. Zhang Bangchang and other treacherous officials asked Yue Fei to pay for the prince's life but was stopped by marshal Zong Ze. With the help of Niu Gao and other friends Yue Fei got out of the city quickly.

《说岳全传》中的故事。 有一年，朝廷比武考试，小梁王和岳飞争夺武状元。小梁王柴桂是柴世宗的嫡系子孙，他早就收买了几个主考官，唯有大元帅宗泽拒绝贿赂。当时考试，一考文才，岳飞作"枪论"，他妙笔生花，一挥而就。小梁王作"刀论"，他心慌，胡乱交了卷。二考射箭，岳飞射时，奸臣张邦昌让

人私动靶子，岳飞不慌不忙，一连九箭，支支中靶心，引起全场喝彩。小梁王不敢比射箭了。三比武艺，岳飞上场比武怕伤了小梁王而担待不起，所以不敢出手，只是躲闪。比了几个回合，岳飞突然跳出场外，来到主考官面前，要求立下"生死文书"方敢再比。张邦昌等奸臣看了方才的几个回合，认为岳飞武艺不行，小梁王必胜，所以答应二人立"生死文书"以后重新较量。再上场时，你杀我砍互不相让。岳飞精神抖擞，沉着应战，只见岳飞虚晃一枪，而后实枪把小梁王挑下马来，结果了性命。张邦昌等奸臣要岳飞偿命，被宗泽阻拦。岳飞在牛皋等兄弟的协助下，飞奔出城。

A Couple That Treated Each Other with Mutual Respect　举案齐眉

This ancient story of Liang Hong and Meng Guang, an affectionate couple who treated each other with the utmost respect has been told over many generations in China. Liang Hong was born in Pingling County, Fufeng Prefecture (in present-day Shaanxi) at the beginning of East Han Dynasty (about 100). His parents died when he was small, and his family fell into decline. But Liang Hong had big ambitions. As he was upright, intelligent, learned and versatile, many rich families admired him and for his fine character and wanted to marry their daughters to him. However, he turned down all proposals of marriage. There was a girl called Meng Guang from a rich family in the same county. She was tall and fat, dark-skinned and ugly . She was 30 years old and not married. Her parents asked her what kind of man she wanted to marry . She said: "I want a good husband like Liang Hong." Later, Liang Hong heard about this and thought he had found a girl who keenly appreciated his talents. So he married Meng Guang. After they were married, Liang Hong took Meng Guang to Wushi City where he had found work. They lived in a hut under the porch of Gao Botong, a rich man there. Whenever Liang Hong finished his work, Meng Guang had already prepared the food. She stood in front of Liang Hong with a lowered head, holding the tray at brow level, to invite her husband to dinner. Gao Botong was surprised when he saw this. "Liang Hong is but a hired laborer, but he receives such respect from his wife. It seems that he is not at all an ordinary person." said Gao Botong. Thus he invited the couple to live in his house. After a while, Liang Hong brought Meng Guang to a remote mountain region in Baling and lived in seclusion there. Liang Hong ploughed the field and Meng Guang weaved cloth. They earned their own living.

描绘梁鸿和孟光夫妻恩爱,相敬如宾的故事。梁鸿东汉初期扶风郡平陵县(今陕西境内)人。他很小就失去父母,家境败落,但他志气很大,为人正直。再加上他聪明过人,博学多识。很多富家人羡慕他的人品高尚,想把女儿嫁给他作妻子,但都被他拒绝了。同县有个叫孟光的富家姑娘,身高体胖,又黑又丑,年已三十还没嫁人。父母问她到底想嫁什么样的人。她说:"我要找一个像梁鸿那样的好丈夫。"后来,这话传到梁鸿的耳朵,梁鸿以为碰到了知音,便娶孟光为妻。婚后,梁鸿带孟光到外做工。住在财主皋伯通廊下的小屋。每到收工回家,孟光早给他做好饭菜,站在梁鸿面前低着头,把饭盘高举齐眉请梁鸿吃饭。皋伯通看后觉得很奇怪说:"梁鸿本是个雇工,却使他妻子这般尊敬,看来绝不是个平常的人。"便请梁鸿夫妻居住在自己家中。后来,梁鸿带着孟光隐居在霸陵深山中,过着男耕女织,自食其力的生活。

This is a story from *Complete Biography of Yue Fei*. In the early Southern Song Dynasty, Yue Fei was upset and anxious at being unable to defeat Lu Wenlong, adopted son of Jin Wuzhu. One night, Wang Zuo, a general who had just defected to the Song Dynasty, devised a plot of faked defection by cutting off one arm. He cut off one of his arms and went to see Yue Fei. "I know you are worried about how to defeat Lu Wenlong. I am going to pretend to surrender to the Jin army and kill Jin Wuzhu and Lu Wenlong," said Wang. Yue Fei had to bite the bullet and nodded in agreement. Wang Zuo arrived at the Jin camp and weepingly told Jin Wuzhu his story: "I had been under Rebel Yang Muo but had to surrender to Yue Fei of the Song Dynasty. When all the generals were discussing the situation yesterday, I, seeing the Song army in a dilemma, persuaded Yue Fei to surrender, who turned down my well-intentioned words, labeled me a traitor and cut off my arm." He took the arm out from the sleeve to prove his words. All this won the trust of Jin Wuzhu. In the Jin camp, Wang found Lu Wenlong's nursing nanny and learned that Lu Wenlong was actually the son of Lu Deng, a Song general who had died at his post resisting against the Jin army. Lu Wenlong, then months old, had been taken away by Jin Wuzhu and raised as his adopted son. One day, Lu Wenlong invited Wang to a dinner. Wang told Lu the story about how his family was murdered. Learning about his family background, Lu Wenlong was determined to defect to Yue Fei. Thereafter, Lu helped the Song Dynasty with one military victory after another.

《说岳全传》中的故事。　南宋初年岳飞为不能取胜金兀术义子陆文龙而烦恼。一夜,刚投宋不久的将领王佐想出"断臂诈降"计谋,他把自己的右臂砍下,去见岳飞说:"我知元帅为破陆文龙发愁,我决心去诈降金兵,找机会杀掉金兀术。"岳飞忍痛答应。王佐来到金营,向金兀术泣说:"我原是绿林杨么之臣,无奈投降大宋,跟随岳飞。只因昨天聚众将议事,小臣见宋军进退两难,便劝岳飞投降,他不听好言,反说我卖国,砍下我的一臂。"说着从袖中拿出断臂,果然取得金兀术信任。陆文龙是宋朝抗金殉难将领陆登的儿子,在陆文龙生下只有几个月时被金兀术掳去收为义子。一天,陆文龙约王佐一起吃饭,王佐借讲故事将真情告知陆文龙。陆文龙知道自己身世后,归降岳飞,并屡立战功。

Index 索 引

Three Kingdoms 《三国演义》

Brotherhood Forged in the Peach Garden
Inner corridor, *Part* I 11
桃园结义 … 一区廊内 …

Cao Cao Presents a Blade
Inner corridor, *Part* I 19
曹操献刀 … 一区廊内 …

Three Heroes Combating Lü Bu
Inside Qingyao Pavilion. 20
三英战吕布 … 清遥亭内 …

Interlocking Stratagems
Inner corridor, *Part* II 26
设连环计 … 二区廊内 …

Lü Bu and Diaochan
Inner corridor, *Part* I 30
吕布戏貂蝉 … 一区廊内 …

Zhang Fei's Apology
Inner corridor, *Part* VI 33
张飞赔罪 … 六区廊内 …

Magic Shot Outside the Military Camp
Inner corridor, *Part* V 35
辕门射戟 … 五区廊内 …

Mi Heng's Denouncement of Cao Cao
Outer corridor, *Part* V 38
击鼓骂曹 … 五区廊外 …

A Leap Over the Tanxi River
Inner corridor, *Part* VI 44
马跃檀溪 … 六区廊内 …

Recommending Zhuge Liang on Horseback
Inner corridor, *Part* I 47
走马荐诸葛 … 一区廊内 …

Three Visits to the Thatched Cottage
Inner corridor, *Part* II 51
三顾茅庐 … 二区廊内 …

Fresh from Thatched Cottage
Inner corridor, *Part* V 54
初出茅庐 … 五区廊内 …

Zhao Yun Saves Young Master
Single-Handedly
Outer corridor, *Part* VI 58
单骑救主 … 六区廊外 …

Jiang Gan Steals a Letter
Outer corridor, *Part* IV 64
蒋干盗书 … 四区廊外 …

To Borrow Arrows with Thatched Boats
Inner corridor, *Part* IV 69
草船借箭 … 四区廊内 …

Liu Bei Crossed the River to
Keep an Appointment
Inner corridor, *Part* II 78
江东赴会 … 二区廊内 …

The Battered-Body Trick
Outer corridor, *Part* II 84
苦肉计 … 二区廊外 …

Cao Cao Sings an Ode with Leveled Spear
Inner corridor, *Part* IV 91
横槊赋诗 … 四区廊内 …

Guan Yu's Loyal Deed of Letting
Cao Cao Run Away
Outer corridor, *Part* III 98
义放曹操 … 三区廊外 …

Liu Bei Returns to Jingzhou
Outer corridor, *Part* II 105
回荆州 … 二区廊外 …

Zhuge Liang Pays a Mourning Call
Outer corridor, *Part* I 110
诸葛亮吊孝 … 一区廊外 …

Night Fight Against Ma Chao
Inside Jilan Pavilion 120
夜战马超 … 寄澜亭内 …

Huang Zhong Takes on the Challenge
Inner corridor, *Part* III 122
黄忠请战 … 三区廊内 …

Guan Yu Floods Seven Armies
Inner corridor, *Part* IV 123
水淹七军 … 四区廊内 …

Scrape the Poison off the Bone
Inner corridor, *Part* V 126
刮骨疗毒 … 五区廊内 …

Winning Over Jiang Wei by
a Clever Stratagem
Inner corridor, *Part* IV 130
计收姜维 … 四区廊内 …

Taking Chencang by Using Clever Strategy
Inner corridor, *Part* III 135
计取陈仓 … 三区廊内 …

Journey to the West 《西游记》

The Tang Priest's Journey for Scriptures
Outer corridor, *Part* II 12
唐僧取经 … 二区廊外 …

Thousand-Mile Eye and
Wind-Accompanying Ear
Inner corridor, *part* II 21
千里眼顺风耳 … 二区廊内 …

Making Havoc in Heaven
Inside Liuzhui Pavilion 40
大闹天空 … 留佳亭内 …

Chaos at the Feast of Peaches
Outer corridor, *Part* III 79
闹蟠桃会 … 三区廊外 …

Leaping Out of the Eight Trigrams Furnace
Inner corridor, *Part* V 85
跳出八卦炉 … 五区廊内 …

Monkey Hit the Lady White Bone Thrice
Inner corridor, *Part* III 86
三打白骨精 … 三区廊内 …

Fighting in the Bottomless Cave
Inner corridor, *Part* IV 92
闹无底洞 … 四区廊内 …

Red Boy Captures Sanzang
Inner corridor, *Part* III 99
智擒唐僧 … 三区廊内 …

Monkey Makes Three Attempts to
Borrow the Plantain Fan
Outer corridor, *Part* V 106
三借芭蕉扇 … 五区廊外 …

Fish Spirit Makes Trouble
Inner corridor, *Part* Ⅵ 111
鱼精作怪 … 六区廊内 …

Outlaws of the Marsh 《水浒传》

Uprooting the Willow Tree
Inner corridor, *Part* Ⅲ 13
倒拔垂杨柳 … 三区廊内 …
The Boar Wood
Inner corridor, *Part* Ⅲ 36
野 猪 林 … 三区廊内 …
Wu Song Beats a Tiger
Outer corridor, *Part* Ⅲ 65
武松打虎 … 三区廊外 …
Li Kui Stirs Up Trouble at Loyalty Hall
Outer corridor, *Part* Ⅴ 67
闹忠义堂 … 五区廊外 …
Shi Qian Steals the Armor
Inner corridor, *Part* Ⅲ 100
时迁盗甲 … 三区廊内 …

A Dream of Red Mansions 《红楼梦》

Seeking Plum Blossoms in Snow
Inner corridor, *Part* Ⅱ 14
踏雪寻梅 … 二区廊内 …
Xiangyun's Drunken Sleep
Outer corridor, *Part* Ⅱ 22
湘云醉卧 … 二区廊外 …
Xiang Ling in Grass Game
Outer corridor, *Part* Ⅵ 28
香菱斗草 … 六区廊外 …
Qing Wen Mends the Cloak
Outer corridor, *Part* Ⅱ 34
晴雯补裘 … 二区廊外 …
Four Fishing Beauties
Outer corridor, *Part* Ⅴ 37
四美钓鱼 … 五区廊外 …
The Third Sister's Suicide
Outer corridor, *Part* Ⅳ 50
三姐自刎 … 四区廊外 …
Homecoming by an Imperial Concubine
Inner corridor, *Part* Ⅲ 55
元妃省亲 … 三区廊内 …
Reading West Chamber
Outer corridor, *Part* Ⅰ 59
读西厢记 … 一区廊外 …
A Crane's Flit Across a Chilly Pool
Inner corridor, *Part* Ⅲ 66
寒塘鹤影 … 三区廊内 …
A Song from "Peony Pavilion"
Distresses a Tender Heart
Outer corridor, *Part* Ⅳ 71
艳曲警芳心 … 四区廊外 …
Two Yu's Listen to Music
Outer corridor, *Part* Ⅴ 73
双玉听琴 … 五区廊外 …
Jia Baoyu in Love
Outer corridor, *Part* Ⅴ 80
宝玉痴情 … 五区廊外 …

A Secret Is Disclosed
Inner corridor, *Part* Ⅲ 101
池露机关 … 三区廊内 …
Daiyu Burns Her Manuscripts
Inner corridor, *Part* Ⅴ 121
黛玉焚稿 … 五区廊内 …

Strange Tales from Make-Do Studio 《聊斋志异》

Chance Meeting with Lady Feng
Inner corridor, *Part* Ⅴ 15
邂逅封三娘 … 五区廊内 …
The Drunken Tao
Outer corridor, *Part* Ⅴ 23
黄英醉陶 … 五区廊外 …
Parrot's Marriage
Outer corridor, *Part* Ⅳ 29
鹦鹉许婚 … 四区廊外 …
A Painted Hide
Outer corridor, *Part* Ⅵ 39
画 皮 … 六区廊外 …
Ying Ning with Plum Blossoms
Inner corridor, *Part* Ⅲ 52
婴宁拈梅 … 三区廊内 …
Princess Yunluo
Inner corridor, *Part* Ⅲ 60
云萝公主 … 三区廊内 …
Hong Yu
Inner corridor, *Part* Ⅳ 70
严父斥子 … 四区廊内 …
How Xiliu Taught Her Children
Inner corridor, *Part* Ⅳ 81
细柳教子 … 四区廊内 …
Two Ghosts Taking Care of Their Mother
Inner corridor, *Part* Ⅳ 93
双鬼侍母 … 四区廊内 …
Shanhu, a Filial Daughter-in-Law
Inner corridor, *Part* Ⅳ 102
珊瑚孝婆 … 四区廊内 …
Gejin and Yuban
Inner corridor, *Part* Ⅴ 112
葛巾玉版 … 五区廊内 …
Lü Wubing
Outer corridor, *Part* Ⅵ 118
吕 无 病 … 六区廊外 …

The Generals of Yang Family 《杨家将》

Mu Guiying Captures Her Man
Inner corridor, *Part* Ⅵ 16
智套宗保 … 六区廊内 …
Yang Paifeng's Combat with Yin Qi
Outer corridor, *Part* Ⅲ 31
杨排风战殷奇 … 三区廊外 …

Tale of the White Snake 《白蛇传》

The Boat Trip and the Borrowed Umbrella
Outer corridor, *Part* Ⅴ 17
游湖借伞 … 五区廊外 …

Love Renewed by the Dilapidated Bridge
Inner corridor, Part IV   32
断桥解冤 … 四区廊内 …

Stealing a Medicinal
Herb to Save Her Husband
Inner corridor, Part IV   42
盗草救夫 … 四区廊内 …

Complete Biography of Yue Fei 《说岳全传》

Yue Fei's Mother Tattooed on His Back
Inner corridor, Part II   45
岳母刺字 … 二区廊内 …

Battle in Zhuxianzhen
Inside Jilan Pavilion   88
大闹朱仙镇 … 寄澜亭内 …

Throwing Xiaoliang Prince Down
from His Horse
Inside Qiushui Pavilion   136
枪挑小梁王 … 秋水亭内 …

Wang Zuo Cuts Off His Arm
Inner corridor, Part VI   139
王佐断臂 … 六区廊内 …

Others 其它

The Eight Immortals Crossing the Sea
Outer corridor, Part III   9
八仙过海 … 三区廊外 …

Qin Xianglian
Inner corridor, Part VI   10
秦 香 莲 … 六区廊内 …

Strict Law Enforcement by Lord Bao
Inner corridor, Part VI   18
包公执法 … 六区廊内 …

The Seven Sages of Bamboo Grove
Insids Qiushui Pavilion   24
竹林七贤 … 秋水亭内 …

Lord Jiang Angles for Fish
Inner corridor, Part IV   25
姜太公钓鱼 … 四区廊内…

Three Talented Literary Men
Inner corridor, Part I   27
文人三才 … 一区廊内 …

Su Wu Herds Sheep
Outer corridor, Part IV   43
苏武牧羊 … 四区廊外 …

Asking for a Longer Life-Span
Outer corridor, Part V   46
赵颜求寿 … 五区廊外 …

Exiting the Hangu Pass
Outer corridor, Part IV   48
老子出关 … 四区廊外 …

Retrieving the Ball with Water
Outer corridor, Part II   49
灌水得球 … 二区廊外 …

Wang Hua Buying a Father
Outer corridor, Part IV   53
王华买爹 … 四区廊外 …

Three County Sheriffs
Inner corridor, Part V   56
三个县令 … 五区廊内 …

The Five Dragons of the Dou Family
Inner corridor, Part IV   57
五子夺魁 … 四区廊内 …

The Imperial Concubine's Charms
Outer corridor, Part IV   61
贵妃出浴 … 四区廊外 …

Zhang Liang Picks Up Shoes for an Old Man
Inner corridor, Part II   62
张良进履 … 二区廊内 …

Laundry Woman Shares Food with Han Xin
Inner corridor, Part IV   63
漂母分食 … 四区廊内 …

King Wu Loses His Life
Outer corridor, Part III   68
吴王毙命 … 三区廊外 …

The Peach Flower Land
Inside Liuzhui Pavilion   72
桃花源记 … 留佳亭内 …

Kong Rong Offering the Pear to Others
Inner corridor, Part V   74
孔融让梨 … 五区廊内 …

Unicorn's Gift
Outer corridor, Part V   75
麒麟献书 … 五区廊外 …

Rescues His Mother by Splitting
the Mountain
Outer corridor, Part IV   76
劈山救母 … 四区廊外 …

Pleasure After Retirement
Inner corridor, Part IV   77
归 田 乐 … 四区廊内 …

Ehuang and Nüying
Outer corridor, Part V   82
娥皇女英 … 五区廊外 …

He and He Immortals
Outer corridor, Part V   83
和合二仙 … 五区廊外 …

Chang'e Flew to the Moon
Inner corridor, Part IV   87
嫦娥奔月 … 四区廊内 …

A Trip of Xuan Zong to the Moon
Inner corridor, Part V   90
玄宗游月宫 … 五区廊内 …

Pointing at Xinghuacun in the Distance
Inner corridor, Part III   94
遥指杏花村 … 三区廊内 …

The Goddess of Luoshui
Outer corridor, Part I   95
洛水女神 … 一区廊外 …

Lu Ji Conceals Oranges in His Clothes
Inner corridor, Part V   96
陆绩怀桔 … 五区廊内 …

The Three Travel-Stained Chivalries
Inner corridor, Part I   97
风尘三侠 … 一区廊内 …

Su Xiaomei Tests Her Bridegroom
Three Times
Outer corridor, Part III   103
三难新郎 … 三区廊外 …

Zhou Dunyi Loves Lotus Flowers
    Inner corridor , Part I   104
敦颐爱莲 … 一区廊内 …

The West Chamber
    Inner corridor , Part V   107
西厢记 … 五区廊内 …

Han Kang Sells Medicinal Herbs
    Inner corridor , Part Ⅲ   108
韩康卖药 … 三区廊内 …

Drawing the Pupils in the Dragon's Eyes
    Inner corridor , Past Ⅲ   109
画龙点睛 … 三区廊内 …

Celestial Maids Scatter Flowers
    Inner corridor , Part V   113
天女散花 … 五区廊内 …

Joint Hearing
    Inner corridor , Part Ⅵ   114
三堂会审 … 六区廊内 …

Carrying His Mother into the Mountain
    Outer corridor , Part Ⅵ   115
背母进山 … 六区廊外 …

The Cowherd and the Girl Weaver
    Inner corridor , Part Ⅲ   116
牛郎织女 … 三区廊内 …

Xizhi Loves Goose
    Inner corridor , Part Ⅱ   117
羲之爱鹅 … 二区廊内 …

Pounding Herbal Medicine in Lanqiao
    Inner corridor , Part Ⅱ   119
蓝桥捣药 … 二区廊内 …

Boya Broke the Fiddle
    Inner corridor , Part Ⅱ   124
伯牙摔琴 … 二区廊内 …

Zhang Chang Does Mascara for His Wife
    Inner corridor , Part Ⅳ   125
张敞画眉 … 四区廊内 …

The Fisherman Kills the Despot
    Inner corridor , Part Ⅳ   127
打渔杀家 … 四区廊内 …

Wenji Pays Homage at Her Father's Grave
    Inner corridor , Part Ⅰ   128
文姬谒墓 … 一区廊内 …

Mi Fu Prostrates Himself Before Stones
    Inner corridor , Part Ⅳ   129
米芾拜石 … 四区廊内 …

The Four Venerable Elders
  from Shangshan Mountains
    Inner corridor , Part Ⅱ   131
商山四皓 … 二区廊内 …

Asking a Child About
  a Recluse Under the Tree
    Inner corridor , Part Ⅳ   132
松下问童子 … 四区廊内 …

The Third Wife Teaches the Son
    Inner corridor , Part Ⅱ   133
三娘教子 … 二区廊内 …

Ma Gu Offers Long Life
    Inner corridor , Part Ⅲ   134
麻姑献寿 … 三区廊内 …

A Couple That Treated Each Other
  with Mutual Respect
    Outer corridor , Part Ⅱ   138
举案齐眉 … 二区廊外 …

◊ West 西   East 东 ◊

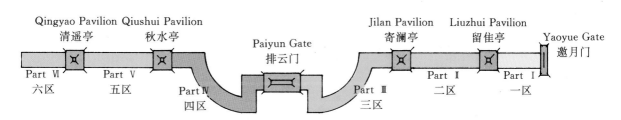

Qingyao Pavilion   Qiushui Pavilion   Jilan Pavilion   Liuzhui Pavilion
清遥亭   秋水亭   寄澜亭   留佳亭   Yaoyue Gate 邀月门
Paiyun Gate 排云门
Part Ⅵ 六区   Part V 五区   Part Ⅳ 四区   Part Ⅲ 三区   Part Ⅱ 二区   Part Ⅰ 一区

A Sketch of the Long Corridor
长廊彩画位置示意图

图书在版编目(CIP)数据

颐和园长廊彩画故事精选:英汉对照/《颐和园长廊彩画
故事精选》编委会编.—北京:外文出版社,1996
ISBN 7－119－01859－0

Ⅰ.颐… Ⅱ.颐… Ⅲ.故事－中国－对照读物－英、汉 Ⅳ.H319.4

中国版本图书馆 CIP 数据核字(96)第 02990 号

外文出版社网页:

http://www.flp.com.cn

外文出版社电子邮件地址:

info@flp.com.cn

sales@flp.com.cn

颐和园长廊彩画故事精选

编委会编

＊

ⓒ外文出版社

外文出版社出版

(中国北京百万庄大街 24 号)

邮政编码 100037

北京百花彩印有限公司印刷

1996 年(16 开)第一版

1998 年第二次印刷

(英汉)

ISBN 7－119－01859－0 /J·361(外)

05000